VITAL SIGNS

VITAL SIGNS

Contemporary American Poetry from the University Presses

Edited by Ronald Wallace   The University of Wisconsin Press

The University of Wisconsin Press
114 North Murray Street
Madison, Wisconsin 53715

The University of Wisconsin Press, Ltd.
1 Gower Street
London WC1E 6HA, England

5   4   3   2   1

Printed in the United States of America

Library of Congress Cataloging-in-Publication Data
Vital signs: contemporary American poetry from the university presses
   Ronald Wallace, editor.
   522 p.   cm.
   Includes bibliographical references.
   1. American poetry—20th century.   2. University presses—
United States.   I. Wallace, Ronald.
PS615.V54   1989
811'.5408—dc20   89-40271
ISBN 0-299-12160-7
ISBN 0-299-12164-X

iv

Contents

Preface

Although I had been secretly enamored of verse since early childhood, memorizing poems like Vachel Lindsay's "The Moon's the North Wind's Cooky" and Lewis Carroll's "The Walrus and the Carpenter" for the sheer pleasure of it, and although I retained an incorrigible enthusiasm for poets I discovered in junior high school—Emily Dickinson and Stephen Crane—despite the best efforts of my teachers and my friends, it wasn't until 1972 that I began to think seriously about trying to publish my own work. My wife and I had just returned to St. Louis from an extended tour of Europe where, in cheap hotels or the back seat of our $200 Morris Minor, I had written a series of travel poems which weren't as bad or as good as I'd thought they might be when we decided romantically to sell everything we owned and buy one-way tickets to London a year earlier. Now we were expecting our first child and, while my wife manned the cash register at a local cleaner's and I sold underwear at Famous Barr Department store, we wondered what we would do with our lives.

One afternoon, on a whim, I decided to visit a librarian who had befriended me in high school when I worked nights at the University City public library shelving books or, more often, surreptitiously reading in the stacks. She wasn't working that day, but on the bulletin board behind the desk a flier caught my eye, announcing the $1,000 United States Award of the International Poetry Forum and the University of Pittsburgh Press. I hadn't thought very seriously about sending my work to book publishers; the New York presses seemed to publish mostly "famous" poets, and the small presses I'd tentatively looked into seemed to have big backlogs or be uninterested in the work of strangers. I had no literary connections or powerful friends. But here was a university press, actually soliciting manuscripts, and offering a $1,000 prize! Vowing to win the United States Award, I retired to an upper room of my mother's house and typed up my first manuscript of poems.

Over the next eight years I submitted evolving versions of that manuscript to every university press and trade press that would read it, receiving encouraging rejections from Paul Zimmer, Stanley Kunitz, Richard Hugo, Beverly Jarrett, and others, until in 1981 *Plums, Stones, Kisses & Hooks* was published by the University of Missouri Press in their Breakthrough Books series. *Tunes for Bears to Dance To* followed from the University of Pittsburgh Press in 1983 (the U.S. Award, alas, had been discontinued) and *People and Dog in the Sun* appeared from Pitt in 1987.

During this period, partly because I was trying to publish my books with university presses, and partly because it seemed to me that that was now where the best books were coming from, I began reading every poetry book that had been published by a university press. My enthusiasm for those books, and my own personal experience with university presses, stimulated me to compile this anthology.

The two central purposes of anthologies—preservation and evaluation—have changed little since Elihu Hubbard Smith articulated them in his *American Poems,* the first American poetry anthology, published in 1793.[1] Smith's first concern was preservation: "to afford a stronger, and more durable security" to poems that might otherwise disappear. In the eighteenth century, all American poetry was published in magazines whose average life was fourteen months. Smith's anthology thus preserved works from extinction. Today, although preservation means selecting from abundance rather than protecting from oblivion, the principle applies. University press books are printed in fairly small editions of 500–2000, and are not always readily available at book stores or even at some larger libraries. Advertising budgets are minimal. Good books, moreover, can get lost in the crowd. Thus, one purpose of this anthology is to preserve poems that might not otherwise be accessible.

Elihu Hubbard Smith's second purpose was "to bring together, in one view, the several poetical productions of the different states. By this means a more certain estimation can be made of the comparative merit of their various writers." The principle of evaluation applies in this anthology as well. Because university presses have from the beginning been especially important in discovering and promoting the work of new poets, this anthology includes the work of many younger writers whose reputations have not yet been securely established. Because university presses have, increasingly in recent years, published the work of well-established poets, this anthology includes the work of many of our most respected older writers. A juxtaposition of these poets, young and old, who have published over the past thirty years, can lead to a "more certain estimation" of their "comparative merit."

Preservation and evaluation are, of course, in some ways contradictory activities. Preservation requires breadth—a large number of poets and poems—while evaluation requires selectivity. Because university presses have published so many good poets over the past thirty years, I have emphasized breadth. But even a selection of 168 poets excludes many fine writers. My original version of the anthology, which was considerably longer, had to be cut to meet publication requirements.

Anthologists are no more exempt from foolishness than anyone else. Rufus Wilmot Griswold, that respected nineteenth-century taste-maker, a hundred years ago summarily dismissed Walt Whitman and quarantined most women from his *The Poets and Poetry of America*. A hundred years from now, or maybe tomorrow, some wiser person may find errors of judgment and taste in this anthology to rival Griswold's. What appears so accomplished and promising now may later look like blind fashion and convention.

I hope that this will not be the case. The poems in this volume have, in fact, survived several rigorous evaluations. In many cases they were originally published in our best literary magazines and then included in books that were selected from among many hundreds of submitted manuscripts. In the case of older books, the poems are those that appealed to me years ago and continue to appeal today. Although there are no transhistorical or universal standards for good poetry, and although an homogeneity of taste may restrict genuine eclecticism, the poems included here have been judged excellent by magazine editors, press editors, and reviewers, as well as myself, over a period of time. In some cases the poets themselves made useful recommendations. In all cases I selected only poets whose work *as a whole* impressed me, and only poems that vitally represented that work. In addition, many of these poems have proved important to my own writing and teaching. I hope that other writers and teachers will find their range and variety to be useful as well as pleasurable. Passion, conviction, intelligence, urgency, honesty, vitality, wit—these are the qualities that moved me, and the qualities that I hope will send the readers of this anthology back to the books from which the selections were made, to read the work whole.

A further purpose of this anthology is to celebrate the commitment of the university press to poetry, by providing a historical overview. Hard data proved more difficult to come by than I had anticipated. Although the Academy of American Poets annual bibliography of poetry has become more comprehensive in recent years, no completely accurate record of poetry books published in the United States is yet available. The university presses themselves have little data on the histories of their poetry series, and often have only incomplete lists of the books they have published. I apologize to any poets whom I may have inadvertently left off the lists.

In many cases I have relied on personal, factual, and historical information obtained through questionnaires I sent to each press and poet included in the book. This anthology would not have been possible without the cooperation of those who took the time to respond to the questionnaires, who made suggestions about particular selections, and who were more than generous about permissions fees.

One question in which I was initially interested involved the "character" or "personality" of individual press poetry series. I had my own intuitive sense of the various series, and I believed that an individual book was often valued according to the particular press that published it. Poets and presses differed widely on this question. While most presses preferred not to answer the question or felt it was irrelevant, many poets agreed that the various series had their own characters. In fact, one reason some poets cited for publishing with university presses was the possibility of having a book in a well-defined series with a clear aesthetic character. Although those series with a strong single editor might be expected to have the most evident character, there was agreement about other of the presses as well. Press series do seem to establish a personality in readers' minds, and the ambiance of the press can help determine a reader's response to a particular book. Thus Princeton was typically described as publishing elegant, cerebral, discursive poetry, that thinks as much as it feels; Missouri was thought of as publishing a more accessible book, featuring more natural description and a more modest voice; Louisiana State University was considered, in part, a "Southern" press, with a special interest in more traditionally formal poetry, and a tendency to more mordant humor; Pittsburgh was described as "eclectic," while favoring the "plain style," and preferring a strong narrative voice. Such assessments, however, finally seemed too vague and intuitive to be particularly useful. What seems evident is that while each series does seem to develop a character, the range of books on any given list makes it impossible to define that character at all precisely. I have therefore decided to leave such speculations to the interested reader.

If this anthology demonstrates anything, it is the richness and diversity of contemporary American poetry, which is healthier than ever. There are no geographical centers, no warring "schools," no one or two dominant voices. Like Adso of Melk in *The Name of the Rose*, as I was reading and rereading the 900 books published by university presses, I became aware not of competing personalities or groups, but of a harmonious "murmuring, an imperceptible dialogue between one parchment and another." This anthology represents poems of all shapes and sizes, all thematic and stylistic persuasions, involved in that great ongoing dialogue.

I considered many possible titles for this anthology before settling on *Vital Signs*. In my self-deprecatory moods I considered calling it *Mulch for Your Begonias* after a line from Peter Meinke's "Recipe": "tear your anthologies into small pieces/ use them as mulch for your begonias and/ begin with your hands." In my self-aggrandizing moods I considered calling it *Enormous Hosanna* after a line from Constance Urdang's "The World Is Full of Poets": "On days like this all the poets of the world/ Might soar to the skies, arm in arm with one another/ Like glorious brothers and sisters, to astonish/ The world, with a single enormous hosanna." I opted for *Vital Signs*, as an affirmation of the vitality and significance of contemporary American poetry. Actually, I don't think the book would make very good mulch. But it does make one damn fine hosanna.

Special thanks to Kathy Dauck for her extensive help with correspond-
ance; to Ruth Evans for her help in typing the manuscript; to Paul Chot-
less for his work in compiling the press lists; to Barbara Hanrahan and
Allen Fitchen for their advice and support; and to Margaret, Molly, and
Emily Wallace.

Notes

1. Here and elsewhere in the *Preface* I am indebted to Alan C. Golding, "A
History of American Poetry Anthologies," in Robert Von Hallberg, *Canons* (Chicago: University of Chicago Press, 1983), pp. 279–307.

VITAL SIGNS

Introduction

1   In the beginning of the great Modernist Period, when Gertrude Stein published *Tender Buttons* (1914), Robert Frost published *North of Boston* (1914) and *Mountain Interval* (1916), H. D. published *Sea Garden* (1916), T. S. Eliot published *Prufrock and Other Observations* (1917), and Ezra Pound published "Three Cantos" (1917), Howard Swayzee Buck, a Yale graduate student, published *The Tempering* (1919) as the inaugural volume in the Yale Series of Younger Poets. Composed largely of Buck's prize-winning undergraduate work, the collection was cited by *The Dial* as "a first book of verse wherein jubilant youthfulness, unwearied even in the poems of war experience, marches to gay pipes with a sweeping stride and an idealism unappalled." [1] Although few readers today would recognize Buck, or any of the other poets included in the early years of the Yale series, Yale's decision to publish original verse has had a dramatic impact on American poetry.

When Clarence Day (author of *Life With Father*) suggested to his brother, George Parmly Day (founder of Yale University Press), that Yale start a poetry series, he proposed "to afford a publishing medium for the work of young men and women who have not yet secured wide public recognition. It will include only such verse as seems to give the fairest promise for the future of American poetry, to the development of which it is hoped that the series may prove a stimulus." [2] If early Yale poets like Howard Buck, Darl Macleod Boyle, Viola Chittenden White, Medora C. Addison, Dean Belden Lyman, Jr., and Harold Vinal seem, in retrospect, not to have fulfilled the Press's hopes, Yale poets from about 1950 on have consistently given "the fairest promise," and the series as a whole has proved to be an incomparable "stimulus."

Under the distinguished editorships of W. H. Auden, Dudley Fitts, and Stanley Kunitz, Yale's "discovery" of such poets as Adrienne Rich, James Wright, W. S. Merwin, John Ashbery, Carolyn Forché, and others, secured its reputation as the most distinguished first book series in the country. In addition to "stimulating" the "development" of American poetry by publishing some of our best poets, Yale's series has served as a model for other university presses. In 1958, at the suggestion of Richard Wilbur, Wesleyan University Press implemented a poetry series which was to become perhaps even more influential than Yale's. With the resolve not to limit itself to first books, Wesleyan inaugurated its series with the publication of four volumes in 1959. Over the years Wesleyan has published more books than any other university press, featuring work by Yale winners and by many of America's most distinguished poets. In 1969, a decade after the inauguration of the Wesleyan series, Norman Holmes Pearson, one of Wesleyan's initial poetry board members, modestly reminisced: "Somehow the publishing of poetry, though not the writing of it, had been in the doldrums. The Wesleyan series helped to stir the air."[3] Stir the air it did, with the work of James Wright, James Dickey, Robert Bly, Marge Piercy, and others who would become some of our most admired and influential established poets.

With the distinguished examples of Yale and Wesleyan as stimulus, and with the proliferation of serious poets and writing programs across the country, over twenty university presses have now established lively poetry series: Louisiana State University in 1964; Massachusetts in 1965; Pittsburgh in 1968; Missouri in 1969; Illinois in 1971; Princeton, Florida, and Carnegie Mellon in 1975; Texas Tech and Virginia in 1976; Johns Hopkins in 1978; Georgia in 1979; Arkansas in 1980; Alabama in 1982; Chicago in 1983; Northeastern in 1984; Wisconsin and Ohio State in 1985; and Iowa in 1987. Most poets would agree that the university presses have kept poetry alive and thriving at a time when many factors are working against it, not the least of which has been the continuing erosion of the trade poetry lists. While few New York presses will now read any new poets at all, university presses read from 500 to 1500 manuscripts annually, publishing about sixty. Thus the responsibility for finding and promoting poets in America has largely fallen to the university presses, as it had to the small presses earlier in the century.

Since 1960, university presses have published over 900 volumes, in recent years surpassing the trade publishers not only in quantity but in quality. According to an interesting recent book-length study by Mary Biggs, among younger writers particularly, university press poets have garnered the lion's share of such awards as the Lamont, the Guggenheim, and the Academy of American Poets.[4] The Pulitzer Prize in Poetry has gone to university press books. It is therefore perhaps not hyperbole when Dan Masterson insists that university presses "have saved poetry in America" and Rita Dove affirms that without them "poetry would all but disappear in this country."

This anthology has three major purposes. First, to provide a rich overview of the best contemporary American poetry irrespective of publisher, age of poet, aesthetic program, or current status in the literary canon. Second, to showcase and celebrate the work of the university presses in discovering and supporting that poetry. Third, tentatively to suggest some questions about American poetry—its democratization, canonization, aesthetics, politics, and sociology—which might be pursued at greater length by other writers.

2   Affixed to the door of my office at the University of Wisconsin, for the delight and edification of passers-by, are several cartoons.

In one, a middle-aged woman, standing at the podium before a large crowd of people says, "Before I introduce tonight's author, I thought perhaps I'd read something of my own."

In another, a frowsy woman in the foreground, holding a bag of groceries as a dark figure in the background gets out of a Rolls Royce and approaches his walled mansion, explains to a friend in a pillbox hat: "He made it big in poetry."

In a third, a man in a hard hat with a noodle-shaped head, a cigarette dangling from his lip, sits at a bar reading aloud from a slim volume. The man on his right holds his nose and clutches his drink; the man on his left stares straight ahead plugging both ears with spaghetti arms; a third man is passed out, his sausage nose limp on the bar. The caption is: "Arthur's poetry reading gets mixed reviews."

In a fourth, a slightly balding, porcine man clings to the side of a mountain, clutching a portfolio. On the thin ledge above him, a frightened man in a lumberjack shirt edges precariously away. The bubble over the first man's head reads: "Would you care to read some of my poetry?"

In a fifth, a woman in a bathrobe, a kerchief tied around her stringy hair, sits in her kitchen reading to her vacuum cleaner, toaster, juicer-blender and coffee pot, arranged attentively on chairs in front of her. The caption notes: "In her spare time, Mrs. Bomblatt writes poetry and reads it to her friends."

In the last, a short man with bug eyes and a big cigar walks behind a tall man with whiskers and an outlandish hat. "You say you're a great poet, Floyd?" says the short man. "Right," replies the tall man. "Then why don't you make any money?" asks the short man. "I'm undiscovered," replies the tall man. "After you're discovered will you make a lot of money?" asks the short man. "We're discussing poetry, not plumbing," retorts the tall man.

These cartoons are all based on two familiar premises: that poets make no money and have no popular audience. The problems of market and audience have been so perennial for poets that they have gained the status of a popular joke, a convention known even to people who neither read nor think much about poetry. Interestingly enough, the cartoons do point to something that poets might like to preserve: the conviction that poets don't *write* for money, or for a particular audience. Robert Bly observes in *Talking All Morning,* "If the poets were on television and were able to reach everyone, I'm convinced that poetry would disintegrate in a matter of five to ten years. They would start thinking . . . not of the relationships they have to the poem, but of their relationship to the audience."[5] Louis Simpson in *A Company of Poets,* taking issue with Walt Whitman's famous statement that great poets need great audiences, agrees: "There can be no such thing as a great audience for poetry. An audience for bad writing—yes! The mark of the bad writer is that he is popular. . . . Real poetry cannot be popular in its own time."[6] If it were possible to write poetry for money and an audience, Bly and Simpson suggest, that poetry would be formulaic and programmatic.

But if the cartoons point up something that may be essential to serious poetry, they also point up something that remains troubling. Although the cartoons are funny, and poets themselves can laugh at them, problems of economics and audience present a very real dilemma for poets and publishers and ultimately for poetry itself: American society seems not to value poetry, and poets seem to be writing largely to themselves; because poetry makes little money and has a limited audience, it fails to compel enthusiastic support from trade publishers or to survive without subsidy.

The situation is, of course, not peculiar to the contemporary period, and the popular notion of a golden age of a large and informed readership for serious poetry is largely a myth. Poets and other serious writers have always had difficulties publishing their books and getting an audience. Walt Whitman had to self-publish *Leaves of Grass,* and when he did, the *Saturday Review* called it "garbage." Even Emerson, who praised the book in a letter, omitted Whitman from his own anthology, *Parnassus.* Emily Dickinson's query to T. W. Higginson at *The Atlantic,* "Are you too deeply occupied to say if my verse is alive?" was met with befuddlement and rejection. Poe self-published his *Poems* in 1831; Frost self-published his first book, *Twilight,* in a two-copy edition in 1894, and had to go to England to publish his more mature work; A. R. Ammons published his first book with a vanity press in 1955.

Other poets went to small presses for their initial book publications. Marianne Moore and T. S. Eliot published with the Egoist Press in London, and Eliot's *Prufrock and Other Observations* took five years to sell out 500 copies. Robert Lowell's first book, *Land of Unlikeness,* was published by the Cummington Press in 1944, and Allen Ginsberg turned to his friend Lawrence Ferlinghetti at City Lights Books to publish *Howl.* Trade publishers remained uninterested in these poets until they had built their reputations and found an audience through self and small press publication. Thus poets, who are stereotypically unworldly, unconcerned with business and commerce, have had to work harder to find publishers and distribute their work than most other writers or artists. In many cases they have started their own presses, and carried books with them as they travelled, foisting poems off on whomever they could.

Trade publishers are not, however, quite the villains they are sometimes made out to be, nor have university presses quite single-handedly saved poetry from extinction over the past thirty years. The popular view is that during the 1960s and 1970s mergers and conglomerate take-overs and the profit motive prompted most New York presses to abandon their poetry programs, and that university presses stepped in to fill the gap. The commercial book-publishing industry, which was thought to be a low-key gentlemanly profession, where personal satisfactions out-weighed financial rewards, was now controlled by such corporate inter-ests as Gulf & Western, which acquired Simon & Schuster, and RCA, which acquired Random House. Caring more for the bottom line than for the good line, businessmen fostered a blockbuster mentality, hustling for best-selling cookbooks, diet plans, sensational political reports, and novels that could be sold to the movies. Although this scenario is more or less true, it is misleading. For one thing, it was hardly a new phenom-enon, and it affected the publishing of poetry, which was small to begin with, much less adversely than is commonly thought.

The romantic view of the gentleman publisher in New York, writing eloquent long letters to his authors, is largely sentimental. As Robert Dana points out in *Against the Grain,* "there is enough evidence in the biographies of T. S. Eliot, Henry Miller, James Joyce, Anaïs Nin, and others to confirm an unsentimental perspective, to suggest that personal indifference to both the plights and triumphs of writers has been all along the prevailing editorial style."[7] And poetry has long been the bastard child. As long ago as 1900, Edmund Clarence Stedman, the first Ameri-can anthologist to give Whitman, Emerson, Poe, and Dickinson their due, noted the "public indifference to the higher forms of poetry," as fiction, since the mid-1870s, had come to dominate the book market at poetry's expense. "While fetching trifles are taken up by the press," Sted-man fondly hoped for "poesy's return to dignity and favor."[8]

Similarly, an enlightening symposium reported in the October 1949 issue of *Poetry* has the clear ring of something that could have been writ-ten (and has been written) about the publishing situation in the 1960s and 1970s or today. Hayden Carruth notes that "the costs of publication have increased sharply, making it more and more difficult to publish cer-tain kinds of books. Several publishers have dropped poetry altogether, others have reduced the numbers of poets on their lists. . . . The evils of the present situation among publishers—the pressures of best-seller sys-tems, advertising schemes, etc.—have spread so far into the literary structure, have affected so many types of writers, that I believe the whole idea of professionalism in writing is endangered." Alan Swallow, founder of Swallow Press, and Albert Erskine, an editor at Random House, were less gloomy about the situation. Swallow urged that "the large foundations should surely revise their plans so that they can support serious publishing . . . and the institutional press (chiefly the university press) needs to support serious publishing of poetry." And Erskine, noting that poets have always had difficulties finding publishers, predicted that "two or three years hence it will probably be easier again for poets to find publishers, because printing costs will have come down."[9]

Come down they did, and by the time most university presses entered the scene, the poetry publishing industry was relatively booming. Buoyed by affluence, an expanding economy, cheap offset printing, and heavy federal spending for social welfare, including public schools, colleges, and libraries, small press and commercial publishers expanded dramatically. Financial and industrial leaders began to think that book publishing might be a good investment, given the promise of an expanding education market and the notion that computer interactive teaching would make the combination of publishers' software with electronics hardware the wave of the future. The energy and optimism evident in the civil rights movement, community organization, anti-Vietnam protest, and the proliferation of writers and writing programs, carried over into the publishing world as well, and in this spirit of enthusiasm trade presses expanded, and hundreds of small presses sprang up all over the country.

In the period 1955–60, the first period for which reliable figures are available, trade presses published, on the average, under thirty single-author new poetry books per year. From 1960–65 the total increased to nearly fifty books per year. In 1966, perhaps in response to the government's commitment of Title II funds to schools and libraries, the figure jumped to over seventy, and from 1966–76, the period when many university press poetry series were getting established, trade presses published an average of over eighty books per year, peaking at one hundred in 1972. Over the past decade, the number of trade press poetry titles has slipped back to around fifty, reflecting rising costs, small returns, and perhaps even the competition of the university presses themselves.[10]

Over the same period, university presses consistently expanded, from a handful of books published annually in the 1950s, to about twenty per year in the early 1970s, forty in the early 1980s, and an average of sixty annually over the past few years. Although most university presses thus established their series when the trade presses were expanding, not decreasing their lists, the trade presses could not have accommodated the wealth of good poetry being written during the period. And in the last decade, while continuing to publish well-established poets, the trade presses have pretty much completely abandoned the publishing of new and mid-career poets to the university and small presses.

University presses began publishing poetry for a variety of reasons: the decision that such publishing was congruent with their mission to publish quality but economically marginal books; the observation that, despite expansion, the trade houses, true to their historical role, still published few or no first books; the mood of expansion in the country as a whole; government support through direct grants to presses, arts boards, and libraries; the growing commitment of the university to creative writing programs; and the sense that the university press was economically suited to publishing poetry.

Originally, of course, the university press was solely the province of the scholarly monograph, often the research of local faculty members. Its visibility in the public world was slight and its profile was low. While criticism of poetry was deemed appropriate, poetry itself was considered to be incongruous with a press's mission. In 1951 when Hayden Carruth, for example, approached the University of Chicago Press about publishing poetry, he was given a flat "no". "An academic press was for the publication of academic materials and that was that."[11] As presses proliferated in the 1950s and 1960s, their range expanded, and they became publishers of academic works from campuses generally.

In the 1960s and the 1970s, an influx of editors and staff from the trade presses, unhappy with the direction New York publishers seemed to be taking, broadened the role of the university press even further. Seeking greater prestige, and recognizing the continuum between creative writing, research, and teaching, presses began the poetry and fiction series that continue today.

At the outset, in the 1960s and early 1970s, the university presses operated more like small presses than trade presses, seeing their role as the discovery of new talent. Their non-profit status, and their ability to attract volunteer labor from faculty members and local poets, enabled them to take the financial risks of publishing new poets that only small presses had traditionally been prepared to take. As Beverly Jarrett of

Louisiana State University Press observes, "Our non-profit status suits us for publishing non-profit poetry. Our dedication to culture *obliges* us to publish poetry." Paul Zimmer concurs, "And just *who* can truly afford to test unknown talent through publication? As the editor of one of the most active poetry lists in the country (Pittsburgh—Zimmer is now at Iowa), I am increasingly aware of how much the burden has fallen to the small press and the university press." [12] With trade presses increasingly unwilling or unable to publish books in editions of 500–2,000 copies, university presses found that that figure suited their smaller operations perfectly. Subsidized often by their universities, and unfettered by the marketplace mentality that characterized larger houses, the university presses could take economic risks.

But the university press was more than just another small press. With so many small presses publishing hundreds of new books annually, poets risked getting lost in the crush. The prestige of the university press name on a book was more likely to gain poets attention and public recognition. If the university press was in some ways a small press, it was a very prestigious small press, discovering those poets who would go on to publish with the trade houses eventually. Thus many of Yale's and Wesleyan's early poets, and some of Pittsburgh's, Missouri's, and Louisiana State University's, went on to publish with trade houses. The system has been likened to that of a baseball farm club that develops a player for the big leagues.

But the commitment of many university press poetry programs was too strong to remain for long in the minor leagues. When New York's expansionary period peaked in 1972, and trade poetry lists began slipping back to the levels of the early 1960s, trade editors were faced with a dilemma. If they were to continue publishing new work by poets they had taken on in the 1950s and 1960s, they would be unable to publish poets new to their lists who had developed reputations through small press and university press publication. Increasingly, the trade presses published only their own poets, and today the doors are virtually closed to poets who are not already on a trade backlist.

Thus, the university press has gradually taken on the original role of the trade press, publishing established poets. With a few bright exceptions, poetry publishing in New York now seems to be in a period of stagnation, while the most exciting work of younger and older poets alike is coming out of the university presses.

Faced with this changing situation, several university presses shifted their programs away from an emphasis on first books. Pittsburgh, for example, under the innovative editorship of Ed Ochester, now publishes one or two first books and four or five "veterans" annually, with at least one book by a poet not previously on the Pitt list. Wesleyan has similarly expanded its program, and Iowa, under the editorship of Paul Zimmer, has recently implemented a series which will publish *only* poets who have already published at least one book. Having begun largely as a small press publisher of poetry, the university press has now surpassed the trade press in success and prestige, moving into the big leagues and winning, if not pennants, then Pulitzers.

There seems to be only one area in which the university press may be inferior to the trade press. Although the economics of publishing poetry in a mass market culture favors the university press, enabling it to publish economically marginal books and keep them in print years longer than any trade press can afford to do, it is economics that also limits the distribution and marketing capabilities. Most poets in this anthology agree that distribution and marketing are the most serious unsolved problems faced by university presses, and most believe that New York presses are better equipped in these areas.

While it is true that trade presses have the capability to distribute and advertise books widely, it is also true that they rarely invest the money in their poetry books to do so, reserving it for more commercial books. In fact, several poets, who have published with both New York and university presses, strongly prefer the latter. Alicia Ostriker, for example, refers to her experience publishing her first book of poems with Holt Rinehart as "a disaster." "Nothing much was done to distribute it, or encourage me. . . . The book was soon remaindered, and, with lightning speed and no forewarning, pulped." Carol Muske's experience with Doubleday was similar. Although Muske praises Sandy Richardson (the editor-in-chief) and Barbara Trainer as strong advocates for poetry, "No promotion at all was done for my book and it was printed on paper you could see through. . . . They printed 6,000 copies of *Skylight* and they told me the computer would kick out any book that hadn't sold at least that amount.

The alternatives at that point would be the remainder bin or the shredder." The experiences of Miller Williams and Robert Wallace at Dutton reinforce the pattern. Dutton let Williams' books go out of print before the reviews were in, and Wallace, who "was treated royally (dinners at expensive French restaurants)" when his first book proved successful, was "rapidly demoted (lunch at a little Italian place around the corner . . . and then just a cup of coffee in the office)" when his second book did less well. Michael Harper's Doubleday book was "out of print in six weeks."

Although a few poets reported that their experience with New York presses was preferable to that with university presses, most noted their frustration with junior editors, lack of press commitment to poetry, unreasonable market expectations, premature shredding and remaindering, and small commitment of the extensive resources available for other books. What this suggests is that trade presses are, finally, no better at marketing and distributing poetry than university presses, and in some ways, may be worse. As Dave Smith observes, "Convinced poetry does not sell, they make little effort to sell it, and it therefore doesn't sell—unless by accident or fad."

The university press may be inferior to the small press in at least one way. Just as the trade press has an economic commitment that prevents it from risking the publishing of new poets, so the university press may have a cultural commitment that prevents it from risking the publishing of the extremely experimental or avant-garde. In fact, several groups of avant-garde poets have recently established their own presses in competition with university presses. The small press will probably remain the source of discovery of avant-garde poets, as the university press tends more toward mainstream work, though some presses do boast some lively experimental poetry on their lists.

Thus, the university press seems ideally suited to publishing poetry. Combining the prestige, visibility, and professionalism of a New York press with the artistic integrity, personal commitment, and non-profit status of a small press, the university press is thriving at a time when there are more and better manuscript collections available than ever before.

In fact, the slippage of poetry from trade presses may have less to do with corporate take-overs and best-seller mentalities, than with pure market competition. According to a 1978 survey of publishing patterns from 1952–77, *Poets & Writers* concluded that "poetry is a staple of the small presses, and the quantity, quality, and distribution facilities of small presses have grown greatly since 1972. The decline in trade hardcover poetry may reflect competition by small presses. Unlike hardcover fiction, hardcover poetry is vulnerable to small press competition because hardcover poetry is not usually carried by bookstores serving the general reading public and thus has little distribution advantage over small press books. Small press books and trade poetry alike are sold primarily to libraries and at special literary bookstores, competing on almost equal footing. . . . Trade hardcovers may have some advantage in getting reviews and library sales, but this seems to be changing." [13] It may be that trade presses just can't compete with university presses in the specialized field of poetry.

Despite New York's lukewarm attitude toward poetry, the present situation seems a healthy one. Together, the trade, university, and small presses publish, on the average, nearly 400 poetry books a year. If trade presses or small presses were suddenly to discontinue their unique contributions to poetry, or if the university presses were unable to expand to meet the needs of the poets who rely on them, poetry would be in trouble once again. But, for now, the balance seems strong.

3   The rise of the university press as a publisher of poetry can be explained, in part, by a shift in perceived mission and by the favorable economic, political, and social conditions of the 1960s and 1970s which gave rise to a general expansion in the publishing business. But it is also importantly dependent on another factor—the concomitant proliferation of graduate and undergraduate programs in creative writing. When Yale University Press initiated its Younger Poets Series in 1919, neither creative writing nor contemporary literature was thought to be an appropriate subject for study in the classroom. Today not only are creative writing and contemporary literature taught in the classroom, but there are nearly 300 degree-granting creative writing programs in the country, and creative writing is becoming a staple of public school curriculums

from the graduate schools to the grade schools. If these creative writing programs haven't solved the problems of market and audience focused by the cartoons described earlier, they have gone a good way toward addressing them.

In the early twentieth century, poets lived on inherited or family money (Jeffers, Hart Crane, George Oppen), professional income (Stevens, Moore, Eliot, Williams), or a miscellaneous combination of friends' largesse and menial jobs (Pound, Lindsay). As long ago as 1842, Rufus Wilmot Griswold argued in his *The Poets and Poetry of America* that poets "should receive as much of the fostering care of government as is extended to the agriculturist or manufacturer," [14] and in the 1949 *Poetry* symposium, Alan Swallow added that "the large foundations should surely revise their plans so that they can support serious publishing as well as individual writers." [15] In 1965, the NEA began supporting individual poets and presses to a degree that would have surprised Griswold and Swallow. Together, the government and the university became the institutional patrons that poets had long hoped for. Although poets were still not making money directly from their poetry, they were making money in related ways—through teaching, directing programs, giving readings, and obtaining grants. Today, most poets in America are connected with universities. Nearly all of the poets in this anthology teach, although several are free-lance writers, one is a professional actor, one a body work therapist, and one an insurance man. Given the opportunities of university and governmental support, the stereotype of the penniless poet may be going the way of the absent-minded professor, the henpecked husband, and the country bumpkin.

It is sometimes argued that such support is somehow bad for poetry, that poets should be "out in the world" gaining experience for their art. It seems doubtful, however, that university life insulates poets from their proper material any more than Eliot, Williams, and Stevens were insulated by their careers in banking and publishing, doctoring, and selling insurance. One has to look fairly hard, in fact, to find any specific material from the professional lives of the great modernists in their writing.

Further, the phenomenon of university teaching and publishing of poetry is really part of an ancient and honorable tradition. As Michael

Heffernan points out, "The earliest Roman poets, even before Vergil and Horace, published their works for distribution among themselves, usually in connection with poetry workshops in academies of master poets who were professional rhetoricians and verse-makers. Pagan Irish poetry flourished in the same way. Monastic scriptoriums were really university presses. So, in a sense, the American university press embodies the oldest publishing tradition." John Barth similarly defends university creative writing programs in a recent *New York Times Book Review* article. According to Barth, the programs are based on ways authors have always acquired "authority"—"first, by paying a certain sort of attention to the experience of life as well as merely undergoing it; second, by paying a certain sort of attention to the works of their great and less great predecessors in the medium of written language, as well as merely reading them; third, by practicing that medium themselves, usually a *lot* . . . ; and fourth, by offering their apprentice work for discussion and criticism by one or several of their impassioned peers, or by some more experienced hand, or by both." [16]

Workshops and creative writing programs do more, therefore, than merely provide a place of employment for poets. They also provide an audience for poetry, and a source of good new poets who will go on to publish with university presses. Poetry readings, which had been stimulated by the Beat Poets in the 1950s, became an active part of the literary curriculum in the 1960s, as poets protested the Vietnam war in verse, reinforcing the social and political dimension of poetry and raising poetry's visibility. Stimulated by this energy and commitment on the part of poets, audiences grew, and more and more students began to write seriously. The university and the writing programs didn't so much create an audience as identify and consolidate one that was already there. Robert Frost affirmed years ago in his introduction to *New Poets of England and America,* "As I often say a thousand, two thousand, colleges, town and gown together in the little town they make, give us the best audiences for poetry ever had in all this world." [17]

Thus the university, through its presses and its writing programs, has become one of the most responsible patrons of both new and established poets from the middle of this century on. The university has become the teacher of poetry and poetry writing, and the publisher, credentialer, and employer of poets. It has provided what poets have longed for: an audience, a livelihood, and an aesthetic and intellectual community. Today there are more magazines and presses publishing poetry, more courses in poetry and poetry writing, more people buying and reading poetry, and more people feeling compelled to attack or criticize poetry and the system that supports it, than ever before.

4   Although there have been complaints that poets have adopted a defensive self-boosterism and self-congratulation in the face of an embarrassment of riches, there is also considerable self-flagellation, as the most cursory glance at any current issue of *The American Book Review,* the *American Poetry Review,* or the *AWP Newsletter* will reveal. Poets are their own biggest detractors, full of self-doubt and mistrust of the system that supports them. Perhaps condemnation is easier than celebration. Perhaps attack is one way of setting oneself apart from the mediocre masses. Or perhaps the critical temper is just the natural consequence of university life, where healthy skepticism and enquiry have always been valued and promoted for their own sake.

Thus, reviewing Paul Carroll's *The Young American Poets,* John Haines writes, "The truth may be that we have no great poets among us today . . . at a time when poetry, or its imitation, has become part of the free enterprise system; it is almost a commodity among us. Workshops, university courses, degrees in creative writing—perhaps never before has there been so great an interest in poetry, so many people trying to write it, so many magazines publishing it, so much money going to support it. . . . So much activity, such a proliferation of talent, might be taken as evidence of great creative vitality, but it can also be seen as an unmistakable sign of decay." [18] Similarly, Robert Bly remarks in *Talking All Morning,* "I was thinking of this only yesterday: that the university system, which seems in the beginning so sweet, where one can go in as a younger poet and find an older poet whom you admire to work with, causes everything to break down. We're living in a swamp of mediocrity, poetry of the Okefenokee, in which a hundred and fifty mediocre books . . . are published every year." [19] Bly would send a poet not to the university, but to a shack in the woods and isolation for two years. Philip Levine sees many university press poetry lists as "full of dead weight" and "mediocrity." Gary Miranda muses, "University presses have kept American poetry alive over the past twenty years, though 'alive' in this case is the equivalent of being on an artificial respirator. American poetry is not healthy, though whether it is terminally ill remains to be seen." And Greg Kuzma, in a vitriolic attack in the September 1986 issue of *Poetry,* places the blame squarely on the whole university poetry network. "The old sweet antagonism between the academic and the creative writer has disappeared. . . . For the serious scholar as well as for the serious poet, the new communion of the rival arts dooms both, since little of any good and worthy work is going to come out of English Departments who have sold their souls to 'creative writing.' . . . What is so special about our current scene—so discouraging—is the terrible vastness of the mass, volume, and weight of mediocrity that afflicts us." [20]

The critics tend to focus the same themes—there are too many poets, the mass of poetry is merely competent or mediocre, the whole system fosters conservatism, boredom, and inbreeding. These are serious charges which can be answered, if not completely refuted, and it is good periodically to be made accountable.

The charge that there are too many poets is the one which, at first, seems most factual and least debatable. Nearly 4,000 poets are now listed in the *Poets and Writers Directory,* and this only includes those poets who have already published work. Paul Zimmer speculates that "There are certainly more poets per square mile in America than at any time in the history of the world." [21] And John Engels worries about the consequences: "Now there are crowds out there—and where are the poet-heroes of yesteryear, the Lowells, Schwartzes, Thomases, Audens, etc.? Lost in the crowds, some would say. They do not necessarily fight their way out of the pack."

And yet, this perception isn't new. In the April 1927 issue of *Poetry,* Associate Editor George H. Dillon painted as gloomy a picture as any contemporary critic could concoct: "One wonders in just what extreme of batik-bound fatuousness this current mania for publication will culminate. The truth is, that it can go no further. The extreme is already reached; the show is over; it is time to ring the curtain down. . . . It is easy to imagine what an unsettling effect such a fad must have on the nation in general. One thinks of book-keepers in Kansas City, and housewives in Milwaukee, suddenly disregarding their daily duties and pinning the faith of their lives to orgiastic day-dreams of poetic fame; of perfectly normal and potentially happy people everywhere suddenly becoming temperamental, melancholy, and restless. One sees innocent-eyed college students flunking their exams in order to write little lyrics about passion and poppies. . . . Indeed, it has become one of our great national pastimes, succeeding such pleasantries as embroidery and anagrams, ping-pong and charades, and ranking with cross-word puzzles." [22] Dillon proposed to pack all the slim volumes *Poetry* had received for review over the year into a truck and dump them into Lake Michigan. In 1938, when the first *Biographical Dictionary of Contemporary American Poets* was published, the editors listed more than 2,000 poets who had published substantial amounts of verse in books and magazines, and referred to "many thousands" of others who were omitted for lack of space or inability to locate the poet. In 1949, Hayden Carruth, then the young editor of *Poetry,* noted that the magazine received approximately 3,000 manuscripts per month, from which they could accept about twenty poems. There seem to have been too many poets in 1927, 1938, and 1949 as well as today, and there probably always will be. It also seems likely that the great poets will, as they have in the past, continue to surface. From the poetry manuscripts submitted to the University of Wisconsin Press in 1985, the first year of our Brittingham Prize in Poetry competition, over half of the twenty finalists we were unable to accept have now been published by other presses. Given the daunting odds, some good manuscripts may never be published, but many of the best do survive.

The claim of "sameness" and mediocrity, which is heavily dependent on personal taste and opinion, is more difficult to answer with assurance. Marieve Rugo notes, "In an area which looks like diversity, there is much sameness." Paul Zimmer speculates that perhaps we live not in a golden or even silver age of poetry, but in an "age of aluminum," an "age of competence." And Donald Hall, in the February 1987 issue of the *AWP Newsletter,* charges that our major contribution to literature is "the McPoem—Ten billion served." [23]

In the 1950s the kind of poetry to which Hall refers was called "academic poetry"—a term that evoked writing that was dull, pedantic, studied, unoriginal, and establishment. "Academic poetry" was the kind favored by the New Critics, and characterized by irony, detachment, wit, learning, and overt technical skill. Robert Lowell called this poetry "cooked," in contrast to the "raw" poetry of the Beats and New York Poets, and Donald Hall's anthology, *New Poets of England and America,* became identified by some as its handbook.

The notion of "academic poetry" no longer applies to many contemporary writers. Ironically, as the poets went into the academy, the academy went out of the poets. But the term has been replaced with an equally derogatory one—"the workshop poem." The workshop poem is a kind of generic minor effort, written off quickly and to some formula, an exercise. It is competent, amiable, and reproducible. It is marked by decorum or propriety, and an off-hand slickness of tone or voice. The language is simple, the images archetypal, the mood personal, the line short and Hemingwayesque, the subject matter mundane and sentimental. The poem is accessible, modest, and symmetrical. There is little discursive thought, or visionary passion, or relentless experimentalism. This kind of poem is, however, not the creation of the workshop; it is the normal route of most young poets. One could easily find poems by Yeats, Frost, and Williams that sound remarkably like "workshop poems," if only because they are not the few major works we know those poets by. Like the great poets of the past, our contemporary poets have written their share of merely competent poems. Time, and anthologies like this one, will tell whether their best work is finally major or minor.

It is true, and arguably lamentable, that the trade and university presses tend to preserve the conservative mainsteam. There is little radical experimentation, little extreme political poetry, little ethnic dialect, little of the avant-garde, little of the flamboyance associated with the great modernists. It remains the important role of the alternative presses and magazines to support such innovative work. Richard Kostelanetz points out in his essay "Avant-Garde," "Some artistic experiments are based upon personal incompetence. When Arnold Schoenberg told his pupil John Cage that he had no talent for harmony, the young man disregarded harmony in his musical experiments; when Gertrude Stein was told her writing was often ungrammatical, she made her principal experiment the possibilities of ungrammatical English. In our time, experiments with insufficiency are more interesting, more heroic, than the exploitation of virtuosity."[24] The workshop is not likely to foster, and the university press is not likely to publish, experiments with insufficiency.

As to the claim that all our poets begin to sound alike, that is probably true in any age, and it is partly what enables literary critics to identify periods of literary history. More interesting, perhaps, than the claim of sameness is the question of what period style and voice we are developing out of the diversity and eclecticism around us, by which we will be characterized in the future.

Finally, it is perhaps instructive to remember that there seems to be a tendency in any period to devalue the work of one's contemporaries as shallow or narrow or in some way not up to the great writers of the past. T. W. Higginson thought Emily Dickinson had a deaf ear; Rufus Wilmot Griswold dismissed Walt Whitman's *Leaves of Grass* as a "gathering of muck"; Louis Untermeyer thought T. S. Eliot's *The Waste Land* was a "pompous parade of erudition." In fact, the criticisms of the poetry scene over the past 150 years are reassuringly familiar. Griswold, in his 1842 anthology, notes that he "accepted more that was relatively poor" because "our poets have generally written with too little preparation, and too hastily, to win enduring reputations."[25] Edmund Clarence Stedman, who included Whitman, Dickinson, Poe, and Emerson in his 1900 anthology, called the period "a twilight interval, with minor voices and their tentative modes and tones."[26] And James Dickey, reviewing Donald Hall's 1958 anthology observed, "Most of these are *occasional* poets; most have been schooled or have learned to pick up pretty nearly any scene or object from memory and make acceptable poetic currency of it."[27]

But the very real and troubling question of the impact of university teaching, funding, and publishing of poetry, remains. When poets themselves become teachers, students, writers, readers, judges, publishers, and promoters, literary power is organized in a way that encourages inbreeding and insularity, and could end up creating a closed system.

5   So far, however, that has not been the case. Although a number of the university press directors polled in my survey held fairly modest views on the influence of university presses on American poetry, it seems

clear that the university presses have had great impact in two areas: their numbers and regional locations across the country have influenced the democratization of poetry, and their submission procedures and editorial policies have opened and directed the poetic canon dramatically.

Not so very long ago if you wanted to be a poet you had to leave the provinces and venture to New York or, perhaps, San Francisco. Then, in the 1960s, with the establishment of writing programs across the country, and with the power in poetry publishing shifting from trade to university presses, poets started staying in the provinces. New York and California were no longer the poetry capitals of America, and what was happening in other parts of the country came to seem as exciting as, or more exciting than, what was happening on the coasts. The number and locations of writing programs and university presses led to a new diversity and pluralism; it was no longer necessary to have literary "connections" to succeed as a writer and find a publisher.

Some years ago, Barry Commoner proposed a visionary solution to the growing energy crisis. Rather than maintaining a few centralized power stations that pumped energy great distances and used up our finite natural resources of coal, oil and gas, Commoner proposed a network of sources, a vast power grid made up of small facilities across the country, using whatever renewable resources were available in the region—solar energy, wind power, the burning of garbage, hydroelectric power, the production of methanol from corn. Everyone, in some way, would be involved in the production of energy. This visionary proposal, not soon to be adopted in this country, is a passable metaphor for what has happened with poetry. The large, centralized power centers (New York, California) and the big producers of energy (Eliot, Pound) have been replaced by a power grid spread across the country (university writing programs and presses). Fred Chappell comments, "The greatest contribution of the university press has been in the prevention of ruling cliques." Elizabeth Spires concurs that "university presses have helped in the democratization of American poetry—*not* in the leveling of literary or poetic standards, but in taking serious poetic endeavor out of the hands of a literary 'elite' and opening up opportunities for those talented poets not necessarily affiliated or connected with an 'academy.'" And Alicia Ostriker concludes, "Part of the health of American poetry at present . . . stems from its diversity. We don't have a single dominant poet or group of poets. . . . We have not a capital city surrounded meekly by the provinces, but a fine array of regional traditions. This state of things satisfies my notion of what the state of the arts should be in a large democracy. Obviously, the university presses have played a great part in creating it."

This democratization does not satisfy everyone, and some detractors have argued that we now have no "great" poets. Indeed, the popular myth of "the great poet" may not survive the democratizing spirit. The notion that the poet is some kind of special being, in touch with mysteries the rest of us can't comprehend, seems a thing of the past. As Richard Hugo points out in *The Triggering Town*, "Giants are not the style of the society, though the wind knows there are enough people who want to create them, and not just a few who want to be them. I think we'll end up with a lot of fine poets, each doing his thing." [28] Philip Levine remarks in *Don't Ask*, "You won't find a man more sensitive than you, you won't find a light and airy spirit. I'm not a 'special case.' I'm a man who is more articulate than most people and one who found something called poetry quite early in life, grew to love it, determined to make it, and because of his stubbornness is some thirty years later still trying." [29]

One can argue that we are not producing immortals. It is harder to argue that we are not producing more poetry of high quality than ever before. It has been suggested, in fact, that if we are not producing a few great poets, we may be producing many poets who together are producing a great poetry. Denis Donoghue, in a 1978 *New York Times Book Review* article, suggests "the current mood enhances the notion of poetry as a collective act rather than an individual assertion. . . . Grandeur, especially of the bardic kind, is out of phase. . . . But for the moment I am not impatient to see American poets jumping off the deep end, playing Hamlet, or competing for a starring role in some sequel to 'The Bridge' provisionally titled 'Ginsberg Two.' " [30] Donoghue may be right, though Dave Smith has listed twenty contemporary poets he considers "great" (ten of whom are in this volume), and I could list a dozen more.

Although many factors have influenced the democratization of poetry over the past twenty-five years, university press editorial policies and selection procedures have been centrally important. Unlike those of some small presses and trade presses in the past, university press selection procedures have fostered democracy, resisting any particular political or aesthetic program that might limit them. As I noted earlier, before the establishment of university press poetry programs, most poets first published with small presses. While these small presses have been instrumental in publishing and promoting some of the best poets of this century, they have often catered to a particular kind of work or a particular group of poets. City Lights, Tibor di Nagy, and Black Sparrow, for example, had their cadre of poets and were unlikely to consider anything that didn't fit the mode. In Robert Dana's *Against the Grain*, John Martin of Black Sparrow Press summarizes what is not an uncommon procedure of small presses: "I published Robert Kelly. . . . And Kelly was pals with Diane Wakoski. And Wakoski was pals with Clayton Eshelman. And Eshelman was pals with Jerome Rothenberg. And Rothenberg was pals with David Antin." [31] If you was not pals with one of these poets, you was not likely be read at all, much less published.

Trade presses have worked in a similar way. James Laughlin of New Directions, for example, admits in Bill Henderson's *The Art of Literary Publishing*, "That's really the way that New Directions has grown. Most of our writers have come to us through the recommendations of another writer friend." [32] Thus, Laughlin's Harvard friend Delmore Schwartz recommended his friends Berryman and Jarrell; Pound recommended Williams; Rexroth recommended Levertov and Rothenberg. Of course, not all trade and small presses have operated in this way, and those that have, have in some cases published our most distinguished and irreplaceable writers.

But when presses refuse even to read new work by writers not recommended to them, the method is exclusive and exclusionary, favoring those who are talented at making powerful connections and knowing the right people. University presses, on the other hand, have gone out of their way to avoid even the appearance of nepotism or favoritism. With few exceptions, university presses have always had open submissions policies, reading manuscripts by anyone who wanted to submit, regardless of pals, affiliations, or aesthetic proclivities.

Open submissions policies, however, have resulted in a major logistical problem for university presses: how to deal fairly with the hundreds of manuscripts which are submitted annually. Some presses now receive between 500 and 1,500 submissions each year, and sheer numbers could work against the poet whose poetry is "difficult," or different, not accessible on a first reading. On the other hand, the bulk of submissions could enable the truly original and unique manuscript to stand out. In any case, the competition is fierce, and anyone who claims it is easy to publish with a good press today hasn't entered what are sometimes referred to as the "sweepstakes."

But the university press series are not finally sweepstakes, because of the meticulous attention given to the selection process. Various presses have adopted various ways of handling submissions. Many presses employ a single series editor who makes decisions himself. Currently James Merrill edits the Yale series, Ed Ochester the Pittsburgh series, Gerald Costanzo the Carnegie Mellon series, Laurence Lieberman the Illinois series, John Irwin the Johns Hopkins series, Miller Williams the Arkansas series, and Thomas Rabbitt and Chase Twichell the Alabama series. The single editor method has the possible disadvantage of a narrow range of selections, reflecting the editor's tastes, but it has the distinct advantage of giving a character to a series, and allowing the kind of risky or idiosyncratic choice that a small press editor might make. Ed Ochester is an articulate spokesman for this method. "Maybe it's because Pittsburgh isn't New York or Bolinas or Iowa City, maybe it's because committees don't make our editorial decisions, but it does seem to me that no other press has a more varied poetry list. I'm not sure, given the divergence of styles and tastes, that I'd like to have all our poets together under one tent for a cocktail party, but I like them together in the catalogue. I like the fact that so many of them are, relatively speaking, loners unsupported by powerful school associations or critical power brokers." [33]

Although most presses employ initial screening readers, some do not. When Stanley Kunitz became editor of the Yale series in 1975, for example, he opted to read all 700 manuscripts himself, fearing that a screener might leave him with conventional, safe choices, while the most original manuscripts would be lost in the shuffle. Similarly, Missouri employs a single judge to read all of its submissions.

Other presses employ a single editor who seeks outside advice and forms a group decision. At Georgia, Bin Ramke confers with an outside judge and the press director, and at Chicago, Robert Von Hallberg confers with two anonymous outside poets.

Wisconsin, Princeton, Northeastern, and Missouri all employ distinguished outside judges, who rotate from year to year. An outside judge provides impartiality (or at least a continual shifting of partialities), and can help ensure variety as the judge changes from year to year. But an outside judge has no ongoing commitment to a particular press or series, and may not be willing, as a single permanent editor would be, to put his or her reputation on the line with an unconventional choice.

Louisiana State University, Wesleyan, and Massachusetts all draw readers from a stable board or pool of poets. Beverly Jarrett says of L.S.U.'s method of selection, "Speaking generously, one might call our review process 'open;' speaking less generously, one might call it 'haphazard.' What these friendly and unfriendly adjectives mean is that we read poetry manuscripts by anybody at almost any time. . . . In order to sustain and strengthen the breadth of our poetry series we've resisted the temptation to rely on two or three outside readers exclusively. There are nearly a dozen established poets whom we regularly call on for readings." [34]

Despite the differences, the selection procedures at nearly all of the university presses are the same in two important ways. Poets, rather than what Dave Smith calls "the typical junior editor in New York: age 24, Vassar B.A., not yet trusted with the 'real work'—fiction or cookbooks," make the decisions; and submissions are open to anyone who cares to submit.

It is interesting to compare two recent and innovative publishing programs, as a final example of the differing premises behind trade and university press publishing. Believing that "democratic procedure for publishing poetry does not produce good books," Daniel Halpern initiated the National Poetry Series in 1978 with a generous subsidy from James Michener and the Ford Foundation, among others. Halpern enlisted five New York presses to participate, and, given the no-risk financial arrangement and the prestige involved, they were only too happy to oblige. In the first years of the series four books were selected annually through a closed process, established poet-judges selecting manuscripts from poets with whom they were familiar. One book was selected in an open competition.

At about the same time the Associated Writing Programs instituted the AWP Award Series in Poetry. Composed of member creative writing programs across the country, the AWP series was founded on the premise, according to Walton Beacham, "that if we consolidate our resources and attract a steady audience for poetry, university and small presses can fill the gap commercial houses have left." Employing an elaborate reading system in which four poets screened the 1500 manuscripts submitted in an open competition to 200, and then those 200 were screened by other poets to 100, and those were screened by others to 25 which went to a final judge, the system was completely open and democratic, using a grass roots method. The winning volume was published, and the AWP then acted as an agent, promoting the other finalists to a network of university presses. A substantial number of AWP finalist books have since been published.[35]

It would be difficult to prove that one of the two methods produced better books. But recently, when asked by Robert Dana in *Against the Grain* how he felt about the National Poetry Series selections, Daniel Halpern confessed that he was "disappointed." He hadn't expected his poet-judges to select their friends.[36] By 1988, several university and small presses had replaced some of the original New York presses, and all five of the National Poetry Series books were selected in an open competition.

6   The democratization of poetry has not pleased everyone. John Haines speaks for a number of people when he asserts in "The Hole in the Bucket," "The notion that this is a time for the small and plentiful poet and not for the major talent seems to limit beforehand the possibilities."[37] It is possible that we find ourselves in the bland country described by Lisel Mueller in "The Fall of the Muse": "Now she is one of us. / She laughs the small laugh of the ordinary. She gives us all equal kisses. / . . . We share the flat bread of affluence."

And yet, democratization has been a useful corrective to some obvious abuses of the past. For one thing, it has opened the poetic canon to poets who had been excluded. The increasing inclusion of poetry by women is an interesting case in point. In his 1848 edition of *The Female Poets of*

America, Rufus Wilmot Griswold explained the necessity of confining women to their own anthology.

> It is less easy to be assured of the genuineness of literary ability in women than in men. The moral nature of women, in its finest and richest development, partakes of some of the qualities of genius. It assumes, at least, the similitude of that which in men is the characteristic or accompaniment of the highest grade of mental inspiration. We are in danger, therefore, of mistaking for the efflorescent energy of creative intelligence that which is only the exuberance of personal 'feelings unemployed.' We may confound the vivid dreamings of an unsatisfied heart, with the aspirations of a mind impatient of the fetters of time, and matter, and mortality. That may seem to us the abstract imagining of a soul rapt into sympathy with a purer beauty and a higher truth than earth and space exhibit, which in fact shall be only the natural craving of affections, undefined and wandering.[38]

Women have continued to be underrepresented in anthologies to the present. Donald Allen's *New American Poetry* includes about 11 percent women; Paris Leary's *A Controversy of Poets* includes about 12 percent; Donald Hall, Louis Simpson, and Robert Pack's *New Poets of England and America* includes about 13 percent; M. L. Rosenthal's *Chief Modern Poets of England and America* includes about 15 percent; Edward Field's *A Geography of Poets* includes about 25 percent; Daniel Halpern's *American Poetry Anthology* includes about 30 percent; Dave Smith and David Bottoms' *Morrow Anthology of Young American Poets* includes about 38 percent.

Of the 900 books published by university presses over the past thirty years, approximately 225 or 25 percent have been by women. In recent years the figure has increased to 40 percent, and this anthology reflects that proportion. Alicia Ostriker observes, "At the present moment, the flying wedge of dissent and quest is composed mainly of women, who collectively are contributing an extraordinary intellectual, emotional, and moral exhilaration to American poetry, and who may be expected to have an impact on its future course."[39]

Although many complex cultural, political, and sociological forces have contributed to the newly-perceived importance of poetry by women, the university press's openness to new voices has been significant. In fact, university press publication of poetry is generally influencing the literary canon in ways that are becoming increasingly apparent. As Barbara Herrnstein-Smith points out in Robert von Hallberg's *Canons,* recent theory has paid relatively little attention to canon formation. New criticism, structuralism, psychoanalytic criticism, reader-response criticism, reception aesthetics, speech-act theory, deconstruction, semiotics, and hermeneutics have mainly been concerned with literary interpretation. The literary scholar, modeling his work on science, strives to be rigorous and objective, basing his method on fact and knowledge. The evaluative critic has come to be seen as an unscientific dilettante, basing his evaluations on suspect taste and sensibility. The literary scholar has been more influenced by the disciplines of linguistics and the philosophy of language than by sociology and economics, which are more broadly concerned with the nature of value and evaluative behavior. When the issue of canon formation does come up, as with feminist criticism, it is often with the purpose of revaluation. And yet canons are formed, whether the process is talked about or not, and over the past twenty-five years the university press has been actively shaping and defining the canon of American poetry.

Press directors and poets are, interestingly, divided on the extent to which this is true. A number of press directors doubt that the university press has had much influence at all over what is written and valued, and a number of poets concur. Predictably, among the poets, the older established poets deny influence, while the younger poets uniformly claim considerable influence. David Wojahn typifies the younger poets when he remarks "Nearly thirty years after Wesleyan started its poetry series, poetry has been more defined and shaped by the university press than by the commercial or small house. I don't see how anyone could see the situation differently."

On the simplest level, university presses have shaped the canon merely by publishing so many books, many of which, one assumes, would not have been published otherwise. It would be difficult to imagine a contemporary poetry scene without James Wright, Adrienne Rich, Marge Piercy, Robert Bly, Henry Taylor, Carolyn Forché, Sharon Olds, Michael Harper, or Rita Dove. The mere recognition of the value of these poets has been immeasurably influential.

But publication by a university press does not merely *recognize* value; in a very real way such publication *confers* and *determines* value. *Where* a work is published not only *promotes* the value of the work, but goes a good way toward *creating* its value. As Herrnstein-Smith notes, "All value is radically contingent, being neither an inherent property of objects nor an arbitrary projection of subjects but, rather, the product of the dynamics of an economic system." [40] And the economics of literary publishing involves more than sales and ledger sheets. For trade publishers, marketability affects the evaluation of a work substantially; for university presses, less affected by the market economy, the personal economies of editors and staff are the determiners of value. Publication is thus a form of pre-evaluation that, in part, determines how a book will subsequently be read and received. The very name of the press on the book acts as a sign of cultural endorsement. The poet thus gains respect, self-respect, and a sense of poetic identity merely by publishing with a distinguished house.

Further, the perceived value of other books on a press's list passes some of that value on to any new book that appears on the list. Thus a first book published in the Yale series is probably valued more highly than a book published elsewhere, not because the book is actually better, but because the Yale list has a longer and more distinguished history.

As a form of pre-evaluation, the academic imprimatur on a book is an important step in its canonization. The university press book is not only likely to be read seriously, it is likely to attract reviews, find its way into anthologies, garner course adoptions, and establish its author's reputation, paving the way to the writing and publication of subsequent books. When the author is thus successful, he or she becomes a model for young writers whose work will reflect in one way or another their response to that model. Barbara Herrnstein-Smith concludes, "the canonical work begins increasingly not merely to survive within but to shape and create the culture in which its value is produced and transmitted and, for that very reason, to perpetuate the conditions of its own flourishing." [41]

Thus the process of canon formation is based in an economy of literary value which begins when an author invests a certain amount of energy and passion in a work until his or her interest is expended, and then continues in the marketplace where the work is further evaluated and perhaps appreciated by judges, editors, publishers, reviewers, librarians, readers, teachers, and students. The author and publisher are central in this economy, producing and determining literary value. By decentralizing, democratizing, and otherwise opening up the selection process, the university press not only democratizes and opens up the canon. It provides a mood of possibility and an encouragement to poets which in turn generates new works for the canon. One might summarize the cycle by altering Walt Whitman's famous pronouncement slightly: to have great poets, you need great publishers.

7   What kind of poetry, then, is being introduced into the canon by the university press? It has become something of a critical commonplace to assert the immense range and variety of contemporary American poetry. No single mode or modes are the standard, and diversity, innovation, and individuality are unquestioned positive hallmarks. Energy and inventiveness are legion. Still, there is always a period style in any period that has life and energy at all, and although this style can become narrow, and will eventually be replaced by something else, its conventions of language, subject, and voice can be isolated and described.

Any literary period can be seen as a continuation of, or a reaction to, one that preceded it. In reaction to late modernism, "academic" poetry, and the New Criticism which valued detachment, paradox, irony, wit, and impersonality, warring groups of poets sprang up across the country, each with its own disciples, publicists, interpreters, magazines, and presses. The formalism and technical virtuosity of the late 1940s and early 1950s gave way to the vigor and iconoclasm of the Beats (Ginsberg, Corso, Ferlinghetti), the "New York" school (Koch, Ashbery, O'Hara), the Black Mountain poets (Olsen, Creeley, Duncan, Levertov), the Confessional poets (Lowell, Plath, Sexton) and others. These groups defined themselves, in part, by attacking the others, and the rift between what Robert Lowell called the raw and the cooked (Beat and academic) came to a head in the "anthology wars" of the late 1950s and early 1960s. It came to be a clear matter of choosing sides—if you were for Ashbery you were against Wright. If you were for Creeley you were against Simpson. Now these poets seem comfortable together in the same anthology.

The premise of the warring "schools" seemed to be that there wasn't room in the poetic canon for everyone, and that someone would have to get out of town before sundown. Given the democratizing effect of creative writing programs and university press poetry series, no one finally got out of town: the groups rather merged or collapsed. The poets of the 1960s, 1970s, and 1980s have not so much rejected the "schools" of the 1950s as assimilated them. There seems to be a new eclecticism, a new catholicity of taste, in which such rigid categories blur. In *Don't Ask,* Philip Levine summarizes the shift in sensibility: "Yes, the split, the rift healed; people realized that it was false. There was a lot of real garbage coming out of academia; There was a lot of real garbage coming out of Haight-Ashbery in San Francisco . . . just extraordinarily silly poems . . . and you realized you couldn't evaluate either group on the basis of the crap it produced. You really had to look at somebody as good as Lowell, as good as Ginsberg, as good as Snyder. And then you saw they had a lot in common." According to Levine, what grew out of the assimilation of these groups was "an American style uncluttered by the silliness you found in the worst Beat poetry or the slavish accommodation of English literary form that you found in the worst academic stuff." [42]

The poets of the 1960s and on did continue to react vigorously against late modernism and the new (and newer) criticism. Believing that modernism had lost poetry what popular audience it may once have had, and that New Criticism's demands for impersonality, complexity, ambiguity, paradox, and allusion had anesthetized poetry, poets embraced the affective, intentional, and pathetic fallacies. The rift between poets and literary theorists continues to this day. With some important exceptions, most poets publishing with university and trade presses today reject modes of disruption, discontinuity, inconsistency, erasure, and incoherence that are valorized by recent theory. In "The Impure Every Time," Marvin Bell remarks, "The critics have gone off into structuralism, post-structuralism, cartographies of misinterpretation, talk about semiotics and hermeneutics—which is to say they have left the scene." [43] Most poets in this anthology would be unhappy with Michael Riffaterre's notion in *Semiotics of Poetry* of poems as riddles, intricate constructions that can be described without reference to the attitudes of a speaker.

In fact, over the past thirty years, mainstream poetry has steadily moved away from any notion of poem as intricate riddle and toward the notion of a poem as the personal utterance of a speaker, often, autobiographically, the poet himself or herself. In his 1952 preface to W. S. Merwin's Yale Younger Poets collection, *A Mask for Janus*, W. H. Auden describes "two classes" of poems: "In the first kind of poem, the overt subject of the poem is a specific experience undergone by the 'I' of the poem at a specific time and place—whether the experience actually occurred to the poet or was invented makes no difference—and the universal significance is implied, not stated directly. In the second kind, the overt subject is universal and impersonal, frequently a myth, and it is the personal experience of the poet which is implied." According to Auden, Frost is an example of the first, and Valery of the second. The dangers of the approaches are that "in uninspired hands, the occasional approach degenerates into triviality and journalism . . . while the mythological approach becomes 'literary' in the bad sense, a mere elegant manifestation of the imaginative work of the dead without any live relation to the present of the writer or his reader." Auden sees the trend in poetry as shifting toward the "mythological" approach and away from the "occasional," and he finds that trend "probably a fortunate one." [44]

Auden was, of course, wrong. American poetry did not take the direction of Merwin's book, and, for that matter, neither did Merwin. The movement has been, instead, strongly toward what Auden called the "occasional," or what we might today call the personal.

Mainstream American poetry of the past thirty years is not primarily a poetry of discontinuity and simultaneity, but of continuity and sequentiality. It is not typically a poetry of surface difficulty, of opacity and complexity, but of surface clarity and accessibility. Dave Smith explains in *Local Assays*, this does not mean "easy verse, transparent speech" but it does suggest "a poem of ordinary human experience enacted dramatically." [45] Although most of our poets now hold graduate degrees, teach in universities, and are published by university presses, they do not flaunt erudition. In most cases, our poets have adopted a strategy of immersion in their experience, rather than suspension above it. Aesthetic distance and impersonality have given way to a more directly personal voice.

Acknowledging their debt to the confessional poets, recent poets have opened the poem up to all kinds of autobiography, not just the extremes of personal experience dramatized by their predecessors. Poets have traced curves of personal growth and change—domesticity, dailiness, responses to political and social conditions. When asked by Larry Levis in an interview, "But maybe there is a special way in which people who read you as a poet think they're really getting *you*," Donald Justice replied, "Actually, I would like to keep that true. When I say *I* in a poem, I would like to be saying what I really do think and believe and have done or seen or experienced."[46] Although Sandra M. Gilbert in "My Name is Darkness" sees "the self-defining confessional genre, with its persistent assertions of identity and its emphasis on a central mythology of the self" as "(at least for our own time) a distinctively female poetic mode,"[47] it has become fairly universal in recent years.

Robert Bly's 1963 essay, "A Wrong Turning in American Poetry," may be seen as a kind of manifesto for this new personalism. In the essay, Bly attacks Eliot's notion of an "objective correlative" and Williams' phrase "no ideas but in things" and argues for "the idea of the poem as infinite concentration of the personality." According to Bly, late modernist

> poetry is also a poetry in which the poem is considered to be a construction independent of the poet. It is imagined that when the poet says "I" in a poem he does not mean himself, but rather some other person—"the poet"—a dramatic hero. The poem is conceived as a clock which one sets going. This idea encourages the poet to construct automated and flawless machines. Such poems have thousands of intricately moving parts, dozens of iambic belts and pulleys, precision trippers that rhyme at the right moment, lights flashing alternately red and green, steam valves that whistle like birds.

Bly concludes, "In the poems of Neruda, Vallejo, Jiminez, Machado, Rilke, the poem is an extension of the substance of the man, no different from his skin or his hands."[48]

There is always the risk with a more personal or autobiographical poetry, as Auden pointed out, of triviality—that the poem will remain merely personal or anecdotal. Dave Smith writes in *Local Assays,* "If the personal poem most interests us, however, it also risks our suspicion as the *merely* anecdoctal, the poem which too easily lacks large authenticity, dramatic resonance, a more-than-egocentric vision. I wanted to write poems in which something lyrical happened but poems whose realistic events would be lenses for seeing the life of the human creature at large." [49] And Marge Piercy concurs in *Parti-Colored Blocks for a Quilt:* "My poetry evolves more directly [than fiction] out of my life and the lives of other people. . . . The validity or the invalidity of the poems is not dependent on whether they're about me or not, but rather whether they're about you." [50] The poem may be autobiographical, but it has to be the *reader's* autobiography.

Of course, there is a wide range of possible "personal voice," from Ashbery's fairly impersonal desire to write not autobiography but just the "forms of autobiography," through Bly's archetypal "deep image" in which the poet's voice merges with the earth's, to the more nearly confessional narratives of Sharon Olds and Carolyn Forché, and the conversation poems of Gary Gildner and Jonathan Holden. If the major mode of contemporary poetry has been the lyric (defined by Northrop Frye as anything short enough to be got into an anthology whole), it is a lyric that has been stretched to include narratives, fictional biographies, excerpts from long poems, character sketches, prose poems, light verse, invective, disquisitions, and discursive meditations, among other things.

It is a lyric which, moreover, has usurped the language of prose. In 1957, after a reading tour, Robert Lowell described his transition to this new style: "I was still reading my old New Criticism religious symbolic poems, many published during the war. I was in San Francisco, the era and setting of Allen Ginsberg, and all about very modest poets were waking up prophets. I became sorely aware of how few poems I had written, and that these few had been finished at the latest three or four years earlier. Their style seemed distant, symbol-ridden and willfully difficult. . . . I felt my old poems hid what they were really about, and many times offered a stiff, humorless and even impenetrable surface. . . . My own poems seemed like prehistoric monsters dragged down into the bog and death by their ponderous armor. I was reciting what I no longer felt. What influenced me more than San Francisco and reading aloud was that for some time I had been writing prose. I felt that the best style for poetry was none of the many poetic styles in English, but something like the prose of Chekhov or Flaubert." [51] Lowell's words were prophetic, and the resources of a colloquial style, of daily conversational prose, with special attention to the nuances and resonances that lurked beneath it, became the rich source of renewed exploration.

It was, in fact, these "prose virtues" that Robert Pinsky argued for in his 1975 book *The Situation of Poetry*. Sharing John Haines's belief that "American poetry lacks ideas," and that "subjective exclamation has largely replaced insight," Pinsky called for a poetry that would transcend the image without abandoning it, would feel free to be discursive. [52] Although abstractions have been taboo in our poetry since Pound's warning to go in fear of them, ideas have never been absent, and in the last decade a new discursiveness seems to have developed. For poets like Pinsky or John Koethe or Pattiann Rogers or Jorie Graham, for example, the vivid personal or autobiographical experience becomes an occasion to meditate on an idea or philosophical question. A passionate intellection is, in fact, a hallmark of the best new poets represented here.

The renewed interest in discursiveness leads perhaps naturally to a renewed interest in traditional forms. If the free-verse lyric seems particularly suited to the brilliant emotional burst, traditional forms seem suited to a more discursive meditation. Although free verse is clearly our major stylistic mode, and will continue to be, the renewed interest in traditional forms has proved to be energizing for many poets.

Most older poets, like James Wright, began writing in highly wrought metrical forms, and then broke with the tradition to develop their uniqueness in free verse. For most younger poets, free verse has been the established norm. Once revolutionary, free verse has now become the fashion. One way for a younger writer to engage in technical experiment, therefore, is to explore the possibilities of forms that seem no longer current or even usable. In fact, the term "formalism" has become something of an aesthetic and political weapon, equated with fascism, conservatism, and boredom. It is the enemy. And yet, the form of the sonnet, the sestina, the villanelle, the couplet, cannot in and of itself carry the weight of this negativity. It is, rather, what is done with the forms that makes them new and enlivening or old and deadening. Richard Wilbur comments in his introduction to Philip Dacey's and David Jauss's recent anthology of contemporary poetry in traditional forms, "good rhyme is not ornament but emphasis, ligature, and significant sound; . . . a good poet is not coerced by any technical means, however demanding they may be; . . . one does not set out to write a quatrain, but rather finds that one is doing so." Or, as Howard Nemerov puts it, "Having to fill up traditional poetic forms is marvelous; it keeps you from being stupider than the law allows." [53]

Given the openness of contemporary poetry it is not surprising to see poets expanding their craft to include forms that had for centuries engaged their valued predecessors. And this renewed interest is not a retreat from the musical phrase to the metronome. The new formalism is not the old formalism. The formal poems in this anthology are handled so deftly and effortlessly, with such conversational manner, personal subject matter, and idiomatic tone, that they seem as "natural" as free verse. Perhaps the old notion of the physiological source of iambic pentameter—that the heart beats in iambs and five times for every breath—has more than an element of truth in it.

In most cases, the traditional forms included in this anthology are used to explore some of our most serious themes—war, pollution, prejudice, human communication—but such forms also lend themselves to humor and light verse. Although light verse has waned in favor since the days when *The New Yorker* routinely published it, humorous poetry has not died or been abandoned. Humor has, in fact, had a central place in American poetry. Although Robert Pack had to apologize for the humorlessness of the poets in his coedited anthology, humor has characterized American poetry from Whitman and Dickinson, though Stevens, Frost, and Berryman, down to the present day. As Robert Frost insisted, "Poetry is play. If you forget that you're a fraud." Our poets have not only not forgotten that, they have made it a central element of their poetry. Sparked in part, perhaps, by the requirements of the public poetry reading, which favors humor, and in part by a basically affirmative stance, contemporary poets embrace satire, irony, whimsy, humor, and play, in ways that Whitman, Dickinson, and Frost would have approved. Like their great predecessors, our contemporary poets are serious but not solemn.

And their seriousness prompts them to do what all great writers attempt to do—with energy and urgency to celebrate the world by describing it; to capture the freshness and vitality of life; to narrow the discrepancy between human experience and human expression. University presses have come a long way since Howard Swayzee Buck published *The Tempering* in 1919. From the publishing of the merely fashionable and forgettable, to the publishing of the major voices of our time, the university presses have been instrumental in assuring the health and vitality of American poetry. Opening the canon to a wide range of rich and exciting voices, they have promoted eclecticism, an accessible personal voice, autobiographical subject matter, a colloquial style, and a renewed interest in discursiveness, traditional forms, and humor.

The selections in this anthology represent the range of contemporary American poetry from minimalism to epic, from free verse to traditional form, from plain conversation to richly embroidered tapestry, from passionate political utterance to intense personal drama, from light verse to tough lyricism. Taken all together the poems convey a clear and vivid picture of what it was like to be alive and vital in the second half of the twentieth century.

In the first half of the twentieth century, the great modernists believed that the poet was a kind of priest, that poetry could take the place of religion, that poetry could save us. We may no longer have such elevated notions of the power of poetry. The poet may be no hero, priest, or savior. Poetry may not save us. But if poetry can't save us, it's at least one thing that makes us worth saving.

Notes

1. Howard Swayzee Buck, *The Tempering* (New Haven: Yale University Press, 1919), reviewed in *The Dial* (May 1920), p. 667.

2. Quoted in Buck, *The Tempering,* n.p. Undocumented historical information and quotations in this introduction are drawn from a survey I conducted in 1987 with all of the university presses and poets included in the anthology.

3. Norman Holmes Pearson, "Introduction," *Decade* (Middletown, Conn.: Wesleyan University Press, 1969), p. xx.

4. Mary E. Biggs, "The Publishing of Poetry, 1950–1980," (Ph.D. diss., University of Chicago, 1985).

5. Robert Bly, *Talking All Morning* (Ann Arbor: University of Michigan Press, 1980), p. 25.

6. Louis Simpson, *A Company of Poets* (Ann Arbor: University of Michigan Press, 1981), p. 37.

7. Robert Dana, *Against the Grain* (Iowa City: University of Iowa Press, 1986), p. xiv.

8. Edmund Clarence Stedman, *An American Anthology* (Boston and New York: 1900), pp. xxxi-xxxii.

9. Hayden Carruth, Alan Swallow, and Albert Erskine, "Poet, Publisher, and the Tribal Chant," *Poetry* 75, no. 1 (October 1949): 22, 55, 30.

10. Statistics are drawn from The Academy of American Poets "Semi-annual Checklists of American Poetry." (Published each spring and fall by the Academy of American Poets, New York.)

11. Hayden Carruth, in Bill Henderson, ed., *The Art of Literary Publishing: Editors on Their Craft* (New York: Pushcart Press, 1980), p. 51.

12. Paul Zimmer, in *The Publication of Poetry and Fiction: A Conference* (Washington, D.C.: Library of Congress, 1977), p. 41.

13. Poets & Writers, Inc., *A Survey of Trade Publishing: Poetry & Fiction 1952–77* (New York: Poets & Writers, 1978).

14. Rufus Wilmot Griswold, *The Poets and Poetry of America* (Philadelphia: Carey and Hart, 1842), p. 7.

15. Alan Swallow, in "Poet, Publisher, and the Tribal Chant," p. 55.

16. John Barth, "Writing: Can It Be Taught?" *The New York Times Book Review* (June 6, 1985): 36.

17. Robert Frost, "Introduction" to Donald Hall, Robert Pack, and Louis Simpson, eds., *New Poets of England and America* (Cleveland: World Publishing Company, 1957), p. 12.

18. John Haines, "The Young American Poets," in *Living Off the Country* (Ann Arbor: University of Michigan Press, 1981), p. 76.

19. Bly, *Talking All Morning*, p. 284.

20. Greg Kuzma, "The Catastrophe of Creative Writing," *Poetry* 147, no. 6 (September 1986): 342, 354.

21. Paul Zimmer, quoted in George Blooston, "Honor Without Profit," *Publishers Weekly* (August 12, 1983): 48.

22. George H. Dillon, "Spring Cleaning," *Poetry* 30, no. 1, (April 1927): 39–40.

23. Donald Hall, "Poetry and Ambition," *AWP Newsletter* 19, no. 3 (February/March 1987): 4.

24. Richard Kostelanetz, "Avante-Garde" in Donald Hall, ed., *Claims for Poetry* (Ann Arbor: University of Michigan Press, 1982), p. 245.

25. Griswold, *The Poets and Poetry of America*, p. 8.

26. Edmund Clarence Stedman, *An American Anthology*, p. xxviii.

27. James Dickey, "In the Presence of Anthologies," in *Babel to Byzantium* (New York: Farrar, Straus and Giroux, 1968), p. 13.

28. Richard Hugo, *The Triggering Town* (New York: W. W. Norton & Co., 1979), p. 33.

29. Philip Levine, *Don't Ask* (Ann Arbor: University of Michigan Press, 1981), p. viii.

30. Denis Donoghue, "Does America Have a Major Poet?" *The New York Times Book Review* (December 3, 1978): 9, 88.

31. John Martin, in Dana, *Against the Grain*, p. 128.

32. James Laughlin, in Henderson, *The Art of Literary Publishing*, pp. 33–34.

33. Ed Ochester, "A Comment from Ed Ochester," *Chowder Review*, nos. 18/19 (Spring-Summer 1983): 200.

34. Beverly Jarrett, "Comments from L. E. Phillabaum, Director, and Beverly Jarrett, Executive Editor," *Chowder Review*, nos. 16/17 (Winter-Spring 1981): 104.

35. Walton Beacham, "Finding Poets Publishers," *Scholarly Publishing* 9, no. 2 (January 1978): 159–166.

36. Daniel Halpern, in Dana, *Against the Grain*, pp. 163–64.

37. John Haines, "The Hole in the Bucket," in Hall, *Claims for Poetry*, p. 131.

38. Rufus Wilmot Griswold, *The Female Poets of America* (New York: James Miller, Pub., 1848), p. 3.

39. Alicia Ostriker, "The Nerves of a Midwife," in Hall, *Claims for Poetry*, p. 322.

40. Barbara Herrnstein-Smith, "Contingencies of Value," in Robert Von Hallberg, *Canons* (Chicago: University of Chicago Press, 1983), pp. 5–39.

41. Ibid., p. 26.

42. Levine, *Don't Ask*, p. 131.

43. Marvin Bell, "The Impure Every Time," in Hall, *Claims for Poetry*, p. 12.

44. W. H. Auden, "Foreword," in W. S. Merwin, *A Mask for Janus* (New Haven: Yale University Press, 1952), pp. vii-viii.

45. Dave Smith, *Local Assays* (Urbana and Chicago: University of Illinois Press, 1985), p. 4.

46. Donald Justice, *Platonic Scripts* (Ann Arbor: University of Michigan Press, 1984), pp. 72–73.

47. Sandra Gilbert, "My Name is Darkness," in Hall, *Claims for Poetry*, p. 118.

48. Robert Bly, "A Wrong Turning in American Poetry," in Hall, *Claims for Poetry*, p. 24.

49. Smith, *Local Assays*, p. xiii.

50. Marge Piercy, *Parti-Colored Blocks for a Quilt* (Ann Arbor: University of Michigan Press, 1982), p. 26.

51. Robert Lowell, quoted in David Kalstone, *Five Temperaments* (New York: Oxford University Press, 1977), pp. 41–42.

52. Haines, "The Hole in the Bucket," p. 131; Robert Pinsky, *The Situation of Poetry* (Princeton: Princeton University Press, 1976).

53. Richard Wilbur, "Foreword," in Philip Dacey and David Jauss, eds., *Strong Measures* (New York: Harper & Row, 1986), p. xx; Howard Nemerov quoted by Dacey, p. 3.

The University of Alabama Press

Although the University of Alabama Press published Sandra M. Gilbert's *In the Fourth World* in 1979, and Rodney Jones's *The Story They Told Us of Light* in 1980, the Alabama Poetry Series was not officially underway until 1982. About 1980 the Press approached Alabama's English department with the idea of initiating a poetry series. Thomas Rabbitt and Dara Wier were the initial editors, but Wier has recently been replaced by Chase Twichell. From the beginning the series has been a cooperative enterprise between the Press and the English department.

The Press publishes two new titles each year, in an edition of between 800 and 1,000 copies, mostly paperback.

Michael Milburn, *Such Silence,* 1989
John Morgan, *Walking Past Midnight,* 1989
Paul Nelson, *The Hard Shapes of Paradise,* 1988
Susan Snively, *Voices in the House,* 1988
Mary Ruefle, *The Lost Costumes,* 1987
Richard Jackson, *Worlds Apart,* 1987
Roy Bentley, *Boy in a Boat,* 1986
Thomas Swiss, *Measure,* 1986
Ralph Burns, *Any Given Day,* 1985
Peggy Shumaker, *Esperanza's Hair,* 1985
John Morgan, *The Arctic Herd,* 1984
Lee Upton, *The Invention of Kindness,* 1984
Marieve Rugo, *Fields of Vision,* 1983
Alberta Turner, *A Belfry of Knees,* 1983
Mary Ruefle, *Memling's Veil,* 1982
Brian Swann, *The Middle of the Journey,* 1982
Rodney Jones, *The Story They Told Us of Light,* 1980
Sandra M. Gilbert, *In the Fourth World,* 1979

Ralph Burns

AND LEAVE SHOW BUSINESS?

This elephant keeper shoved a hose up
the ass of an elephant every day. He
told a man. The man said, *So why don't*
you quit? And the keeper said, *You have*
to understand: elephant bowels are fragile,
you only spray a little and shit flies
all over. . . . And the man said, *I understand,*
I think, someone has to, but why don't you
quit? And the keeper said, *And leave show*
business? I don't know who first told me,
You'll die someday, you can't live forever.
I don't know who took my hand and said,
Some things, not all things, are possible.
At a state mental hospital where I work
I asked a patient once what he remembered.
Everything. Everything that ever happened.
Thinking back, incompletely, I think
I must've disbelieved his ease, his willingness
to witness all his loss always, so I asked,
just having heard the stupid elephant joke:
Anything about elephants? pets? He had a dog:
Bean, Bingo, something like that. And he walked
him every day on a leash and they bought
a hamburger every day on South Harrison
or North Harrison, somewhere in Shelbyville.
I asked where the dog was. He said he loved
him so much he'd drink out of the river
and the dog would too, he loved him
so much. I have to admit I had to say
something and of course there was nothing
to say. His head was down as he drank.
The water was sweet. Easily I left him
alone to walk myself out of the river
of sense. I remember riding shotgun

in a truck with my Uncle Ralph across flat
Kansas. He said something. I said, *Really?*
And he said, *Hell yes boy, do you think
I'd lie? Why do you always say really?*
And I didn't know, God help me, I don't
know. He was my uncle. He wouldn't lie.
Truth is I hadn't been listening,
but watching the long rows pass my window,
I was busy being elephant keeper
and elephant, the hose inside, the dog
that drank with a man, and the river, where
everything is equal, is possible, where
I knew I'd die someday and live without
sight or sound or touch, possibly forever.

Sandra M. Gilbert

HER LAST SICKNESS

Sailing the long hot gulf
of her last sickness,
out past the whispering beach,
she saw the town lights dim.
What were those voices shouting in her head?
She was their sentence, they were hers.
Words ripped at her ribs
like multiplied hearts, until
she drowned in that intolerable pulse.

Now riding the slow tide
she's dumb as driftwood, sheds
her last light skins of thought
easily as October.
Mouthing the great salt flow,
black with it, white with its foam,

she's picturesque—no more than a design
on the packed sand, hieroglyph
from another land.

———

The Suits

We're your shadows, your discarded skins,
your dark nurses and your tweedy mistresses.
No matter what you do, we retain you
like the stripped synapses of a computer.

On summer afternoons we exhale you
in the quiet of the closet
while you're practicing the deadman's float
at the country club.

All night
when you lie naked in your bed
(dreaming of feathers)
we bear the imprint of your shape
like the hammock in your mother's back yard.

No matter where you go
we wait for you,
wait and wait, patient
as grandfathers on the porch of a nursing home.

The best of us, the oldest and wisest,
you've almost forgotten:
the sharkskin with padded shoulders that you
put on for your first job interview,
the navy flannel with a special lining
that you wore for your bar mitzvah:

those two
will wait forever,

wait and wait at the back of the closet
where hangers multiply
and it's never morning.

Marieve Rugo

TRANSLATION

I tell you, old friend, all our talk
of my language for yours proves
it can't be done. There is no symmetry
in the syntax of needs, the tenses of touch.
Think of, say, French, that luminous skin
on few words with multiple meanings—
desire, tenderness, regret. And English,
all flavor, meter of consonants, the click
of certainties—*debts, fear, wife*.

By now, you must understand our love
was a long conversation with absences.
The grammar we trusted has fallen apart
into my verbs of distance, your memories'
inexact nouns. Conditional shrivels
to imperfect past. At the junctures of speech
nothing matches. I think of your mouth,
and what our clotted tongues never said.

Peggy Shumaker

CALVINISM

When the knob on my calf
reached the size of an egg,
my mother held a double-edged blade
in the blue-gas flame.

Look away when I lance it,
she did too, so the putrid spray
hit only her earlobe and the left lens
of her glasses. I misheard her, *abscess,*
and pictured instead, in my leg,
the bottomless hole
sinners fall into, evil ones
cast into my leg, and me
walking around with muscles full
of other folks' deceptions.
No wonder the teakettle screamed,
I did too, as the packs boiled away
layer after layer. My cooled skin
peeled away easily as bologna
once you find the edge.
Remind me to change the wick.
Every day accordian-pleated pressed gauze
tempted the poison out of the wound
until the morning the dressing came away
clean as it went on, and I knew
about limbo, a dance involving a broomstick
and flesh bending back, and I knew about belief,
and the boiling oblivion.

The University of Arkansas Press

The University of Arkansas Press Poetry Series began with the inception of the Press in 1980. The series, edited by Miller Williams, publishes two or three books per year, in an edition of 500 cloth and 1500 paper.

John Ciardi, *Echoes*, 1989
James McAuley, *Coming and Going*, 1989
William Trowbridge, *Enter Dark Stranger*, 1989
John Ciardi, *Poems of Love and Marriage*, 1988
Billy Collins, *The Apple that Astonished Paris*, 1988
Michael Heffernan, *The Man at Home*, 1988
Dan Jaffe, *Round for One Voice*, 1988
Debra Bruce, *Sudden Hunger*, 1987
Harry Humes, *Ridge Music*, 1987
David Citino, *The Gift of Fire*, 1986
Leon Stokesbury, *The Drifting Away*, 1986
John Ciardi, *The Birds of Pompeii*, 1985
Dan Masterson, *Those Who Trespass*, 1985
R. S. Thomas, *Poems of R. S. Thomas*, 1985
John Ciardi, *Selected Poems*, 1984
George Garrett, *The Collected Poems of George Garrett*, 1984
Debra Bruce, *Pure Daughter*, 1983
Sarah Henderson Hay, *Story Hour*, 1982
Ronald Koertge, *Life on the Edge of the Continent*, 1982

Debra Bruce
_____

Hey Baby

Some men can strip
a woman down, while
they put a building up.
A whistle, a look—

One hoot from him as he dangles
from a moving crane, and off
go my clothes, and I am all ass,
ass, flaring with every step.
My body gets so hot so fast
it burns the air everywhere
with shapes of me but only he
can see them.

Chances are there's nothing hard
on him but his hat. Still,
what I feel makes my nipples burn,
and not with lust, or love.

John Ciardi
_____

True or False

Real emeralds are worth more than synthetics
but the only way to tell one from the other
is to heat them to a stated temperature,
then tap. When it's done properly
the real one shatters.
                              I have no emeralds.
I was told this about them by a woman
who said someone had told her. True or false,
I have held my own palmful of bright breakage
from a truth too late. I know the principle.

Two Egrets

On Easter morning two egrets
flew up the Shrewsbury River
between Highlands and Sea Bright

like two white hands
washing one another
in the prime of light.

Oh lemons and bells of light,
rails, rays, waterfalls, ices—
as high as the eye dizzies

into the whirled confetti
and rhinestones of the breaking blue
grain of lit heaven,

the white stroke of the egrets
turned the air—a prayer
and the idea of prayer.

Was a Man

Ted Roethke was a tearing man,
    a slam-bang wham-damn tantrum O
from Saginaw in Michigan
    where the ladies sneeze at ten below
but any man that's half a man
    can keep a sweat up till the freeze
    gets down to ninety-nine degrees.
    For the hair on their chests it hangs down to their knees
      in Saginaw, in Michigan.

Ted Roethke was a drinking man,
 a brandy and a bubbly O.
He wore a roll of fat that ran
 six times around his belly O,
then tucked back in where it began.
 And every ounce of every pound
 of that great lard was built around
 the very best hooch that could be found
  in Saginaw, in Michigan.

Ted Roethke was an ath-a-lete.
 (So it's pronounced in Michigan.)
He played to win and was hard to beat.
 And he'd scream like an orangutan
and claw the air and stamp his feet
 at every shot he couldn't make
 and every point he couldn't take.
 And when he lost he'd hold a wake,
  or damn you for a cheat.

Sometimes he was a friend of mine
 with the empties on the floor O.
And, God, it's fun to be feeling fine
 and to pour and pour and pour O.
But just to show we were not swine
 we kept a clock that was stopped at ten,
 and never started before then.
 And just to prove we were gentlemen
  .we quit when it got to nine.

Ted Roethke was a roaring man,
 a ring-tailed whing-ding yippee O.
He could outyell all Michigan
 and half the Mississippi O.
But once he sat still and began
 to listen for the lifting word,
 it hovered round him like a bird.

And oh, sweet Christ, the things he heard
    in Saginaw, in Michigan!

Now Roethke's dead. If there's a man,
    a waking lost and wanting O,
in Saginaw, in Michigan,
    he could hear all his haunting O
in the same wind where it began
    the terrors it could not outface,
    but found the words of, and by grace
    of what words are, found time and place
        in Saginaw, in Michigan.

David Citino
————

EINSTEIN, PLACENTA, THE CAVES OF LASCAUX

The natural universe moves to precise rhythms:
Einstein died at 1:15 a.m. E.S.T. on April 18, 1955,
while speaking frantic German to a New Jersey nurse
who, though she knew only English, still comprehended
two hands seizing the sheets, the jaw stricken slack,
eyes turning up zeros. Each percentage point rise
in the annual national unemployment rate produces
an additional 320 suicides. Nature works in five ways:
gravity (through the agency of the as-yet-undiscovered,
the graviton), electromagnetism (which can be explained
only by assuming that the energy of each photon
equals the frequency of the light multiplied
by Planck's constant h), the strong force (gluons),
the weak force (the Z and W particles we've only just found),
and the human force (or belief), so powerful after all
that it can for example propel women and men
through the exact replica of the caves of Lascaux
of the Aurignacio-Perigordian period (c.14,000-c.13,500 B.C.)

located a stone's throw from the real Paleolithic thing
already damaged irreparably by the same force.
All such movements of matter into energy, energy to matter
are of course influenced by what we know of love and fear,
as when, for example, in my twelfth grade biology class
in Cleveland at St. Ignatius High School
when the Jesuit instructor tossed onto the lab table
the still warm placenta bloody as sunrise
in its clear plastic bag, eight youngsters, 1/3 of the class,
left the lab and ran directly to the room marked *Men*.

George Garrett

LITTLE MOVIE WITHOUT A MIDDLE

The big bad abstractions are back in town again.
Tall, slope-bellied, shaded by wide-brimmed hats,
dragging their huge shadows by the heels, they swagger
down the empty street. A hound dog rises from his snooze
near the swinging doors of the Red Eye Saloon and slinks away
without even pausing to stretch, boneless as poured water.
Chink-a-chink-a-chink, bright spurs warn the dusty world.
Beneath an enormous sombrero, a Mexican crosses himself,
and then continues to snore more loudly than before.
Acting more on inspiration than logic,
the Sheriff pins his tin star on the Town Drunk
and runs to catch the last stagecoach for California.

Meanwhile into a sunny plaza ghostly with fountains
here come generalizations in full dress uniforms,
all lavish in polished leather and brass buttons, tilting,
nearly topheavy with medals, these brilliant officers
of the old regime. *Oompah-oompah-oompah* blares a band
while the crowds wolf down bananas and chocolate bars,
buy every balloon and pound palms raw with sweaty applause.

Now cut directly to the inevitable moment
when the smoke is finally clearing away and there they are,
heels up and spurs down, those generalizations,
hanging conventionally from the streetlamps and phone poles.

Their rows of medals make a tinkly music.
See also, flat as oriental rugs along the street,
those are abstractions who once were fast on the draw.
While buzzards circle like homesick punctuation marks,
the simple and specific common nouns come forth again
to clean up mess and mark the spot for scholars
        (*oh oompah-oompah, chinka-chink*)
with a row of gravestones grinning like false teeth.

Ronald Koertge
———

GRETEL

said she didn't know anything about ovens
so the witch crawled in to show her
and Bam! went the big door.

Then she strolled out to the shed where
her brother was fattening, knocked down
a wall and lifted him high in the air.

Not long after the adventure in the forest
Gretel married so she could live happily.
Her husband was soft as Hansel. Her
husband liked to eat. He liked to see
her in the oven with the pies and cakes.

Ever after was the size of a kitchen.
Gretel remembered when times were better.
She laughed out loud when the witch
popped like a weenie.

"Gretel! Stop fooling around and fix
my dinner."

"There's something wrong with this oven,"
she says, her eyes bright as treasure.
"Can you come here a minute?"

———

SIDEKICKS

They were never handsome and often came
with a hormone imbalance manifested by corpulence,
a yodel of a voice or ears big as kidneys.

But each was brave. More than once a sidekick
has thrown himself in front of our hero in order
to receive the bullet or blow meant for that
perfect face and body.

Thankfully, heroes never die in movies and leave
the sidekick alone. He would not stand for it.
Gabby or Pat, Pancho or Andy remind us of a part
of ourselves,

the dependent part that can never grow up,
the part that is painfully eager to please,
always wants a hug and never gets enough.

Who could sit in a darkened theatre, listen
to the organ music and watch the best
of ourselves lowered into the ground while

the rest stood up there, tears pouring off
that enormous nose.

———

Two Men

and two women were racing. Sometimes
a man won, sometimes a woman.

In the course of this event, the contestants
grew fond of one another. The men
were ashamed of themselves, however,
and each chose a wife.

Now the teams raced. Sometimes one team
won, sometimes the other.

"Let's make this more interesting,"
said the men and they gave one of the women
a Norge and a Hoover and a Singer to carry.
The other had to hold a baby and every
so often douche or shave her legs without
stopping and without putting down the baby.
Sometimes one of the women won, sometimes
the other.

"Let's get in on this," said the men
and they sprinted to the wire, looking back
over their shoulders and laughing.

"It's all over," they said, "we won."
But the women kept on
coming.

The University of California Press

For several decades the University of California Press has published poetry in translation, but not original poetry. During the 1970s the Press developed a plan to publish editions of works by modern poets who seemed "wrongly inaccessible." Such collections are published from time to time in editions of 2,000. Works selected for publication depend on the taste of the Press staff and close advisors. With editions of Zukovsky, Olson, and Creeley, California has concentrated on the objectivist school.

Charles Olson, *The Maximus Poems,* 1983
Robert Creeley, *The Collected Poems of Robert Creeley,*
   1945–1975, 1982
Louis Zukofsky, *A,* 1978
Kenneth Burke, *Collected Poems, 1915–1967,* 1968

Robert Creeley

———

I KNOW A MAN

As I sd to my
friend, because I am
always talking,—John, I

sd, which was not his
name, the darkness sur-
rounds us, what

can we do against
it, or else, shall we &
why not, buy a goddamn big car,

drive, he sd, for
christ's sake, look
out where yr going.

———

JOY

I could look at
an empty hole for hours
thinking it will
get something in it,

will collect
things. There is
an infinite emptiness
placed there.

THE LANGUAGE

Locate *I*
love you some-
where in

teeth and
eyes, bite
it but

take care not
to hurt, you
want so

much so
little. Words
say everything.

I
love you
again,

then what
is emptiness
for. To

fill, fill.
I heard words
and words full

of holes
aching. Speech
is a mouth.

Charles Olson

I, Maximus of Gloucester, to You

By ear, he sd.

But that which matters, that which insists, that which will last
where shall you find it, my people, how, where shall you listen
when all is become billboards, when all, even silence, is
when even the gulls,
my roofs,
when even you, when sound itself

> Where, Portygee Hill, she sang
> and over the water, at Tarr's
> (the water glowed, the light west,
> black, gold, the tide
> outward at evening
>
> The fixed bells rang, their voices
> came like boats over the oil-slicks,
> like milkweed hulls
>
> And a man slumped,
> attentionless,
> against pink shingles
>
> > (sea city

2

one loves only form,
and form only comes
into existence when
the thing is born

born of yourself, born
of hay and cotton struts
of street-pickings, wharves, weeds
you carry in, my bird

       of a bone of a fish
       of a straw, or will
       of a color, of a bell
       of yourself, torn

       (o bird
       o kylix, o
       Antony of Padua
       sweep low, bless
       the roofs,
       the gentle steep ones
       on whose ridge-poles the gulls sit,
       from which they depart

       And the flake-racks
       of my city

   3
love is form, and cannot be without
important substance (the weight, say, 50 carats, each one of us,
    perforce,
our own goldsmith's scale (feather to feather added,
and what is mineral, what is curling hair, what string
you carry in your nervous beak, these
make bulk, these, in the end, are
sum

              (o my lady of good voyage
              in whose arm,

in whose left arm rests no boy
but a carefully carved wood, a painted
schooner
       a delicate mast, a bow-sprit
              for forwarding

4

the underpart is, though stemmed, uncertain
is, as sex is, as moneys are, facts
to be dealt with as the sea is, the demand

that they be played by, that they only can be, that they must
be played by, said he coldly,
the ear

But love is not easy,
and how shall you know,
New England, now
that pejorocracy is here, now
that street-cars, o Oregon, twitter
in the afternoon, offend
a gold-black loin?

how shall you strike,
swordfisherman, the blue-red back
when, last night, your aim
was mu-sick, mu-sick, mu-sick
and not the cribbage game?

       (o Gloucesterman,
       weave your birds and fingers
       new, your roof-tops
       clean shat on, racks
       sunned on

American, braid
with others like you, such
extricable surface
as faun and oral satyr lesbos vase
o kill kill kill kill kill
those
who advertise you
out

   5
in, the bow-sprit, bird, beak
in, the act is in, goes in, the form
what holds, what you make, what is
the object, strut, strut

what you are, what you must be, what you can
right now hereinafter erect

               Off-shore, by islands in the blood, I,
                  Maximus, tell you
               (as I see it, over the waters, from this place
               where I am, where I hear, where I can still
                  hear

               from where I carry you a feather
               as though, sharply, I picked up,
               in the first of morning delivered you,
               a jewel, it flashing
               more than a wing, than any old romantic
                  thing
               than memory, than place, than any thing
                  other than

               that which you also carry, than that which is
               (call it a nest) around the bend of, call it
               the next
               second

Carnegie Mellon University Press

The Carnegie Mellon University Press Poetry Series was founded by Gerald Costanzo in 1975. The Press emerged from the small press publishing of Three Rivers Press and *Three Rivers Poetry Journal* which were inaugurated in 1972. The name change, along with a higher volume of publishing (more titles, full-length as opposed to chapbooks, clothbound editions), resulted from Costanzo's desire to procure a distributor, to generate more funds, and to reach a wider audience. The Carnegie Mellon series is the only university press series to have come directly out of small press publishing.

The initial aim of the series was to publish poets in their thirties and forties who had placed their work in periodicals, but who had not yet published a first volume. The policy changed as the series evolved, and now Carnegie Mellon publishes first books, subsequent books by poets on their list, and books by established poets not on their list. The Press publishes approximately six books per year in editions of 500 cloth and 2,000 paper. The series is edited by Gerald Costanzo, and distributed by Harper & Row.

Michael Cuddihy, *Out of the Old Ruins,* 1989
Gregory Djanikian, *Falling Deeply Into America,* 1989
David Keller, *Land That Wasn't Ours,* 1989
Thomas Lux, *Sunday,* 1989
Jay Meek, *Stations,* 1989
Carol J. Pierman, *The Age of Krypton,* 1989
Eve Shelnutt, *Recital in a Private Home,* 1989
Dave Smith, *The Fisherman's Whore,* 1989
Robert Wallace, *The Common Summer,* 1989
Michael Waters, *The Burden Lifters,* 1989
Franz Wright, *Entry in an Unknown Hand,* 1989
T. Alan Broughton, *Preparing to Be Happy,* 1988

Mekeel McBride, *Red Letter Days,* 1988
Ed Ochester, *Changing the Name to Ochester,* 1988
Thomas Rabbitt, *The Abandoned Country,* 1988
Judith Root, *Weaving the Sheets,* 1988
Dara Wier, *The Book of Knowledge,* 1988
Gillian Conoley, *Some Gangster Pain,* 1987
Peter Cooley, *The Van Gogh Notebook,* 1987
Richard Harteis, *Internal Geography,* 1987
Lawrence Raab, *Other Children,* 1987
Vern Rutsala, *Ruined Cities,* 1987
Kim R. Stafford, *Places and Stories,* 1987
Rita Dove, *Thomas and Beulah,* 1986
Ruth Fainlight, *Fifteen to Infinity,* 1986
Brendan Galvin, *Seals in the Inner Harbor,* 1986
Jim Hall, *False Statements,* 1986
C. G. Hanzlicek, *When There Are No Secrets,* 1986
C. D. Wright, *Further Adventures With You,* 1986
Anne Bromley, *Midwinter Transport,* 1985
Michael Dennis Browne, *Smoke from the Fires,* 1985
Stephen Dunn, *Not Dancing,* 1985
Mark Jarman, *Far and Away,* 1985
Paula Rankin, *To the House Ghost,* 1985
Michael Waters, *Anniversary of the Air,* 1985
Greg Djanikian, *The Man in the Middle,* 1984
Jonathan Holden, *Falling from Stardom,* 1984
David James, *A Heart Out of this World,* 1984
Jay Meek, *Earthly Purposes,* 1984
Ed Ochester, *Miracle Mile,* 1984
Dara Wier, *All You Have in Common,* 1984
Robert Wallace, *Girlfriends and Wives,* 1984
Peter Cooley, *Nightseasons,* 1983
Rita Dove, *Museum,* 1983
Mekeel McBride, *The Going Under of the Evening Land,* 1983
Eve Shelnutt, *Air and Salt,* 1983
T. Alan Broughton, *Dreams Before Sleep,* 1982

C. G. Hanzlicek, *Calling the Dead,* 1982

Anne S. Perlman, *Sorting It Out,* 1982

Kim R. Stafford, *The Granary,* 1982

Primus St. John, *Love Is Not a Consolation, It is a Light,* 1982

Stephen Dunn, *Work and Love,* 1981

Richard Harteis, *Morocco Journal,* 1981

Mark Jarman, *The Rote Walker,* 1981

Elizabeth Libbey, *Songs of a Returning Soul,* 1981

Paula Rankin, *Augers,* 1981

Vern Rutsala, *Walking Home from the Icehouse,* 1981

John Skoyles, *A Little Faith,* 1981

Rita Dove, *The Yellow House on the Corner,* 1980

Jim Hall, *The Mating Reflex,* 1980

Jay Meek, *Drawing On the Walls,* 1980

H. L. Van Brunt, *And the Man Who was Traveling Never Got Home,* 1980

Dara Wier, *The 8-Step Grapevine,* 1980

T. Alan Broughton, *Far from Home,* 1979

Peter Cooley, *The Room Where Summer Ends,* 1979

Philip Dow, *Paying Back the Sea,* 1979

Mekeel McBride, *No Ordinary World,* 1979

Robert Wallace, *Swimmer in the Rain,* 1979

James Bertolino, *New & Selected Poems,* 1978

Michael Dennis Browne, *The Sun Fetcher,* 1978

Stephen Dunn, *A Circus of Needs,* 1978

Elizabeth Libbey, *The Crowd Inside,* 1978

Philip Dacey, *How I Escaped from the Labyrinth and Other Poems,* 1977

Jim Hall, *The Lady from the Dark Green Hills,* 1977

Paula Rankin, *By the Wreckmaster's Cottage,* 1977

H. L. Van Brunt, *For Luck: Poems 1962–1977,* 1977

Stephen Dunn, *Full of Lust and Good Usage,* 1976

Jay Meek, *The Week the Dirigible Came,* 1976

T. Alan Broughton, *In the Face of Descent,* 1975

Ann Hayes, *The Living and the Dead,* 1975

Peter Cooley

Last Conversation

When I am old, nodding by the fire,
the lamplight turned down low inside my eyes,
come to visit me some night, late.
Just walk in, you'll know how.

I'll grip the chair, speechless at first
to see you, your face floating through the arms
you stretch toward me, burning on yourself.
Speechless, I'll cry. But that will pass.

And we'll have tea, you'll start to talk,
your words swaying up the stairs again
where I first took a step, my hand in yours.
The hall is very dark. I'm not afraid.

Mother, forgive me if I doze off
and don't come back. Just slip away.
Your last words at the banister will be enough
if I should wake up. Even if I don't.

Philip Dacey

Form Rejection Letter

We are sorry we cannot use the enclosed.
We are returning it to you.
We do not mean to imply anything by this.
We would prefer not to be pinned down about this matter.
But we are not keeping—cannot, will not keep—
    what you sent us.
We did receive it, though, and our returning it to you
    is a sign of that.

It was not that we minded your sending it to us
     unasked.
That is happening all the time, they
     come when we least expect them,
          when we forget we have needed or might yet need them,
     and we send them back.
We send this back.
It is not that we minded.
At another time, there is no telling . . .
But this time, it does not suit our present needs.

We wish to make it clear it was not easy receiving it.
It came so encumbered.
And we are busy here.
We did not feel
     we could take it on.
We know it would not have ended there.
It would have led to this, and that.
We know about these things.
It is why we are here.
We wait for it. We recognize it when it comes.
Regretfully, this form letter does not allow us to elaborate
     why we send it back.
It is not that we minded.

We hope this does not discourage you. But we would not
     want to encourage you falsely.
It requires delicate handling, at this end.
If we had offered it to you,
     perhaps you would understand.
But, of course, we did not.
You cannot know what your offering it
     meant to us,
And we cannot tell you:
There is a form we must adhere to.
It is better for everyone that we use this form.

As to what you do in future,
     we hope we have given you signs,

that you have read them,
that you have not mis-read them.
We wish we could be more helpful.
But we are busy.
We are busy returning so much.
We cannot keep it.
It all comes so encumbered.
And there is no one here to help.
Our enterprise is a small one.
We are thinking of expanding.
We hope you will send something.

Rita Dove

POMADE

She sweeps the kitchen floor of the river bed her husband saw fit
to bring home with his catfish, recalling
a flower—very straight,
with a spiked collar arching
under a crown of bright fluffy worms—
she had gathered in armfuls
along a still road in Tennessee. Even then
he was forever off in the woods somewhere in search
of a magic creek.

It was Willemma shushed the pack of dusty children
and took her inside the leaning cabin with its little
window in the door, the cutout magazine cloud taped to the pane
so's I'll always have shade. It was Willemma
showed her how to rub the petals fine
and heat them slow in mineral oil
until the skillet exhaled pears and nuts and rotting fir.

That cabin leaned straight away
to the south, took the very slant of heaven
through the crabgrass and Queen Anne's Lace to

the Colored Cemetery down in Wartrace. Barley soup
yearned toward the bowl's edge, the cornbread
hot from the oven climbed in glory
to the very black lip of the cast iron pan . . .
but Willemma stood straight as the day
she walked five miles to town for Scotch tape
and back again. Gaslight flickered on the cockeyed surface
of rain water in a galvanized pail in the corner
while Thomas pleaded with his sister
to get out while she still was fit.

Beebalm. The fragrance always put her
in mind of Turkish minarets against
a sky wrenched blue,
sweet and merciless. Willemma could wear her gray hair twisted
in two knots at the temples and still smell like travel.
But all those years she didn't budge. She simply turned
one day from slicing a turnip into a pot
when her chest opened and the inrushing air
knocked her down. *Call the reverend, I'm in the floor*
she called out to a passerby.

Beulah gazes through the pale speckled linoleum
to the webbed loam with its salt and worms. She smooths
her hair, then sniffs her palms. On the countertop
the catfish grins
like an oriental gentleman. Nothing ever stops. She feels
herself slowly rolling down the sides of the earth.

Stephen Dunn

WEATHERMAN

Tonight I've decided to tell you, friends,
how much bad weather excites me.
I love the way it moves
state to state, and though I seem to rejoice

when it blows out to sea, that's just showbiz,
I'd like it to perch off the Carolinas
or double back across the nation,
and I know some of you feel the same.
Something in me responds to a low
and I'm sorry, I can watch the footage
from tornado damage all evening.
I know you too like to see cars off the road,
families disconnected, I know when you sigh
and say "How sad" your heart is thumping
to a tune you hardly understand. Friends,
this is a communication tonight,
not a broadcast. Here in the East
where no weather originates, where everything
moves toward us and so little arrives;
here, where we're forced to watch things
break up, or swerve toward Erie, what is it
that has turned in us, that has turned in me?
All I know is I can't deny the secret
happiness when a system moves across Nebraska
as I thought I would, paralyzing North Platte,
the National Guard called out, wind chill
(just the words *wind chill*) plunging
into my imagination. And you who live out there
where weather is a fact of life, don't you
secretly love it and look forward to it,
don't you love to survive it? And I mean *love*.
When I lived in Minnesota half my life
was the weather. A blizzard was me
and the blizzard. A tornado meant
the southwest corner of my basement
huddled with loved ones. Never have I been
so happy. It is we in the East I worry about;
only in August when the hurricanes wend up
from the Bahamas are our bodies truly connected
to our minds. Only then can devastation
make our lives less academic, only then

can we trace a path that leads directly
to ourselves.

So tonight I wanted to confess to you,
voyeurs and participants alike,
I wanted to let you know I know
the deep thrill of a five day forecast,
of a science so inexact
we learn to trust accident after accident.
Believe me, the scattered highs across
the country will not arrive
any time close to schedule. And they will not
give you any lasting pleasure. Frankly,
I'll be bored if a system, say, out of Manitoba
doesn't push in and complicate everything.
Right now there's a disturbance around the Panhandle
that could be a big one. In the days ahead
I'll follow it for you, I'll watch it the way
a Christian Scientist watches virulence in a leg wound,
and if things turn bad or something perverse
gets into me, I'm sure you'll understand
that's how things are and I am,
that's the weather, some of the time.

Elizabeth Libbey

———

HELPMATE

after "Love Song: I and Thou" by Alan Dugan

Love, float into me for sleep's sake.
You're the body, the future.
I'm the house. Let's
put away the tools we used
for nailing down the marriage.

The bed might have looked better
hung on the wall.
Nothing would have worked out.

I love the neighborhood, the bureau drawers.
I love the care of the children,
the folding and putting away, the care
with which the children
say good night gently, go to their cars, and speed away.

Even if the home collapses
it is too well-practiced to fail for sure.
There will be no way to tell.

Mekeel McBride

A Blessing

*"Freely chosen, discipline
is absolute freedom."*
            —Ron Serino

1.
The blue shadow of dawn settles
its awkward silks into the enamelled kitchen
and soon you will wake with me into the long
discipline of light and day—the morning sky
startled and starred with returning birds.
You half-whisper, half-sigh, "This will never stop."
And I say, "Look at the constellations
our keys and coins make, there,
on the polished sky of the dresser top."

2.
From what sometimes seems an arbitrary
form or discipline often come two words

that rhyme and in the rhyming fully marry
the world of spoons and sheets and common birds
to another world that we have always known
where the waterfall of dawn does not drown
even the haloed gnat; where we are shown
how to find and hold the pale day moon, round
and blessed in the silver lake of a coffee spoon.

Ed Ochester

COOKING

Peel the shrimp, cut the pak choi
on the bias, shred the peppers.
If you wipe the mushrooms
I'll slice them with the chef's knife,
cut the pale breast of chicken into matchsticks,
the mild onion into rings,
start the oil smoking in the pan;
sesame oil is better,
but you can use safflower.

I love you.
And I'm gabbling & cutting
because I think you're happy, too.
Give me a plate. I'll pour wine,
the hell with the thin glasses,
a cup will do.

When I was young I was tonguetied
and I can't remember when the men
in my family
didn't sit, stare at their plates
and shovel, silent as though they'd learned
they'd just contracted syphilis.
And the women, who cooked for love,
beamed.

I think that's why I learned to cook,
so my hands would have something to do.
It's not that they didn't have words,
it's that they didn't trust them.
I mean my hands, and my fathers and uncles.
They never read *Gatsby,* but they believed in him.
They wanted to make money, to take their rich shirts
out of the drawer and spill them across the bed
so someone would say, "what beautiful,
what beautiful shirts." It was cleaner
than talking, or cooking, if you could never
say anything gracefully.

So I learned to love steamy windows, and
I can cook better than my mother.
I can talk better than my father.
And I've always loved pouring wine,
twist it off neatly, or if there's nothing better
put a big jug of Gallo on my shoulder
and without spilling a drop
glug out shots in a cup.
I like my voice and hands.
Over dinner, they meet your hands.

THE HEART OF OWL COUNTRY

Whatever blossoms is rooted
in the dark as, item,

the delicate purple comfrey flower
supported by a brutish taproot

that powers itself into the subsoil
and splits the shale a dozen feet

beneath me, so that the bumblebees
tumble in a drunken frenzy here, and

item, how if I tend my loneliness,
which is no rarer than yours,

friend, I grow stronger,
so that my fists open, and the garden

becomes a natural metaphor for what
we have always known:

that only by going deeply
as possible into our dark

can we discover ourselves
to others, and even though

the stutterer I have always been
would like to say, "we will never

die" I know that we will utterly
except for what we yield to friends

or progeny—that's the garden part—
and I remember now what I'd forgotten

for years, how, once, when we were
driving to my mother's, in New York State,

at twilight passing through a large marsh
my daughter said *look!* and in every dead

tree there was an owl, hundreds of them,
stupid in the light, like a faculty senate,

staring uncomprehendingly at the swamp
and the cars on the interstate, so still

one could have knocked them off their
perches with a stick and my daughter

screamed, delighted, "this must be
the heart of owl country!" and it

was: those soft fists of feathers
waiting for their hour, long

after we'd passed lifting into the spring air
on their solitary flights, each silent

in its large community, alert and perfect.

Paula Rankin
———————

SIDESHOWS

We call them depraved
for what they sell:
Deformity.

We want to say
to the fattest of fat men:
Surely there is something else
you could do
to feed such hunger;
Bearded lady, it would only take a shave.

But then not everyone
can toss fluorescent nipples
and catch them easily as coins
or display the ambiguities of his sex
unabashed. Perhaps these too are callings?

If you have enough quarters,
they will show you everything

you'd only guessed at
from Hermaphrodite's shadow
on the side of the tent
to the glassed-in fetus
of a beast child who
if he never sees his cut
of suckers' money,
will live as long as a memory
when the canvas drops
and its tenants slip into trucks
leaving the fields full of squashed cups
but no trail

though we go back for days
with more quarters.

Robert Wallace

I GO ON TALKING TO YOU

We're getting the divorce—
I am, I'm the one who wants to;
you don't, you're reluctant, you merely agree.
But I stand in the door, or at the bottom
of the fire escape
or I come back up the fire escape.
Though it's settled and what I want to do,
I go on talking to you.

Afterwards, too, by myself by the window,
I keep on asking
why, if you love me, you do what you do.
I watch your lights, and argue
my way down through the seven levels
of your history of lies.
The clock shrugs. Almost two.
I go on talking to you.

Maybe keeping on talking is what love does.
It's what I have to do.
Outside his building at five, parked
in the vapor-lights' peachy hue,
in the lull after I know you won't be leaving
now till morning, and you're sleeping
by him (or doing what lovers do),
I go on talking to you.

Dara Wier

———

LUCILLE'S KUMQUAT–COLORED KIMONO

lies on her chest of drawers,
highboy
dusty with baby powder,
pins,
hairballs rolling across
veneer.

This morning the bedroom
steams.

On the neck of her dress
Ernie's sweat,
not quite the color
of her kimono, dries
like pork drippings.

Everything is wet.

Damp enough to warp.

Her face
hot as a jimmied lock
keeps kissing him,
moving his mouth.

Every wrinkle shows.

Ernie goes on to work,
Lucille bends low,
ironing nuisance out.

———

MIDGE IN THE MORNING

Purely a perched peach, pretty
as a water blister,
supine on her green satin pillow,
her froggy prince's price
nowhere too much.

She is serene as a kitchen match
soon to be struck.
Her brush rollers bristle, each
wire mesh another crawfish trap.
In fact.

Her hair turns a fire
of stinging caterpillars,
pirouettes a jumping
teapot top, white, hot, rollicking,
a blister propped ringing, stung,
steaming, lickety-split.

The University of Chicago Press

The University of Chicago Press published poetry periodically in The Phoenix Poets Series from 1960 to 1975, when the series was discontinued. The series was revived in 1983, with the purpose of providing a publishing opportunity for poets who "desired to challenge reigning fashions." Robert von Hallberg, with the help of two anonymous advisors, edits the series, which considers manuscripts by invitation only. Chicago publishes one or two books per year, in editions of 1,500–2,000 paper and 500 cloth.

Donald Davie, *To Scorch or Freeze*, 1989
Jim Powell, *It Was Fever That Made The World*, 1989
Eleanor Wilner, *Sarah's Choice*, 1989
Paul Lake, *Another Kind of Travel*, 1988
Howard Nemerov, *War Stories: Poems About Long Ago and Now*, 1987
Alan Shapiro, *Happy Hour*, 1987
Turner Cassity, *Hurricane Lamp*, 1986
Anne Winters, *The Key to the City*, 1986
Howard Nemerov, *Inside the Onion*, 1984
Eleanor Wilner, *Shekhinah*, 1984
David Ferry, *Strangers*, 1983
Alan Shapiro, *The Courtesy*, 1983
Howard Nemerov, *Sentences*, 1980
Howard Nemerov, *The Collected Poems of Howard Nemerov*, 1977
Howard Nemerov, *The Western Approaches*, 1975
Elder Olson, *Olson's Penny Arcade*, 1975
Howard Nemerov, *Gnomes and Occasions*, 1973
Ben Belitt, *Nowhere But Light*, 1970
Henry Rago, *A Sky of Late Summer*, 1969
Ben Belitt, *The Enemy Joy*, 1964

Elder Olson, *Collected Poems,* 1963
Howard Nemerov, *The Next Room of the Dream,* 1962
Revel Denney, *In Praise of Adam,* 1961
Isabella Gardner, *The Looking Glass,* 1961
Howard Nemerov, *New and Selected Poems,* 1960

Howard Nemerov

ADORATION

When I report at the funerals of friends,
Which happens nowadays oftener than it did,
I am astonished each time over again
At the fucking obsequiousness addressed to God:
O Thou, &c. He's killed this one already,
And is going to do the rest of us
In His own good time, then what in the world
Or out of it's abjection going to get
For either the dead or their smalltime survivors?
Who go to church at ordinary times
To pray to God, who does not go to church.

As for those masses and motets, no matter:
He happens to be tone deaf (or is it stone deaf?
My hearing's not so good either). But once in a way
The music takes me, if it doesn't Him,
The way Bach does the Et In Terra Pax,
Or Mozart does the Tuba Mirum, where
We doomed and damned go on beseeching anyhow.
Does He, when He hears that heavenly stuff, believe?
And at the Lacrimosa does He weep for us?
No end, my friends, to our inventiveness:
God doesn't matter. Adoration does.

BECAUSE YOU ASKED ABOUT THE LINE BETWEEN PROSE AND POETRY

Sparrows were feeding in a freezing drizzle
That while you watched turned into pieces of snow
Riding a gradient invisible
From silver aslant to random, white, and slow.

There came a moment that you couldn't tell.
And then they clearly flew instead of fell.

BEGINNER'S GUIDE

They stand in the corner, on a shadowy shelf,
Field Books of This, Beginner's Guides to That,
Remainders of an abdicated self
That wanted knowledge of no matter what.

Of flowers, was it? Every spring he'd tear
From their hiding-places, press and memorize
A dozen pale beginners of the year
That open almost among the melting snows,

And for a month thereafter rule his realm
Of small and few and homey in such minds
As his, until full summer came to whelm
Him under the flood and number of her kinds.

Or birds? At least the flowers would stand still
For amateurs, but these flighty alightings
Would not; and as he still refused to kill
In confirmation of his rarer sightings

The ornithologists were not his dish,
And he made do with sedentary birds
Who watched his watching as it were their wish
To check with Peterson, pictures and words.

And even so, before he got them straight
As like as not they'd not be there at all.
On the wings and wits God gave 'em they'd migrate;
"Confusing Fall Warblers" were, each Fall, his fall.

The world would not, nor he could not, stand still.
The longest life might be too short a one
To get by heart, in all its fine detail,
Earth's billion changes swinging on the sun.

His last attempt he made upon the stars,
And was appalled, so many more of them
There were since boyhood that astronomers
Preferred a number to an ancient name.

And if, as The Beginner was advised
To do, he bought himself a telescope,
The host of stars that must be memorized
So mightily increased, he'd lose all hope.

Was it a waste, the time and the expense,
Buying the books, going into the field
To make some mind of what was only sense,
And show a profit on the year's rich yield?

Though no authority on this theme either,
He would depose upon the whole that it
Was not. The world was always being wider
And deeper and wiser than his little wit,

But it felt good to know the hundred names
And say them, in the warm room, in the winter,
Drowsing and dozing over his trying times,
Still to this world its wondering beginner.

Alan Shapiro

MEZUZAH

A small case containing a parchment scroll on which a portion of Deuteronomy is written, attesting to God's everlasting love. It is said whoever breaks open the Mezuzah and removes the sacred scroll will incur God's everlasting retribution.

Though unable to imagine
how harm could fit in there,
in that tiny case,
I thought I knew enough
to stay afraid.
               But once,
moving through the quiet house,
I thought, if I can't hear
my own steps, how can God?
And in the laundry room,
by the dryer humming out its heat,
the thick air,
itself, a kind of linen
covering me, unseen,
unnoticed, I knelt down,
and all I was supposed to fear
I crushed
          with my mother's iron.
The little parchment, speckled
with marks too small to read,
fell out . . .
            and nothing happened:
only the washer jerked
into its spin, and made me wait
a little longer
for my blood to turn to salt,
for my hands to wither,
                    for pain.
But nothing happened.

　　　　　　And later,
playing with my friends, I knew
there was no mark of Cain
upon my forehead, no
lightning come to split me
like a tree.
　　　　　　Only something else,
from then on,
wouldn't go away, kept me
up late at night, damaging
my prayers, till even they no longer tamed
the dark
world of my room:
I knew God's wrath, all right,
His retribution coiled,
forever,
in my questioning.

Eleanor Wilner

THE CONTINUOUS IS BROKEN, AND RESUMES

Adam made the world
stand still so he could name it: the woods
intelligible as thought expressed
in leaves, and when they would not stay
forever green, he took the fall
and turned its gold to parable. And the long slither
of the snake became his dread
uncoiling in the grass. And when, obsessively, the same
thought kept repeating in his head
and in his ears, the trees filled up with locusts
throbbing—so shrill the birds
took off. The rock was his fixed idea;
the creation, to continue, required
his attention. The seasons he made gods
and, as the storms announcing spring

tear limb from limb, the holy ground
was smirched with blood to breed
the soft uncurl of seedlings. This murder
he called Orpheus, Dionysus, Jesus. Man
set it going, his matins
made the sun come up; if he forgot to dance,
the rain grew stubborn. His sin
had such effect that it could blight
the earth, bring on eclipse, rot the fruit
before it ripened. The great god he created
walked among the tents, his sandals opened
fissures in the ground, his touch
made the hills smoke. When Adam slept
the world grew still, mute as a great
organ whose towering pipes require
a little pair of hands
to move the air in thunder.
And how he dreamed of closure: obsessed
with falling curtains, heroic couplets,
and the absolute chord of amens.
Now everywhere he walks, the world is mute.

When he has passed, the birds pick up the notes
where they had dropped them, the wind begins again
to call soft speech from the leaves,
and the deer, seeing the woods deserted
by all but the sea-green light,
walk out into the clearing.
And the ocean nearing the shore
heaves a sigh of relief
and a great shudder goes through the swells,
as when a wind lightly passes.
And the sun, as the earth turns by it,
writes its changing shadows on the land.
Everything speaks of itself:
the fireflies in their code of light—
short flashes, the long dark in between;
the sand, grain by grain, is a pure reiteration;

the earth takes up again its ceaseless
conversation, picking up where it left off—
as a stream, after the agitation of the rapids,
where it was interrupted by the rocks,
flows on again, lyrical
as laughter, with the sheer delight
that can't be called indifference,
without the least concern for whether
anyone is out there, listening.

———

EMIGRATION

There are always, in each of us,
these two: the one who stays,
the one who goes away—
Charlotte, who stayed in the rectory
and helped her sisters die in England;
Mary Taylor who went off to Australia
and set up shop with a woman friend.
"Charlotte," Mary said to her, "you are all
like potatoes growing in the dark."
And Charlotte got a plaque in Westminster
Abbey; Mary we get a glimpse of
for a moment, waving her kerchief
on the packet boat, and disappearing.
No pseudonym for her, and nothing
left behind, no trace
but a wide wake closing.

Charlotte stayed, and paid and paid—
the little governess with the ungovernable
heart, that she put on the altar.
She paid the long indemnity of all
who work for what will never wish them well,
who never set a limit to what's owed

and cannot risk foreclosure. So London
gave her fame, though it could never
sit comfortably with her at dinner—
how intensity palls when it is
plain and small and has no fortune.
When she died with her unborn child
the stars turned east
to shine in the gum trees of Australia,
watching over what has sidetracked evolution,
where Mary Taylor lived
to a great old age, Charlotte's letters in a box
beside her bed, to keep her anger hot.

God bless us everyone until we sicken,
until the soul is like a little child
stricken in its corner by the wall; so there is
one who always sits there under lamplight
writing, staying on, and one
who walks the strange hills of Australia,
far too defiant of convention for the novels
drawn daily from the pen's "if only"—
if only Emily had lived,
if only they'd had money, if only
there had been a man who'd loved them truly . . .
when all the time there had been
Mary Taylor, whom no one would remember
except she had a famous friend named Charlotte
with whom she was so loving-angry,
who up and left to be a woman
in that godforsaken outpost past
the reach of fantasy, or fiction.

The University Presses of Florida

The University Presses of Florida include the University of Central Florida, Florida International University, and Florida State University. Of these, the University of Central Florida has the most active poetry series, publishing two books per year. The Contemporary Poetry Series began in 1975 under the editorship of Roland Browne, and is currently edited by Judith Hemschemeyer.

Lynn Butler, *Planting the Voice,* 1989
Daryl Chinn, *Soft Parts of the Back,* 1989
Rebecca McClanahan Devet, *Mrs. Houdini,* 1989
Barbara Greenberg, *The Never-Not Sonnets,* 1989
Roald Hoffman, *Allotropy,* 1989
William Hathaway, *Looking into the Heart of Light,* 1988
Ron Smith, *Running Again in Hollywood Cemetery,* 1988
Rebecca McClanahan Devet, *Mother Tongue,* 1987
Don Stap, *Letter at the End of Winter,* 1987
Roald Hoffman, *The Metamict State,* 1987
Richard Michelson, *Tap Dancing for the Relatives,* 1985
CarolAnn Russell, *The Red Envelope,* 1985
Lola Haskins, *Planting the Children,* 1983
Hannah Kahn, *Time, Wait,* 1983
Michael McFee, *Plain Air,* 1983
Gerald Duff, *Calling Collect,* 1982
Nicholas Rinaldi, *We Have Lost Our Fathers,* 1982
George Bogin, *In a Surf of Strangers,* 1981
Robert Siegel, *In a Pig's Eye,* 1980
Van K. Brock, *The Hard Essential Landscape,* 1979
Susan Hartman, *Dumb Show,* 1979

Malcolm Glass, *Bone Love,* 1978
Edmund Skellings, *Face Value,* 1977
David Posner, *The Sandpipers,* 1976
Edmund Skellings, *Heart Attacks,* 1976

Robert Siegel

In a Pig's Eye

> *Hickamore, Hackamore,*
> *Why do you sigh?*
> *I saw my true love*
> *In a pig's eye.*

She couldn't (or could she?)
live with the three chins,
the mouth that took the world
to its plush accordion,
Dutch seas of gravy, a cigar
angling, the *Titanic*'s last stack
above its foundering hulk.

His hands over the omelet were
immaculate, the nails' white
quarter moons dancing, while one
big opal seemed to feast an eye
on her through coffee, mints,
and velvet gastronomic sigh.
(She resolved she couldn't!)

Pushing the table back, he was
Atlas shrugging off the world,
Napoleon rolling it toward the stars—
so complete his every gesture.
How odd, she laughed, all this!
The man was obscene, selfish.
Smiling, his wet lips pursed

to a primrose. Yet, squeezing into
cabs, puffing up red-carpeted stairs,
he courted her—she let herself
be courted—those two jowls hemispheres
into which all fell left

or right. A diamond big as a parfait
he said, his red tongue winking.

Rice salted down the two of them
in the dark car that glided home
to the earthquake of his bed,
where for a moment sweet terror
stalked her, rabbit in a white field.
Then the sun fell on her and the moon and, oh,
she danced above the seas a light rain,
and, tasted, drunk, folded to the earth,
slept quiet as his rib again.

The University of Georgia Press

Although the University of Georgia Press had published poetry sporadically before Paul Zimmer moved from Pittsburgh to direct the Press in 1978, it is Zimmer who deserves the credit for initiating the current active series. Modeling the series in part on the one he started at Pittsburgh, Zimmer worked nights and weekends to keep it going until 1984 when he moved on to Iowa and passed the editorship to Bin Ramke, then a visiting writer at Georgia. When Ramke moved to Denver he took the editorship with him, continuing to make joint decisions on manuscripts with Malcolm Call, the press director, and an anonymous outside reader. Georgia publishes four books per year, two by new poets, and two by veterans, in editions of 500 hardback and 1,000 paper.

J. T. Barbarese, *Firewood Talk,* 1989
Caroline Knox, *To Newfoundland,* 1989
Phillis Levin, *Temples and Fields,* 1988
Jacqueline Osherow, *Looking for Angels in New York,* 1988
Alastair Reid, *Weathering,* 1988
Donald Revell, *The Gaza of Winter,* 1988
Arthur Vogelsang, *Twentieth Century Women,* 1988
Joseph Duemer, *Customs,* 1987
Karen A. Fish, *The Cedar Canoe,* 1987
Sydney Lea, *No Sign,* 1987
Susan Stewart, *The Hive,* 1987
Richard Cole, *The Glass Children,* 1986
Wayne Dodd, *Sometimes Music Rises,* 1986
Gary Margolis, *Falling Awake,* 1986
Aleda Shirley, *Chinese Architecture,* 1986
X. J. Kennedy, *Cross Ties,* 1985
Terese Svoboda, *All Aberration,* 1985
Bruce Weigl, *The Monkey Wars,* 1985

Lynn Emanuel, *Hotel Fiesta,* 1984
Michael Heffernan, *To the Wreakers of Havoc,* 1984
Conrad Hilberry, *The Moon Seen As a Slice of Pineapple,* 1984
Caroline Knox, *The House Party,* 1984
Michael Pettit, *American Light,* 1984
Laurie Sheck, *Amaranth,* 1984
Paul Zarzyski, *The Make-up of Ice,* 1984
Dannie Abse, *One-Legged on Ice,* 1983
John Engels, *Weather-Fear: New and Selected Poems,
1958–1982,* 1983
Brendan Galvin, *Winter Oysters,* 1983
Gary Margolis, *The Day We Still Stand Here,* 1983
Jim W. Rivers, *Proud and On My Feet,* 1983
Tony Connor, *New and Selected Poems,* 1982
Myra Sklarew, *The Science of Goodbyes,* 1982
Franz Douskey, *Rowing Across the Dark,* 1981
John Engels, *Vivaldi in Early Fall,* 1981
Bin Ramke, *White Monkeys,* 1981
Marcia Southwick, *The Night Won't Save Anyone,* 1981
Susan Astor, *Dame,* 1980
Gerald W. Barrax, *An Audience of One,* 1980
Brendan Galvin, *Atlantic Flyway,* 1980
Michael Heffernan, *The Cry of Oliver Hardy,* 1979
Mary Swander, *Succession,* 1979
Hayden Carruth, *The Bloomingdale Papers,* 1974

Susan Astor

THE COUPLING

During meals I used to watch them:
Her stirring and muttering,
Him spooning and sucking,
Both of them busy and undistractible,
Both stoking him with a concocted fuel
Of borscht and chunks of meat
And cucumber
And pumpernickel bread.
From their odd cooperation and intentness,
I knew his hunger was important.

All afternoon he would be in the cellar
Bent at the grinding wheel.
Sometimes I was allowed to stand and watch,
And while I saw him spark the knives to life,
I could always hear her thudding just above us
In her boxy shoes,
Canning her overripe cherries, thinking her slow thoughts.
I could not understand how they connected;
They seemed to have only their oldness in common.

Then once at a Bar Mitzvah
When he was flushed with unaccustomed wine,
Responding to a bout of dirty jokes
I heard him say with pride,
"When I was young I was a bull."
And I believed him,
Saw him black and sleek
Stamping out his demands in the tall grass.

The only time I ever heard her reminisce
It was about the farm in Russia
When she was a girl
And about the animals she left behind.

In particular, it was about a cow,
A cow with feelings "just like a person."
When she told me the story, she had cried,
And later I had cried when I recalled
The times I'd heard him say "old cow, old stupid cow"
About her underneath his breath.

But now, perhaps a little drunk myself,
I saw them in a field a century away,
Him snorting and erect with strength and need
Charging at her from behind,
Her grazing steadily on thick hoofs,
Not looking back,
Squatting slightly in her awkward way,
Bracing herself to take the full brunt of his love.

Lynn Emanuel

――――――

THE PHOTOGRAPH OF RAMONA POSING WHILE FATHER SKETCHES
HER IN CHARCOAL

Father is transforming Ramona
Into a streamline of flesh
Smudging the nipple with his thumb
In the tough, awkward way
Children rub their eyes when tired.
The sea is smooth as oiled stone again
Between Cagnes-sur-Mer and Cap Bénat
And the shadows full of models' empty shoes
Because this is 1938 and the tedium and heat
Of the Côte D'Azure.
Even Ramona is boring in the slick
Cool silver of her flesh.
Life is not pretty
Although she does not believe it.

This girl whose gold tooth
Father polished with his tongue
Could make anyone forget the wild buttocks of Rubens
And fill the fields with weeping painters
For whom the world has become a studio
Of beautiful forgeries.
Life is not pretty
Although they do not know it yet—
And in that heat
And the streets full of Germans.

John Engels

———

JOYCE VOGLER IN 1948

That beautiful pale girl with yellow hair
than whom I shall not other love, nor half so much,
stood with me waiting for the Portage Bus,
hands in her pockets, collar up against the wind,

and grinned at me, and laughed. But I
was worried: it was late, the bus
was late, or I may
have missed it altogether, and

my mother would be waiting up,
and I would not see this girl again forever;
and that has been
the terrible, slow truth of it, not wish, not love

recalling me to that night when the wind,
sweet with catalpa blossom, swelling
and softening, drifting her yellow hair
across my face, broke sternly on us. Now,

in the monstrous wake of passage, I give up
to no less love than did not understand before
the flesh intent on its own timely bearing.
The night hums crazily with wind and trees,

and birds fly, as if it were full day.
I see her laugh at me. I look away,
I crane to see the whole black empty length
of Portage Avenue—and there, at the end,

is the late, the final bus,
ablaze with yellow light,
just turning out from the billowing night
at the far end of the street; for always

time worried me, though always
I was home in time.

Brendan Galvin
———

THE BIRDS

Seeing them corner above fields,
black stars across the morning,
sometimes you'd gladly relinquish
weight of your self-possession
to hover three feet from anything
and be classified rare-to-occasional,

to desert glyph-printed snows one day,
a dot in a quick ellipsis across inlets,
your eyes alert
for heat wavering off savannahs.

Whatever their thoughts, they are never edged
with the scalloped green of money;

no bird violates another
with the inflections of small print;
singular or flocked,
they aren't compared with sheep.

Watching them, you see how their
third step in air
is hardest,
how it puts the boiled-egg face
on every day to flight.
Master it and it's goodbye to everyone
scrubbing at shadows.
You could live on nothing down
and pay only if caught,
you wouldn't be
a lentil in life's great stew anymore.
Think of freely backsliding, of countering
the food-gatherer's monotony
with the new indirection of your ways.
You could perform the herring gull's
high-stepping run,
his oyster drop on the uprise
and brief earth touch
to shake the essence from the broken shell.
You could be hang gliding
above ice piled in harbors like
white grand pianos,
or breasting thermals where sun
rousts vagrant ground fog.

You could be
the least tern who plucks
the edge of the sea's potlatch,
or the egret in its pool
like your spirit's sudden cry at sloughed confusion.

Michael Heffernan

THE CRAZYMAN'S REVIVAL (#6)

When it got specially bad he began to think
He thought about the sick dog by the road
he found one time and put a bullet in its head
He thought about the spot that bullet made
on the dog's brow, wonderfully round and pink
He thought about the things he knew for sure
how men were lonely and lived lonely lives
how even the sun was lonely and on fire
He thought about the cry of Oliver Hardy
how he would dance with dread and tweedle his derby
and send his clear soprano up from all his tonnage
whenever the deadly husband with the knives
the murderous sailor or their own relentless wives
were about to do him and his pal some permanent damage

DAFFODILS

It wasn't the daffodils so much
as the idea of them that got
me. I was wandering by in my
own lonely manner like a cloud in the sky
feeling ugly and grim when out
of nowhere up blossomed a clutch

of yellow daffodils by the curb.
Bright things they were, good and sweet,
and I knew I liked them better than
music or money or my girl's friendly skin
the way they stood there by the street
nicer and newer and simpler

by far than anything I had seen
all morning. Oh it was fine
to know them! I said, You daffodils
put me in mind of the clean white windowsills
of a kitchen when I was nine
one April Saturday in 19

52—my grandmother's kitchen,
her fingers dangling with dough,
the odor of pie in the oven,
the windows white as the windows of Heaven,
as if the air were bright with snow,
and someone outside them, watching.

————

FAMOUS LAST WORDS

Is it a question, then, of getting up
the will to move from one place to the next?
I'm undecided, largely, at the start,
as always, though I guess I'm apt to see
a good bit better once I've had a drink.
It's still too soon for that yet. I can wait.

Sometimes I have to laugh: the more you wait,
the more you end up wishing you could up
and have a look at what will happen next.
Where did it ever get you, from the start,
the time or two you said you'd wait and see,
when all you really wanted was to drink

it all in, all of it, in one long drink
that would relieve you of the need to wait
for the Right Moment? A man's time is up
too soon in this quick world. As for the next,
I think I have a theory: first you start
to notice how you can't move, think, or see,

and this alarms you, so you try to see
what a person has to do to get a drink
in this place. No one drinks here, so you wait
a long time trying to figure out what's up—
a very long time, well into the next
two or three thousand years, until you start

to feel more lonely than you were to start
with, and you stay this way forever. See,
I'm realistic. And I need a drink.
The will to move is only the will to wait
in different terms: moving is when you're up
and ready for whatever happens next;

waiting is what you do when you're the next
in line and several others got the start
on up ahead of you and you can see
their dust rise off them. If I had a drink
instead of breakfast, I could stand the wait.
They'd probably like to know what held me up.

Maybe they'll send a man up here to see
what keeps me waiting. Maybe he'll say I'm next.
Maybe he'd like a drink before we start.

Conrad Hilberry

———

THE WOMAN WHO WAS READY TO DIE

Unmistakably, the picture showed the mound
under her skull fixing its tentacles
in the grey rocks. The doctor circled around
the news, but she had guessed it. A sudden ease
moved through her like the wash of waves. Her grass
would somehow mow itself this summer. Her children
would untangle their own marriages.
There would be no more choices, no more men.

Yet when her face came loose, when her blood forgot
its language, she took up kitchen knives and fought
the squid. She slashed his watery belly, cut
at the fat arms that reached down and undid
the buttons of her body. When he brought
his mouth to hers, she tore his lips, she spat.

X. J. Kennedy

Ars Poetica

The goose that laid the golden egg
Died looking up its crotch
To find out how its sphincter worked.

Would you lay well? Don't watch.

Nude Descending a Staircase

Toe upon toe, a snowing flesh,
A gold of lemon, root and rind,
She sifts in sunlight down the stairs
With nothing on. Nor on her mind.

We spy beneath the banister
A constant thresh of thigh on thigh—
Her lips imprint the swinging air
That parts to let her parts go by.

One-woman waterfall, she wears
Her slow descent like a long cape
And pausing, on the final stair
Collects her motions into shape.

Charles Martin

TERMINAL COLLOQUY

O where will you go when the blinding flash
Scatters the seed of a million suns?
And what will you do in the rain of ash?

I'll draw the blinds and pull down the sash,
And hide from the light of so many noons.
But how will it be when the blinding flash

Disturbs your body's close-knit mesh,
Bringing to light your lovely bones?
What will you wear in the rain of ash?

I will go bare without my flesh,
My vertebrae will click like stones.
Ah. But where will you dance when the blinding flash

Settles the city in a holy hush?
I will dance alone among the ruins.
Ah. And what will you say to the rain of ash?

I will be charming. My subtle speech
Will weave close turns and counter turns—
No. What will you say to the rain of ash?
Nothing, after the blinding flash.

Bin Ramke

THE OBSCURE PLEASURE OF THE INDISTINCT

Under light soft as seawater, sounds
brush lightly past: shiver of laughter
from a pale woman's flimsy neck,

the rustle of linen under your own
hand resting on the table. You bite
into the dark meat of the pheasant,
you almost scream—you would,
were it not for your exquisite
parentage. Nestled in the stained
crevice of a molar a piece
of lead, shot, twice brutally painful:

and for a second time the bird flies
in your mind, and the long stiff
feathers brush the long brown leaf
on a cold autumn morning. Then
a sip of Pouilly-Fuissé, cool
on the tongue, soothing. Sounds
from the kitchen again are muffled, vague.

Paul Smyth

———

ROAD CONSTRUCTION

Each morning I'd start the compressor, a yellow HERMES,
And pack the shank in grease. The hammer weighed
Ninety-five pounds while the drivers stood in threes
Nodding and spitting, lean, relaxed, well-paid.
The thickfaced foreman muttered studying
His rolled out blueprint's eight abstracted lanes.
His brute D9's ate hills, and they could wring
Fierce arias from rock by treads and chains.

My job was drilling holes for dynamite,
Staying slightly ahead of the highway's thrust.
I traded days for pay. I hated night.
Hunched in the din, in the clouds of granite dust,
My jackhammer beating deeply into the ledge,
I labored at the future's crumbling edge.

Barry Spacks

MALEDICTION

You who dump the beer cans in the lake;
Who in the strict woods sow
The bulbous polyethylene retorts;
Who from your farting car
With spiffy rear-suspension toss
Your tissues, mustard-streaked, upon
The generating moss; who drop
The squamules of your reckless play,
Grease-wrappers, unspare parts, lie-labeled
Cultures even flies would scorn
To spawn on—total Zed, my kinsman
Ass-on-wheels, my blare-bred bray
And burden,

            may the nice crabs thread
Your private wilds with turnpikes; weasels'
Condoms squish between your toes,
And plastic-coated toads squat *plop*
Upon your morning egg—may gars
Come nudge you from your inner-tube,
Perch hiss you to the bottom, junked,
A discard, your dense self your last
Enormity.

The University of Illinois Press

The University of Illinois Press Poetry Series began in 1971 when Laurence Lieberman proposed the idea to Richard Wentworth, then associate director and editor at the Press. Wentworth was receptive to publishing poetry, having been director of the Louisiana State University Press when its poetry series was initiated in 1964. Lieberman and Ralph Mills, both in the English department at the University of Illinois at Chicago, served as coeditors until Mills dropped out in the mid-1970s. Currently, Lieberman continues as poetry editor, and the Press publishes two or three books per year in editions of 1,000 to 1,500 paperback copies.

Dennis Schmitz, *Eden*, 1989
Michael Van Walleghen, *Blue Tango*, 1989
Paul Zimmer, *The Great Bird of Love*, 1989
Philip D. Church, *Furnace Harbor: A Rhapsody of the North Country*, 1988
William Olson, *The Hand of God and a Few Bright Flowers*, 1988
Nance Van Winckel, *Bad Girl, with Hawk*, 1988
T. R. Hummer, *Lower-Class Heresy*, 1987
Frederick Morgan, *Poems: New and Selected*, 1987
Sylvia Moss, *Cities in Motion*, 1987
Steven Berg, *In It*, 1986
Alice Fulton, *Palladium*, 1986
Phyllis Thompson, *The Ghosts of Who We Were*, 1986
Robert Wrigley, *Moon in a Mason Jar*, 1986
Michael S. Harper, *Dear John, Dear Coltrane*, 1985
John Knoepfle, *Poems from the Sangamon*, 1985
Nathaniel Mackey, *Eroding Witness*, 1985
Emily Grosholz, *The River Painter*, 1984
Michael S. Harper, *Healing Song for the Inner Ear*, 1984
T. R. Hummer, *The Passion of the Right-Angled Man*, 1984

Josephine Miles, *Collected Poems, 1930–83,* 1983
Jim Barnes, *The American Book of the Dead,* 1982
Sydney Lea, *The Floating Candles,* 1982
Frederick Morgan, *Northbook,* 1982
Stephen Berg, *With Akhmatova at the Black Gates,* 1981
Dave Smith, *Dream Flights,* 1981
Michael Van Walleghen, *More Trouble with the Obvious,* 1981
Sydney Lea, *Searching the Drowned Man,* 1980
Josephine Miles, *Coming to Terms,* 1979
Frederick Morgan, *Death Mother and Other Poems,* 1979
Dave Smith, *Goshawk, Antelope,* 1979
James Whitehead, *Local Men,* 1979
Michael Anania, *Riversongs,* 1978
Dan Masterson, *On Earth as It Is,* 1978
Michael S. Harper, *Images of Kin,* 1977
Frederick Morgan, *Poems of the Two Worlds,* 1977
Dave Smith, *Cumberland Station,* 1977
Virginia R. Terris, *Tracking,* 1977
Michael Borich, *The Black Hawk Songs,* 1975
Michael S. Harper, *Nightmare Begins Responsibility,* 1975
Michael Van Walleghen, *The Wichita Poems,* 1975
Josephine Miles, *To All Appearances,* 1974
Robert Bagg, *The Scrawny Sonnets and Other Narratives,* 1973
Phyllis Thompson, *The Creation Frame,* 1973
Richard Emil Braun, *The Foreclosure,* 1972
Michael S. Harper, *History is Your Own Heartbeat,* 1971

Alice Fulton

Everyone Knows the World Is Ending

Everyone knows the world is ending.
Everyone always thought so, yet
here's the world. Where fundamentalists flick slideshows
in darkened gyms, flash endtime mess-
ages of bliss, tribulation
through the trembling bleachers: Christ will come
by satellite TV, bearing millennial weather
before plagues of false prophets and real locusts
botch the cosmic climate—which ecologists predict
is already withering from the green-
house effect as fossil fuels seal in
the sun's heat and acid rains
give lakes the cyanotic blues.

When talk turns this way, my mother speaks in memories,
each thought a focused mote in the apocalypse's
iridescent fizz. She is trying to restore a world
to glory, but the facts shift with each telling
of her probable gospel. Some stories have been
trinkets in my mind since childhood, yet what clings is not
how she couldn't go near the sink
for months without tears when her mother died,
or how she feared she wouldn't get her own
beribboned kindergarten chair, but the grief
in the skull like radium
in lead, and the visible dumb love like water
in crystal, at one with what holds it. The triumph

of worlds beyond words. Memory entices because ending is
its antonym. We're here to learn
the earth by heart and everything is crying
mind me, mind me! Yet the brain selects and shimmers
to a hand on skin while numbing the constant
stroke of clothes. Thoughts frame and flash
before the dark snaps back: The dress with lace tiers

she adored and the girl with one just like it,
the night she woke to see my father
walk down the drive and the second she remembered
he had died. So long as we keep chanting the words
those worlds will live, but just
so long, so long, so long. Each instant waves
through our nature and is nothing.
But in the love, the grief, under and above
the mother tongue, a permanence
hums: the steady mysterious
the coherent starlight.

———

PLUMBLINE

In Memoriam: John Callahan, my grandfather

The world could snore, wrangle, or tear
itself to atoms while Papa sat
unnettled, bashful, his brain
a lathe smoothing thoughts civil
above fingers laced and pink

as baby booties; Papa, who said of any gambler,
roughneck, drunkard, just "I don't think much
of him," and in stiff denims
toted his lunchpail's spuds
down a plumbline of twelve-hour shifts:

farmed, lumbered, and cow-kicked,
let the bones knit their own
rivet, oiled big wheels that bullied
water uphill, drank stout, touched animals only
unawkwardly, drove four-in-hand, and sired six.

My ideas are dumb: a fizz
mute and thick as the head on a beer

he once thought, who never thought
such clabber could whiz through
genes and seed and speak.

Michael S. Harper

NIGHTMARE BEGINS RESPONSIBILITY

I place these numbered wrists to the pane
watching white uniforms whisk over
him in the tube-kept
prison
fear what they will do in experiment
watch my gloved stickshifting gasolined hands
breathe *boxcar-information-please* infirmary tubes
distrusting white-pink mending paperthin
silkened end hairs, distrusting tubes
shrunk in his *trunk-skincapped*
shaven head, in thighs
distrusting-white-hands-picking-baboon-light
on this son who will not make his second night
of this wardstrewn intensive airpocket
where his father's asthmatic
hymns of *night-train,* train done gone
his mother can only know that he has flown
up into essential calm unseen corridor
going boxscarred home, *mamaborn, sweetsonchild*
gonedowntown into *researchtestingwarehousebatteryacid*
mama-son-done-gone me telling her 'nother
train tonight, no music, no breathstroked
heartbeat in my infinite distrust of them:

and of my distrusting self
white-doctor-who-breathed-for-him-all-night
say it for two sons gone,
say nightmare, say it loud
panebreaking heartmadness:
nightmare begins responsibility.

115

Sydney Lea

FOR MY FATHER, WHO HUNTED

. . . great as is the pleasure of becoming acquainted with the stars and planets,
greater still the joy of recognizing them as friends, returning after absence. . . .
                                        —*A Beginner's Star Book*

A late beginner, I was struggling with
an early chapter: "Learning to Observe."
I have no faith in stars, in omens—nothing
there prepared me for the uncle's phone call

or the nothings sent back from the hospital,
laid out: a watch, a dollar nine in coin;
yet I hold, despite disastrous evidence,
a faith in language: *planet*, say,

from dim old names for *wanderer*. It has no place
that's certain like the stars'. Come near,
it kindles in the sky; or, wandered off,
it loses glory: that I've learned

is "occultation." Now all detail shines,
with a trace of brightness recognized,
though words obscure: the pheasant's fire
of feather in the dark of afternoon;

river waves rebounding noon's white slap;
the pickerelweed at false dawn flickered orange
above my spread of decoys.   All
have, in your absence, influence; and down,

as if to swing a leg across our log fence,
climbs Orion.   Or minutiae
rise up in mind and air: your wallet
spilling silver and your watch

in constellation, sweep hand sweeping back
the seconds, minutes fallen down.

Dan Masterson

———

FOR A CHILD GOING BLIND

I have awakened her
when the sky was at its blackest,
all stars erased, no moon to speak of,
and led her down the front path
to our dock, where we'd swim to the raft,
finding it by touch
fifty or sixty strokes from shore.

And sit
listening to things, the movement of water
around us drawing us closer, a hunched
double knot of child and father
hearing all there is to hear,
close beneath bats who see without sight,
whose hunger is fed by darkness.

The neighbors see her often in the woods,
on hands and knees, smoothing the moss
where it spreads in the shade, marvelling
at the tongues of birds, the stained petal
of the dogwood, the vein of color
skirting the edge of an upturned stone.

This morning she awoke to the first flash
of the magnolia, and will save the petals

as they fall, their purpled lids
curling white on the lawn.

We meant to tell her how the rainbows come,
how they close into shadows,
how we would be there nonetheless;
we meant to tell her before
they arrived at supper this evening,
rimming everything in sight.

She wonders if we see them
cupping the stars, the kitchen lamp,
each other's face, and we say
we do.

Dave Smith

───

Night Fishing for Blues

Fortress Monroe, Virginia

The big-jawed Bluefish, ravenous, sleek muscle slamming
into banked histories of rock
    pile, hair-shaggy pier legs, drives
    each year to black Bay shallows, churns,

       fin-wheels, convoys, a black army, blue

stained sequins rank after rank, fluting bloodshot
gill-flowers, sucking bitter land water, great Ocean
Blues with belly-bones ringing like gongs.

      Tonight, not far from where Jefferson Davis

hunched in a harrowing cell, gray eyes quick
as crabs' nubs, I come back over planks
deep drummed under boots, tufts of hair

floating at my ears, everything finally right
    to pitch through tideturn and mudslur
    for fish with teeth like snapped sabers.

        In blue crescents of base lights, I cast hooks

baited with Smithfield ham: they reel, zing,
plummet, coil in corrosive swirls, bump on
scum-skinned rocks. No skin divers prowl here,

      visibility an arm's length, my visions

hand-to-hand in the line's warp. A meat-
baited lure limps through limbs nippling the muck,
silhouettes, shoots forward, catches a cruising Blue

      sentry's eye, snags and sets

case-hardened barbs. Suddenly, I am not alone:
    three Negroes plump down in lawn chairs, shudder-
    casting into the black pod plodding under us. One

      ripples with age, a grandmotherly obelisk,

her breath puffing like a coal stove. She swivels
heavily, chewing her dark nut, spits thick juice
like a careful chum.

        When I yank the first Blue
she mumbles, her eyes roll far out on the black-
blue billowing sea-screen. I hear her canting

      to Africa, a cluck in her throat, a chain

song from the fisherman's house. I cannot
understand. Bluefish are pouring at me in squads.
I haul two, three at a time, torpedoes, moon-shiners,
jamming my feet into the splintered floor, battling
whatever comes. I know I have waited
a whole life for this minute. Like purple dreams

      graven on cold cell walls, Blues walk over

our heads, ground on back-wings, grind their teeth.
They splash rings of blue and silver around us, tiaras
of lost battalions. I can smell the salt of ocean
runners as she hollers *I ain't doing so bad
for an old queen.* No time to answer. Two

      car-hoods down her descendants swing sinewy arms

in Superfly shirts, exotic butterflies: I hear them
pop beer cans, the whoosh released like stale breath
through a noose no one remembers. We hang

      fast flat casts, artless, no teasing fishermen,

beyond the book-bred lures of the pristine streams,
speeded-up, centrifugal, movie machines rewound
too far, belts slipped, gears gone, momentum

      hauling us back, slinging lines, winging wildly

as howitzers. Incredibly it happens: I feel
the hook hammer and shake and throw my entire weight
to dragging, as if I have caught the goddamndest

      Blue in the Atlantic. She screams: *Oh my God!*

Four of us fumbling in beamed headlight and blue
arclight cut the hook from her face. Gnats butterfly,
nag us: I put it in deep and it must be gouged out
like a cyst. When it is free, I hear Blues not yet

dead flopping softly. I tell her it is a lucky
thing she can see. She mops blood blued over
gold-lined teeth and opens her arms so her dress

billows like a caftan. She wants

nothing but to fish. I hand her her pole, then cast
as far as I can. She pumps, wings a sinker and hooks
into flashing slop and reels hard. In one instant both

our lines leap rigid as daguerreotypes; we have

caught each other but we go on for the blue blood of
ghosts that thrash in the brain's empty room.
We pull at shadows until we see there is nothing, then
sit on the shaky pier like prisoners. Coil after coil
we trace the path of Bluefish-knots backward,

unlooping, feeling for holes, giving, testing,

slapping the gnats from our skins. Harried, unbound,
we leap to be fishers. But now a gray glow
shreds with the cloud curtain, an old belly-fire

guts the night. Already the tide humps around

on itself. Lights flicker like campfires in duty windows
at Ft. Monroe. She hooks up, saying *Sons they done*
let us go. I cast once more but nothing bites. Everywhere

a circle of Blues bleaches, stiffens

in flecks of blood. We kneel, stuff styrofoam
boxes with blankets of ice, break their backs
to keep them cold and sweet, the woman gravely
showing us what to do. By dawn the stink has passed

out of our noses. We drink beer like family.

All the way home thousands of Blues fall from my head,
falling with the gray Atlantic, and a pale veiny light
fills the road with sea-shadows that drift in figure

   eights, knot and snarl and draw me forward.

ON A FIELD TRIP AT FREDERICKSBURG

The big steel tourist shield says maybe
fifteen thousand got it here. No word
of either Whitman or one uncle
I barely remember in the smoke
that filled his tiny mountain house.

If each finger were a thousand of them
I could clap my hands and be dead
up to my wrists. It was quick
though not so fast as we can do it
now, one bomb, atomic or worse,
one silly pod slung on wing-tip,
high up, an egg cradled
by some rapacious mockingbird.

Hiroshima canned nine times their number
in a flash. Few had the time
to moan or feel the feeling
ooze back in the groin.

In a ditch I stand
above Marye's Heights, the book-
boned faces of Brady's fifteen-year-old
drummers, before battle, rigid
as August's dandelions
all the way to the Potomac
rolling in my skull.

If Audubon came here, the names
of birds would gush, the marvel
single feathers make
evoke a cloud, a nation,
a gray blur preserved
on a blue horizon, but
there is only a wandering child,
one dark stalk snapped off
in her hand, held out to me.
Taking it, I try to help her
hold its obscure syllables
one instant in her mouth,
like a drift of wind
at the forehead, the front door,
the black, numb fingernails.

Michael Van Walleghen

MORE TROUBLE WITH THE OBVIOUS

A baby bird has fallen from its tree and lies feebly peeping dead center
of the bright circle under our streetlight. What is there to do but bring it
in? We dutifully prepare a shoebox, then mix up the baby food and
hamburger of an old routine we know by heart, the ritual we've learned
as children—but the truth is, in all the years since child- hood, neither
my wife nor I can remember having saved a single bird. We won't save
this one either, trembling weakly now on the kitchen table, refusing to
do so much as open its beak for our ridiculous food.

It lives with us two days, then dies suddenly in my hand—of "heart
attack" my neighbor says. "Young birds like that almost always die of
heart attack." He says this pounding nails in his porch and I believe him.
In fact, I feel stupid for having mentioned it at all. A heart attack. Of
course. The best thing would have been not to touch it. Perhaps it would
have found a place to hide; and then, in the morning, its mother might

have flown down to feed it. In any case, it's dead now and buried in the garden. The same garden, by the way, from which my neighbor's cat wrestled a live snake once into the hubbub of our barbecue.

But then I seem to have always had trouble with the obvious. Once, when a friend died, and after my parents had told me he had died, I came around the next morning anyway to call him out for school. His mother came to the door weeping and told me Orville couldn't go to school that day. I felt as if I had been walking in my sleep. I knew my parents hadn't lied, and I certainly knew what death meant; but somehow, until that moment, I must have thought it was just a dream I'd had. At school, another friend said he thought Orville died from eating donuts every night for supper. I had no trouble at all believing that. By then, donuts made about as much sense as anything.

A baby bird has fallen from its tree . . . someone you love perhaps is dying in another city. There must be something we can do. I remember one Sunday Orville and I got down on our knees in an alley and asked the Blessed Mother for a kite. When we found a rolled-up kite in the next ashcan with the rubber bands still on it, we *knew* it was a miracle. And we were glad, of course; but neither one of us, I think, was overwhelmed. We just believed in miracles and thought they happened all the time. We thought the birds we found needed milk and bread. We thought when they got big they would be our friends, do us wonderful favors, and keep us company forever.

James Whitehead

A LOCAL MAN REMEMBERS BETTY FULLER

Betty Fuller cried and said, Hit me.
I did. Which made her good and passionate
But Betty Fuller never came. Fate
Decreed that Betty Fuller would not see
The generosity a lively house
And loyal husband bring. She lost her mind
In Mendenhall. She got herself defined
As absolutely mad. A single mouse
Caused her to run exactly down the line
Of a wide road, running both north and south
With execrations pouring from her mouth.

She's out at Whitfield doing crazy time
And she can't possibly remember me
Among the rest. I'm satisfied she can't.

Robert Wrigley

HEART ATTACK

Throwing his small, blond son
into the air, he begins to feel it,
a slow-motion quivering, some part
broken loose and throbbing with its own pulse,
like the cock's involuntary leaping
toward whatever shadow looms in front.

It is below his left shoulder blade,
a blip regular as radar, and he thinks of wings
and flight, his son's straight soar and fall
out of and into his high-held hands.
He is amused by the quick change
on the boy's little face; from the joy

of release and catch, to the near terror
at apex. It is the same with every throw.
And every throw comes without
his knowing. Nor his son's. Again
and again, the rise and fall, like breathing,
again the joy and fear, squeal and laughter,

until the world becomes a swarm of shapes
around him, and his arms
go leaden and prickled, and he knows
the sound is no longer laughter
but wheezing, knows he holds his son
in his arms and has not let him fly

upward for many long moments now.
He is on his knees, as his son stands,
supporting him, the look on the child's face
something the man has seen before:
not fear, not joy, not even misunderstanding,
but the quick knowledge sons

must come to, at some age
when everything else is put aside—
the knowledge of death, the stench
of mortality—that fraction of an instant
even a child can know, when
his father does not mean to leave, but goes.

Indiana University Press

The Indiana University Press Poetry Series was initiated in 1952 with the publication of Samuel Yellen's *In the House and Out,* and ceased publication in 1978 with David Wagoner's *Who Shall Be the Sun?* Yellen, a professor of English at Indiana University, served as editor for the entire term of the series. Indiana has the distinction of having published probably the bestselling university press poetry book in history—Theodore Roethke's *Words for the Wind,* which sold 60,000 copies before rights reverted to Doubleday. The series terminated, in part, because of competition from other university presses.

David Wagoner, *Who Shall Be the Sun?* 1978
David Wagoner, *Collected Poems, 1956–1976,* 1976
John Woods, *Striking the Earth,* 1976
David Wagoner, *Riverbed,* 1972
John Woods, *Turning to Look Back: Poems 1955–1970,* 1972
Samuel Yellen, *The Convex Mirror,* 1971
Sandra McPherson, *Elegies for the Hot Season,* 1970
Rolfe Humphries, *Coat On a Stick,* 1969
David Wagoner, *New and Selected Poems,* 1969
John Woods, *Keeping Out of Trouble,* 1968
Charles G. Bell, *Songs for a New America,* 1966
David Wagoner, *Staying Alive,* 1966 (1980)
John Woods, *The Cutting Edge,* 1966
Rolfe Humphries, *Collected Poems,* 1965
Samuel Yellen, *New and Selected Poems,* 1964
Joanne DeLongchamps, *The Hungry Lions,* 1963
Babette Deutsch, *Collected Poems, 1919–1962,* 1963
Theodore Roethke, *Words for the Wind,* 1963
David Wagoner, *The Nesting Ground,* 1963
Conrad Aiken, *Brownstone Eclogues,* 1962

Carolyn Kizer, *The Ungrateful Garden,* 1961
John Woods, *On the Morning of Color,* 1961
Jack Hirschman, *A Correspondence of Americans,* 1960
Josephine Miles, *Poems, 1930–1960,* 1960 (1979)
Babette Deutsch, *Coming of Age,* 1959
David Wagoner, *A Place to Stand,* 1958
Richard Aldrich, *An Apology Both Ways,* 1957
Charles G. Bell *Delta Return,* 1956
Kenneth Fearing, *New and Selected Poems,* 1956
Neil Weiss, *Changes of Garments,* 1956
Josephine Miles, *Prefabrications,* 1955
John Woods, *The Deaths at Paragon, Indiana,* 1955
Kenneth Slade Alling, *Kingdom of Diagonals,* 1954
Padraic Colum, *The Vegetable Kingdom,* 1954 (1984)
Walker Gibson, *The Reckless Spenders,* 1954 (1967)
Donald Campbell Babcock, *New England Harvest,* 1953
David Wagoner, *Dry Sun, Dry Wind,* 1953
Samuel Yellen, *In the House and Out,* 1952

Babette Deutsch

DISASTERS OF WAR: GOYA AT THE MUSEUM

Streets opening like wounds: Madrid's. The thresh
Of resistance ends before a tumbling wall;
    The coward and the cursing sprawl
    Brotherly, one white heap of flesh
    Char-mouthed and boneyard black.
A woman, dragged off, howls—a lively sack
Of loot. An infant, fallen on its back,
Scowls from the stones at the Herodian lark.
Light is the monster fattening on this dark.

If shadow takes cadavers for her chair,
Where fresh fires glare life lifts a wolfish snout.
    Bruised and abused by hope, the rout,
    Turning, is gunned across the square
    And scattered. Rope, knife, lead
Slice prayer short. A lolling head
Grins, as with toothache. Stubbornly, the dead
Thrust forward like a beggar's senseless claw.
What is scrawled there in acid? THIS I SAW.

Beyond the Madonnas and marbles, Goya's brute
Testament pits itself against the hush
    Of the blond halls, the urbane crush—
    Against the slat-eyed, the astute,
    Craning, against the guard, who yawns.
And pits itself in vain: this dark, these dawns,
Vomit of an old war, things the nightmare spawns
Are pictures at an exhibition. We
Look, having viewed too much, and cannot see.

Sandra McPherson

KEEPING HOUSE

I never intended this.
Just a house clean, sharp as a knife.
None of this poltergeist
Leaking and cracking and smudging, not

The silver mink
Mildew fuzzing the window frame,
Electric cords ribbon-
Worming behind the phonograph. Bolshevik

Insects insist
We share space, squat
In corners previously bare, strain
Through screens,

Warm on the hot plates
Of windows. Around the ceiling
Our isolate spider runs
Like a train.

So spring breaks—breaks in!
The walls crawl
Where cellophane light blinks
Among shadows

Of willow leaves bursting their buds.
Honey-pot ants decorate the pane
Like ankhs a pyramid.
They are brimful.

The house is brimful.
Eden, pure Eden is chasing us.
The baby is pounding her bars
To get out.

The names of things—sparks!
I ran on them like a component:
Henries, microhenries, Blue
Beavers, wee wee ductors:
Biographer of small lives,
Of a plug and his girl named Jack,
Of Utopian colonies which worked—
Steel, germanium, brass, aluminum,
Replaceables.
        Outside, afloat, my words
Swung an arm charting the woman
Who was the river bottom.

We tried, beyond work, at work,
To keep what we loved. Near
Christmas I remember the office
Women trimming their desperately
Glittering holy day trees. And,
Just as I left, the company
Talent show, the oils and sentiment
Thick on still lifes and seacoasts,
The brush strokes tortured as a child's
First script. Someone
Had studied driftwood; another man,
The spray of a wave, the mania
Of waters above torpedoes.

Theodore Roethke

ELEGY FOR JANE
My Student, Thrown by a Horse

I remember the neckcurls, limp and damp as tendrils;
And her quick look, a sidelong pickerel smile;
And how, once startled into talk, the light syllables leaped for her,
And she balanced in the delight of her thought,
A wren, happy, tail into the wind,
Her song trembling the twigs and small branches.
The shade sang with her;
The leaves, their whispers turned to kissing;
And the mold sang in the bleached valleys under the rose.

Oh, when she was sad, she cast herself down into such a pure depth,
Even a father could not find her:
Scraping her cheek against straw;
Stirring the clearest water.

My sparrow, you are not here,
Waiting like a fern, making a spiny shadow.
The sides of wet stones cannot console me,
Nor the moss, wound with the last light.

If only I could nudge you from this sleep,
My maimed darling, my skittery pigeon.
Over this damp grave I speak the words of my love:
I, with no rights in this matter,
Neither father nor lover.

My Papa's Waltz

The whiskey on your breath
Could make a small boy dizzy;
But I hung on like death:
Such waltzing was not easy.

We romped until the pans
Slid from the kitchen shelf;
My mother's countenance
Could not unfrown itself.

The hand that held my wrist
Was battered on one knuckle;
At every step you missed
My right ear scraped a buckle.

You beat time on my head
With a palm caked hard by dirt,
Then waltzed me off to bed
Still clinging to your shirt.

The Waking

I wake to sleep, and take my waking slow.
I feel my fate in what I cannot fear.
I learn by going where I have to go.

We think by feeling. What is there to know?
I hear my being dance from ear to ear.
I wake to sleep, and take my waking slow.

Of those so close beside me, which are you?
God bless the Ground! I shall walk softly there,
And learn by going where I have to go.

Light takes the Tree; but who can tell us how?
The lowly worm climbs up a winding stair;
I wake to sleep, and take my waking slow.

Great Nature has another thing to do
To you and me; so take the lively air,
And, lovely, learn by going where to go.

This shaking keeps me steady. I should know.
What falls away is always. And is near.
I wake to sleep, and take my waking slow.
I learn by going where I have to go.

David Wagoner

—————

BEAUTY AND THE BEAST

Men wept when they saw her breasts, squinted with pain
At her clear profile, boggled at her knees,
Turned slack-jawed at her rear-view walking away,
And every available inch of her hair and skin
Had been touched by love poems and delicious gossip.
The most jaundiced and jaded people in the village
Agreed with the Prince: young Beauty was a beauty.

But through the long day he doused and plucked his roses,
Drained and refilled his moat, or caulked his dungeons,
And all night long he clocked the erring planets,
Pondered the lives of saints like a Latin-monger,
Or sat up half-seas over with sick falcons,
While Beauty lingered in her sheerest nightgowns
With the light behind her, wilting from sheer boredom.

"You're a bore!" she said, "Prince Charming is a bore!"
She cried to the gaping seamstresses and fishwives.
"He's a bore!" she yelled to the scullions and butcher's helpers.

"That tedious, bland, preoccupied, prickling Princeling
Is a bore's bore!" she told the bloody barbers
And waxy chandlers leaning out to watch her
Dragging her rear-view home to Mother and Father.

But deep in the woods, behind a bush, the Beast
Had big ideas about her. When she slipped by,
Hiking her skirts to give her legs free sway
And trailing a lovely, savage, faint aroma
Fit to unman a beast, the Beast said, "Beauty,
Come live with me in the bushes where it's chancy,
Where it's scare and scare alike, where it's quick and murky."

She looked him over. Though the light was patchy,
She could see him better than she wanted to:
Wherever men have skin, the Beast had hair;
Wherever men have hair, he had black bristles;
Wherever men have bristles, he grew teeth;
And wherever men have teeth, his snaggling tusks
Lapped over his smile. So Beauty said, "No thank you."

"You'd be a sweet relief. I'd gorge on you.
I'm sick of retching my time with hags and gorgons.
You're gorgeous. Put down my rising gorge forever."
She remembered her mother whispering: *The Beast
Is a bargain. It's a well-known fact that, later,
He turns into a Prince, humble and handsome,
With unlimited credit and your father's mustache.*

*So all you have to do is grin and bear him
Till the worst is over.* But Beauty felt uncertain.
Still, after the Prince, it seemed like now or never,
And maybe all men were monsters when they saw her,
And maybe the ugliest would teach her sooner.
Her heart felt colder than a wizard's whistle:
She said, "You Beast, how can I say I love you?"

With horny fingers caressing everything
Available on the little world of her body,

The Beast then took her gently, his rich odor
Wafting about them like the mist from graveyards,
And Beauty began to branch out like a castle
Taller than trees, and from the highest tower
She loosened her long hair, and the Beast climbed it.

When he was spent, he lay beside her, brushing
Leaves from her buttresses, and said, "I love you."
She shrank back to herself and felt afraid.
"You'll change into something much more comfortable
Now that you've taken me," she said. "I know:
You'll be transformed to someone like Prince Charming."
"I'm always like this," he said, and drooled a little.

"If you're going to change, change now," she told him, weeping.
"Peel off that monster suit and get it over."
"I wear myself out, not in," he said. "I'll love you
In all the worst ways, as clumsily as heaven."
"Thank God," she said. And Beauty and the Beast
Stole off together, arm in hairy arm,
And made themselves scarce in the bewitching forest.

THE POETS AGREE TO BE QUIET BY THE SWAMP

They hold their hands over their mouths
And stare at the stretch of water.
What can be said has been said before:
Strokes of light like herons' legs in the cattails,
Mud underneath, frogs lying even deeper.
Therefore, the poets may keep quiet.
But the corners of their mouths grin past their hands.
They stick their elbows out into the evening,
Stoop, and begin the ancient croaking.

Report from a Forest Logged by the Weyerhaeuser Company

Three square miles clear-cut.
Now only the facts matter:
The heaps of gray-splintered rubble,
The churned-up duff, the roots, the bulldozed slash,
The silence,

And beyond the ninth hummock
(All of them pitched sideways like wrecked houses)
A creek still running somewhere, bridged and dammed
By cracked branches.
No birdsong. Not one note.

And this is April, a sunlit morning.
Nothing but facts. Wedges like halfmoons
Fallen where saws cut over and under them
Bear ninety or more rings.
A trillium gapes at so much light.

Among the living: a bent huckleberry,
A patch of salal, a wasp,
And now, making a mistake about me,
Two brown-and-black butterflies landing
For a moment on my boot.

Among the dead: thousands of fir seedlings
A foot high, planted ten feet apart,
Parched brown for lack of the usual free rain,
Two buckshot beercans, and overhead,
A vulture big as an eagle.

Selective logging, they say, we'll take three miles,
It's good for the bears and deer, they say,
More brush and berries sooner or later,
We're thinking about the future—if you're in it
With us, they say. It's a comfort to say

Like *Dividend* or *Forest Management* or *Keep Out.*
They've managed this to a fare-thee-well.
In Chicago, hogs think about hog futures.
But staying with the facts, the facts,
I mourn with my back against a stump.

John Woods

I Only Have One Cavity

We were told, as crosseyed children,
our eyes would stick that way.
We were told that chocolate
would make our teeth fall out
and that playing with ourselves
would lead to hell and madness.

You were told that looking straight
would lead to permanent sanity,
that eating organic would clear the blood
of war and oppressive sexuality
and that playing with yourself
is really serious work.

We exchange these manifestoes.
The squint and the liberated eye
find the world's teeth
enough to go around, and each night,
each night, we lie down in ourselves
and set the alarms.

When You Stop Growing

I'm not getting any taller.
A closet full of artifacts:
pants with 24-inch knees,
one double-breasted suit,
wide ties.

True, I'm using more belt.
But look, down inside
the skin, a child,
wiseacre, full of street cant
and knives, is clawing up
to see out of the eyeholes.

You Can't Eat Poetry

This poem will cost you.
It will not register Black voters in Georgia.
It will not wash oil from ducks.
This poem will starve the big-bellied babies
in Angola, if they send it.
It .. will .. not .. get .. off .. the .. page
to convince the President
that loaded guns are dangerous
and should be kept out of the hands
of infants and senile demagogues.
This poem will not feel around under your dress
down by the lake. It will not be generous
with its time, nor forgive. It can't be
warmed up at midnight after the skating
nor charm the miser out of his hole
nor proclaim amnesty. It's words,
God damn it, it's words.

The University of Iowa Press

After founding the University of Pittsburgh Press Poetry Series in 1967, and the University of Georgia Press Poetry Series in 1978, Paul Zimmer moved to the University of Iowa Press where he founded the Iowa Poetry Prizes in 1987. Two $1,000 prizes will be funded through 1989 by the University of Iowa Foundation for second and subsequent books submitted in an open competition. Originally, responsibility for screening manuscripts and judging the contest was divided between the Iowa Writers Workshop and the Press, but starting in 1989 the Press will administer the program by itself.

Bill Knott, *Outremer,* 1989
Mary Ruefle, *The Adamant,* 1989
Elton Glaser, *Tropical Depressions,* 1988
Michael Pettit, *Cardinal Points,* 1988

Elton Glaser

―――――

RED BEANS & RICE

This town is full of Tabasco
and clarinet players named Sidney,
grasshopper ethics with a catfish smile.
We are always kind to strangers, because
that's where the money comes from—greenbacks
gushing out of Dallas, a trickle of small change
from Toledo. Even the clouds cooperate,
backing up when the sun wants an easement
or rushing rain down to keep the oysters happy.
We measure love on a sliding scale, not like
those hardshell women and peckerwoods upstate
where nobody sucks on grain liquor and bangs
the bottom of a lard can while the radio
cracks out another sloppy chorus of Frogman Henry
crooning "Is You Is Or Is You Ain't My Baby?"
But come Sunday, we balance on our knees,
strippers and street cleaners in the same pew, listening
with our heads shut tight so the sermon
won't use up the rest of the week. The other days, too,
have their mottoes and regalia: Mondays are made
for sidemeat steaming on a mound of rice
and red beans, the ugly child that only his mother loves;
Tuesday breaks once a year, a fat riot, a freaks' parade
before forty slow days of denial; Wednesday stays home,
a bubble of nothing dead center
in the spirit level; Thursdays blunder around
like a blind paraplegic on a whoopee crutch,
no cure except suicide or Friday, when seafood
heals whatever hurts us: okra gumbo for the dispossessed,
blue crabs and crawfish for the idiots, fantail shrimp
spread out to ease the insulted and the injured.
And Saturday nights, thank God, we all get sick again.
If summer's hot scenes make us too lazy
to live, we don't mind, the funerals here

are worth dying for—a ruckus of bells and old priests
praying for cool weather in the afterlife, and sometimes
the wild umbrellas, drumgrunts and trumpets
of a streetband raising the dust, the whole spook show
swinging through laments as a limousine
drives off to deposit you in a vault guarded by
a stone angel standing on the roof, his heavy wings
closed behind him like the last exit out of paradise.

—New Orleans, 1981

Michael Pettit
———————

MIGHTY SEBASTIAN BACH

At the ornate Sheridan Opera House
in tiny Telluride, Colorado
it's standing room only.
Some hoity chamber music ensemble from L.A.
has fled here into the cool mountains
with their flutes and violins,
their oboes, cellos, and whatnot
to play a plaintive sonata or two,
a ticklish concerto for harpsichord.
There's danger in listening
to Bach played live before your eyes—
the music would transport you
but the musicians cannot.
The harpsichordist hovering over his keys
in a wicked way. Violinists screwing up
their faces as if in anguish.
Balding cellist bored as he saws away.
All of them, you see, are
inescapably human, inescapably fleshy,
like you and the fellows to the left
and right of you. What anchors
our bodies are.

So you bless the A Minor
solo for flute and the flutist,
a woman so clearly taken by the lilting
line of Bach she follows completely,
her slim arms ascending, peaking
as her whole body sways under the silver flute
her lips kiss as she is lifted,
inescapably, into the dark rafters
of the Opera House, seeking
release, a way into the cool blue skies
above the mountains above the town—
no longer here, not yet there,
but lost above evergreens and lovely
snowy peaks—not yet ready, maybe never
ready, to descend, slowly,
by measures and single notes,
to this earth again.

The Johns Hopkins University Press

The Johns Hopkins Poetry Series was initiated in 1978, in connection with an anniversary of The Writing Seminars, the nation's second oldest creative writing program. John Irwin has edited the series since its inception. Submissions are by invitation only, and the Press publishes one or two books per year in editions of 2,000 cloth and paper volumes.

Charles Martin, *Steal the Bacon,* 1987
John Hollander, *In Time and Place,* 1986
Wyatt Prunty, *What Women Know, What Men Believe,* 1986
Adrien Stoutenburg, *Land of Superior Mirages,* 1986
David St. John, *Hush,* 1985
Gibbons Ruark, *Keeping Company,* 1983
Wyatt Prunty, *The Times Between,* 1982
Barry Spacks, *Spacks Street,* 1982
Philip Dacey, *The Boy Under the Bed,* 1981
Robert Pack, *Waking to My Name,* 1980
John Hollander, *Blue Wine and Other Poems,* 1979

Philip Dacey

THE LAST STRAW

One minute the camel was standing there,
    then it was not. I said it was her
straw that did it, she said it was mine.
    The fact is, if any one
of all those previous straws had been withheld,
    the camel would not now be dead.
So who can assign responsibility? Better
    just to say the spine by nature
was defective. I still hear its crack
    and shudder. I've heard jokes
about the sound, and I've laughed, because
    they were funny, but unless
you know the experience, you laugh too easily.
    The camel, as camels go, was a beauty,
less scruffy than most, and we had even begun to admire
    the hump. It was like a tower
inside which someone noble waits for rescue.
    If that someone flew
out when the camel fell in a heap before us,
    I didn't notice.
The mystery to me is why we did it,
    pile straw like that.
Maybe we thought camels needed a burden,
    to develop character, or that one
straw plus one straw plus one straw et cetera
    added up to a good way
to pass the time, our little game. More than
    likely, we did it for no reason
at all, a reflex, a gesture as of the arm
    of a sleeper. What could be the harm,
we must have thought, each piece was so light.
    It's true that now we can see straight
ahead, whereas before we always had to peer

around, over, or under
that domesticated mass God designed
   not to sink in sand.
Still, I had begun to see patterns, a map
   even, on that skin, when I got up
close enough, though I hadn't figured out where
   North was. And I'll always remember
a look the camel gave me once: those great
   dark eyes wouldn't let
me go until I had translated them into
   this: "I am the master, you
are the beast I prepare for desert-
   duty." I was hurt
into a kind of joy. She, who put the straws
   on with me, no doubt has
a different camel-story to tell than mine.
   Every day now I see it shine
ahead of me, an oasis of witness,
   the sum of her days,
and watch it, as I approach, disappear
   into the burning air.

Wyatt Prunty
————

TO ED, WITH ALZHEIMER'S

The little comedies came first,
The car keys lost, your way forgotten,
Names transposed on a floating list
Of friends who never coalesced.

Then the ocean turned your stare to miles,
Gray weather where your people slept
More heavily than before, flexed smiles
Buoying their faces when they met.

Today, your aviary eyes sweep over
Surfaces never touched; the future tense,
Suspended like a child's balloon, hovers
In your quiet room as a paid expense.

You have set your general grin
Against our noise, each thing its type,
And now we follow your thin
Transpositions,
                the fragile traps
You place to catch our names,
                        like bells
Marking the waves of voices in a room
With bad acoustics.

WHAT DOESN'T GO AWAY

His heart was like a butterfly
dropped through a vacuum tube,
no air to lift it up again;
each time the fluttering began,
he opened his eyes, first seeing
his family staggered around the bed,
then seeing that he didn't see.
While he died, the nurses wouldn't budge,
blood pressure gone too low, they said.

I, who used to play bad jokes on him,
my laughter in his shaking head,
bent and held his hand and talked *Lamaze,*
"your breathing, concentrate on your breathing."
And he did, like a well coached athlete,
believing I could get him through
his heart's slow, syncopated pains.
I do not know how long we worked that way,
but after he died I couldn't straighten up.

"Your breathing, concentrate on your breathing,"
instead of, "I love you. Thank you."
A respirator tube put down his throat
made what I'd said to him ridiculous.
One last practical joke, an off-speed pitch
I'll never retrieve.

Gibbons Ruark

Essay on Solitude

During his pain, Rilke dreamed solitude
An uncrumpled angel sleeping in the breast.
Forgive me, companion lying fast beside me
In the light, breathing morning, I tell you he dreamed wrong.

Human solitude is a slender single wing,
The only thing born whole, undamaged, lovely,
For all that flaring like a feathered wound.

Though we move in an appreciation
Of the sunlight, the sunlight will lengthen, stain,
And blind stagger out, saying its name was morning.
Think of all the heart-dark solitaries we have known:

Think of that dead cousin, lover of anything
That worked, who oiled his rifle till the bullet
Slept in the chamber, and then woke it up.

His curled hair kissed his ear like a feather.
Think of that live cousin, stunned by polio,
Father and mother wreckage in the small-town bars,
Whose ruined legs flop above the foot-rests of the wheelchair

He is dollying down the rampway to the school
Ballet. His face is rapt at the clumsiest
Of dancers, his gone legs wrapped in a rug.

Think of how it took our handsome old friend
All his life or merely one unbloodied hour
To slow his breath to sleep, emptying the doorway
That he leaned and laughed in. Think of the summer running,

His running with it, edging the shallow surf-foam,
Arms swinging loosely, shoulderblades surfacing,
Flashing at us briefly, one at a time.

What can we turn to from that sunburst back?
Sunlight through the empty doorway glitters on
The trefoil leaves of the green oxalis, the small
Wood sorrel I brought you on a whim a solid year

Of our days ago, that still lives, that folds its leaves
At the first sign of darkness, that opens them
Secretly as eyelids at first dawning.

We fall asleep dreaming of company.
If we are not the perishing stars of flowers
That come and go in a little cloud of leaves,
At least we are the leaves themselves, folding, unfolding

Near our friends the others folded up forever.
Each is one leaf hovering near another
Dreaming two leaves can fly out of darkness.

Leaves fall out of light. Each solitude owns
A simple death shawl dreaming in some darkness
Its raveled hemline grazes the earth like a wing.
It hurts to think between us we have a pair of them.

David St. John

HUSH

For My Son

The way a tired Chippewa woman
Who's lost a child gathers up black feathers,
Black quills & leaves
That she wraps & swaddles in a little bale, a shag
Cocoon she carries with her & speaks to always
As if it were the child,
Until she knows the soul has grown fat & clever,
That the child can find its own way at last;
Well, I go everywhere
Picking the dust out of the dust, scraping the breezes
Up off the floor, & gather them into a doll
Of you, to touch at the nape of the neck, to slip
Under my shirt like a rag—the way
Another man's wallet rides above his heart. As you
Cry out, as if calling to a father you conjure
In the paling light, the voice rises, instead, in me.
Nothing stops it, the crying. Not the clove of moon,
Not the woman raking my back with her words. Our letters
Close. Sometimes, you ask
About the world; sometimes, I answer back. Nights
Return you to me for a while, as sleep returns sleep
To a landscape ravaged
& familiar. The dark watermark of your absence, a hush.

Louisiana State University Press

The Louisiana State University Press Poetry Series began in 1964 by publishing two books per year, and now publishes six, making it one of the more active poetry series in the country. Over the years the series has been edited by Richard Wentworth, Charles East, Les Phillabaum, Lloyd Lyman, and, since 1977, by Beverly Jarrett. Manuscripts receive an in-house reading and an external reading by one of a pool of poets not associated with the university. Books are published in editions of 500 cloth and 750–1,000 paper.

Betty Adcock, *Beholdings,* 1988
Fred Chappell, *First and Last Words,* 1988
Margaret Gibson, *Out in the Open,* 1988
Daniel Hoffman, *Hang-Gliding from Helicon,* 1988
Elizabeth Morgan, *Parties,* 1988
David R. Slavitt, *Equinox and Other Poems,* 1988
Kelly Cherry, *Natural Theology,* 1988
Dick Allen, *Flight and Pursuit,* 1987
Susan Ludvigson, *The Beautiful Noon of No Shadow,* 1987
Martha McFerren, *A Contour for Ritual,* 1987
Julia Randall, *Moving in Memory,* 1987
Dabney Stuart, *Don't Look Back,* 1987
James Applewhite, *Ode to the Chinaberry Tree and Other Poems,* 1986
Margaret Gibson, *Memories of the Future,* 1986
Lisel Mueller, *Second Language,* 1986
Bin Ramke, *The Language Student,* 1986
David R. Slavitt, *The Walls of Thebes,* 1986
Miller Williams, *Imperfect Love,* 1986
Fred Chappell, *Source,* 1985
William Hathaway, *Fish, Flesh, & Fowl,* 1985
John Stone, *Renaming the Streets,* 1985

Henry Taylor, *The Flying Change*, 1985
Marilyn Miller Waniek, *Mama's Promises*, 1985
Dick Allen, *Overnight in the Guest House of the Mystic*, 1984
Fred Chappell, *Castle Tzingal: A Poem*, 1984
Susan Ludvigson, *The Swimmer*, 1984
William Mills, *The Meaning of Coyotes*, 1984
Bink Noll, *The House*, 1984
Herbert Scott, *Durations*, 1984
Betty Adcock, *Nettles*, 1983
James Applewhite, *Foreseeing the Journey*, 1983
Wallace Fowlie, *Characters from Proust*, 1983
Richard Lattimore, *Continuing Conclusions*, 1983
Anthony Petrosky, *Jurgis Petraskas*, 1983
David R. Slavitt, *Big Nose*, 1983
Miller Williams, *The Boys On Their Bony Mules*, 1983
Margaret Gibson, *Long Walks in the Afternoon*, 1982
William Harmon, *One Long Poem*, 1982
William Hathaway, *The Gymnast of Inertia*, 1982
Terry Randolph Hummer, *The Angelic Orders*, 1982
Dabney Stuart, *Common Ground*, 1982
Al Young, *The Blues Don't Change*, 1982
Fred Chappell, *Midquest: A Poem*, 1981
Susan Ludvigson, *Northern Lights*, 1981
David R. Slavitt, *Dozens: A Poem*, 1981
Dave Smith, *Homage to Edgar Allen Poe*, 1981
Radcliffe Squires, *Gardens of the World*, 1981
Miller Williams, *Distractions*, 1981
Fred Chappell, *Earthsleep: A Poem*, 1980
Wayne Dodd, *The Names You Gave It*, 1980
Robert Hershon, *The Public Hug*, 1980
Lisel Mueller, *The Need to Hold Still*, 1980
R. M. Ryan, *Goldilocks in Later Life*, 1980
John Stone, *In All This Rain*, 1980
Jimmy Santiago Baca, *Immigrants in Our Own Land*, 1979
Fred Chappell, *Wind Mountain: A Poem*, 1979
Margaret Gibson, *Signs*, 1979

William Mills, *Stained Glass,* 1979
Richard Stansberger, *Glass Hat,* 1979
Timothy Steele, *Uncertainties and Rest,* 1979
Fred Chappell, *Bloodfire: A Poem,* 1978
Rosanne Coggeshall, *Hymn For Drum: A Poem,* 1978
Joyce Carol Oates, *Women Whose Lives are Food, Men Whose Lives are Money,* 1978
David R. Slavitt, *Rounding the Horn,* 1978
Marilyn Nelson Waniek, *For the Body,* 1978
Kelly Cherry, *Relativity: A Point of View,* 1977
O. B. Hardison, *Pro Musica Antiqua,* 1977
Dabney Stuart, *Round and Round: A Triptych,* 1977
Miller Williams, *Why God Permits Evil,* 1977
Judith Moffett, *Keeping Time,* 1976
Robert Morgan, *Land Diving,* 1976
Lisel Mueller, *The Private Life,* 1976
Joyce Carol Oates, *The Fabulous Beasts,* 1975
William Mills, *Watch For the Fox,* 1974
Dabney Stuart, *The Other Hand,* 1974
James B. Hall, *The Hunt Within,* 1973
Miller Williams, *Halfway from Hoxie,* 1973
David R. Slavitt, *Child's Play,* 1972
Fred Chappell, *The World Between the Eyes,* 1971
Edgar Simmons, *Driving to Biloxi,* 1968
Miller Williams, *A Circle of Stone,* 1964

Fred Chappell

JUNK BALL

By the time it gets to the plate
it's got weevils and termites.

Trying to hit Wednesday with a bb gun.

Sunday.

Or curves like a Chippendale leg or
flutters like a film unsprocketed or
plunges like Zsa Zsa's neckline or
sails away as coy as Shirley Temple

                                        (or)

Not even Mussolini could make
the sonofabitch arrive on time.

MY FATHER WASHES HIS HANDS

I pumped the iron handle and watched the water
Cough his knuckles clean. Still he kept rubbing,
Left hand in his right like hefting a baseball;
The freckles might have scaled off with the clay.
But didn't. They too were clay, he said, that mud
The best part maybe of apparent spirit.

"What spirit?" I asked,
                        He grinned and got the soap
Again and sloshed. A bubble moment I saw
Our two faces little in his palm,
"The Spirit of Farming," he said, "or the Soul of Damnfool."

Our faces went away and showed his lifeline.
"Damnfool why?
                    "A man's a fool in this age
Of money to turn the soil. Never a dime
To call his own, and wearing himself away
Like a kid's pencil eraser on a math lesson.
I've got a mind to quit these fields and sell
Cheap furniture to poor folks. I've got a mind
Not to die in the traces like poor Honey."
(Our jenny mule had died two weeks before.)
"A man's not the same as a mule," I said.

He said, "You're right. A man doesn't have the heart . . .
We buried Honey, me and Uncle Joe,
While you were away at school. I didn't tell you.
Two feet down we hit pipe clay as blue
And sticky as Buick paint. Octopus-rassling,
Uncle Joe called it. Spade would go down
Maybe two inches with my whole weight behind
And come up empty. Blue glue with a spoon.
I soon decided to scale down the grave.
I told him straight, *I'm going to bust her legs
And fold them under.* His face flashed red at once.
*My God, J. T., poor Honey that's worked these fields
For thirteen years, you'd bust her legs?* I nodded.
She can't feel a thing, I said. He says,
By God I do. I told him to stand behind
The truck and stop his ears. I busted her legs.
I busted her legs with the mattock, her eyes all open
And watching me crack her bones and bulging out
Farther slightly with every blow. These fields
Were in her eyes, and a picture of me against
The sky blood-raw savage with my mattock.
I leaned and thumbed her eye shut and it was like
Closing a book on an unsatisfactory
Last chapter not pathetic and not tragic,
But angrifying mortifying sad.

The harder down I dug the bluer I got,
And empty as my shovel. It's not in me
To blubber, don't have Uncle Joe's boatload
Of whiskey in my blood yet. Heavy is how
I felt, empty-heavy and blue as poison.
So maybe it's time to quit. The green poison
Of money has leached into the ground
And turned it blue . . . That grave is mighty shallow
That I dug, but I felt so out of heart I couldn't
Make myself go farther and farther down.
I stopped waist-high and we built up a mound
That will soak away by springtime and be level."

"Are you really going to quit the farm?" I asked.
"I wouldn't quit if I could get ahead,
But busting my behind to stay behind
Has got to be the foolishest treadmill a man
Could worsen on. The farm can wait; there's money
To be made these days, and why not me?
Better me than some cheap crooks I know of,
And that's a fact."

        "Whatever you say," I said,
"It's kind of sad, though . . . And now old Honey's gone."
"*Gone?* Six nights in a row I'd close my eyes
And see her pawing up on her broken legs
Out of that blue mud, her suffering hindquarters
Still swallowed in, and in her eyes the picture
Of me coming toward her with my mattock;
And talking in a woman's pitiful voice:
Don't do it, J. T., you're breaking promises. . . .
And wake up in a sweat. Honey's not gone,
She's in my head for good and all and ever."
"Even if you quit the farm?"
           "Even if."

I handed him the towel. He'd washed his hands
For maybe seven minutes by the clock,

But when he gave it back there was his handprint,
Earth-colored, indelible, on the linen.

THE STORY

Once upon a time the farmer's wife
told it to her children while she scrubbed potatoes.
There were wise ravens in it, and a witch
who flew into such a rage she turned to brass.

The story wandered about the countryside until
adopted by the palace waiting maids
who endowed it with three magic golden rings
and a handsome prince named Felix.

Now it had both strength and style and visited
the household of the jolly merchant
where it was seated by the fire and given
a fat gray goose and a comic chambermaid.

One day alas the story got drunk and fell
in with a crowd of dissolute poets.
They drenched it with moonlight and fever and fed it
words from which it never quite recovered.

Then it was old and haggard and disreputable,
carousing late at night with defrocked scholars
and the swaggering sailors in Rattlebone Alley.
That's where the novelists found it.

Kelly Cherry

FISSION

I
The atoms buzz like bees,
Splendiferously. Trees
Spring into leaf and light
Kisses night good-bye.

II
Here's rain and grassblade!
Made for each other—
I seem to see you in shade
And sun, the trickiest weather.

III
A solitary fly
Sews the sky around my head,
Stitching with invisible thread.
Time is this needle's eye.

IV
You lie, you lie.
I unstopper my veins and drink
My heart dry.
Call me Alice. I shrink.

V
I split. I spin through space at full
Tilt, keel, careen, smash, and mushroom
Into smoke beside your oaken heart.
Death does us part.

FORECAST

The bombs are not falling yet—
Only snow, wet snow, thick snow. Storybook snow.
Yet like most of us, I keep waiting for the bombs.
We know that one day the weatherman will say,
Good morning, America! Dress warmly.
Stay indoors if you can. Try not to drive.
And now for the outlook. Observe
Our wonderful satellite photograph:
In this area, we expect a high-pressure area
Of MX missiles, and over here, to this side
Of the Rockies, something is brewing,
Something radioactive. But cheer up.
This is only the outlook. Weather is wonderful;
It can always change. For today,
Your typical air masses are cold but stable,
And the SAC umbrella remains furled
In the closet of its silos, underground bases,
And twenty-four-hour sky-watches. Today
We have snow, wet snow, thick snow. Storybook snow.
Today we are going to live happily ever after.

SHARKS

"' . . . [A]ll angel is not'ing more dan de shark well goberned.' "
—Fleece in *Moby-Dick*

You have to keep them under close watch.
They attack without warning, sudden as a squall,
underslung jaws swinging loose on the gilled latch

like a baby getting ready to bawl
its head off. Treading time, they circle the sole
survivor, never doubting he'll fall

from grace soon enough, dizzied by their sunlit shoal.
Light yaws and tacks, blown back against his battered vision
by the wind their fins wake. Whole

days drift by, like seaweed. Though history seems to shun
him, and sunburn raises blisters on his mouth,
he sucks salt from the Pacific Ocean

as a baby pulls a breast. Sharks swim south
of Paradise, around the Cape of Sin,
but he who clings like a barnacle to the lessons of his youth

earns the salute of a scaly fin.
He may yet teach a school of hammerheads
to dance on the head of a pin.

Margaret Gibson

THE ONION

Mornings when sky is white as dried gristle
and the air's unhealthy, coast
smothered, and you gone
                              I could stay in bed
and be the woman who aches for no reason, each day
a small death of love, cold rage for dinner,
coffee and continental indifference
at dawn.
                    Or dream lazily a market day—
bins of fruit and celery, poultry strung up,
loops of garlic and peppers. I'd select one
yellow onion, fist-sized, test its sleek
hardness, haggle and settle a fair price.

Yesterday, a long day measured by shovel
and mattock, a wrestle with roots—
calm and dizzy when I bent over to loosen my shoes
at the finish—I thought
                              if there were splendors,
what few there were, knowledge of them
in me like fire in flint,
I would have them . . .
                              and now I'd say the onion,
I'd have that, too. The work it took,
the soup it flavors, the griefs
innocently it summons.

RADIATION

A Call to Worship

Stand in the sun long enough to remember

that nothing is made without light
spoken so firmly
our flesh is its imprint.

Whirlpool nebula, the eye of the cat, snow
crystals, knotholes, the X-ray diffraction
pattern of beryl—all these echo the original

word that hums in the uncharted mind.
Listen and answer.

Responses

If the corn shrinks into radiant air and our bread
is a burning cinder
                like chaff we will wither and burn

If the thrush and oriole vanish, borne off in the wind,
unhoused and barren
                we forget how to sing and to mourn

If our cities and mountains fall into the fields
and sleep with the stones

how can we leaf through old photographs and letters
how summon our lives
                our hands will be smoke

Confession

The bomb exploded in the air above the city destroyed hospitals
markets houses temples burned thousands in darkened air in radiant air
hid them in rubble one hundred thousand dead. As many lived were
crippled diseased they bled from inside from the mouth from sores in
the skin they examined their children daily for signs scars invisible one
day might float to the surface of the body the next red and poisoned
risen from nowhere

We made the scars and the radiant air
We made people invisible as numbers.
We did this.

An Ancient Text

There is a dim glimmering of light
unput out in men. Let them walk, let them walk
that the darkness overtake them not.

Private Meditation

(Shore birds over
the waves dipping and turning their wings together,
their leader invisible, her signal their
common instinct, the long work of years
felt in a moment's flash and veer—

we could be like that.)

Common Prayer

And when we have had enough profit and loss
enough asbestos, coal dust, enough slick
oil and dead fish on the coast; enough
of the chatter and whine and bite
of stale laws and the burn
of invisible ions

then we are ready to notice
light in the gauze of the red dragonfly's wing
and in the spider's web at dusk; ready to walk
through the fallen yellow leaves, renaming
birds and animals.

We will not forget our dead.
We sharpen the scythe until it sings loud
our one original name.

William Hathaway
———

FEAR ROW

First we marched only in dark and whispers,
then muttered echoless in trenches
oozing our brothers, those stinking sleepers

who were once green and scared wayfarers.
For them too it was cheers and wenches
before they marched only in dark and whispers.

Like ghosts afraid of day, shadowless creepers,
we accepted slime, rejected human touches,
and oozed freely with our stinky, sleeping brothers.

Now, that morning still, or again propped near
any bugle, or when a party-fool mentions
war, marching in first dark and whispers

should I remember a snow of tattered papers?
A fast amazing light, one word, one wrench
of pain and we walked in dark and whispers.

Who dives for the floor anymore at firecracker
time? See those "problems" on hospital benches,
stinking sleepers who ooze with whispers
as if their dark march could make us brothers.

T. R. Hummer

THE RURAL CARRIER DISCOVERS THAT LOVE IS EVERYWHERE

A registered letter for the Jensens. I walk down their drive
Through the gate of their thick-hedged yard, and by God there they are,
On a blanket in the grass, asleep, buck-naked, honeymooners
Not married a month. I smile, turn to leave,
But can't help looking back. Lord, they're a pretty sight,
Both of them, tangled up in each other, easy in their skin—
It's their own front yard, after all, perfectly closed in
By privet hedge and country. Maybe they were here all night.

I want to believe they'd do that, not thinking of me
Or anyone but themselves, alone in the world
Of the yard with its clipped grass and fresh-picked fruit trees.
Whatever this letter says can wait. To hell with the mail.
I slip through the gate, silent as I came, and leave them
Alone. There's no one they need to hear from.

The Rural Carrier Resists Temptation

Angie Lloyd, like something slipped loose from heaven,
She's so good looking, comes down from her house trailer wanting
To buy a book of stamps. I'm ready with it when
She gets to me. Every Monday morning
We meet like this. It's a hell of a way to live,
A hell of a thing to live with. She reaches in
The car window, holds out a five. I give
her what she needs, lay it on the soft white skin

Of her upturned palm. Then I'm ready to make her
Change. I let her have it, slow but right.
She walks away satisfied. I watch her out of sight
Wondering if there's anything she can't shake.
But then I think, after all, I've gone this far
With her. Things could be worse than they are.

Susan Ludvigson

A Bargain at Any Price

Daily I go to the carpet warehouse.
The men think I can't make up my mind.
But the truth is, I have fallen in love
with the young ex-football player
who lights the dingy room with his hair.
Even machines can't help him add,
so we spend hours figuring and refiguring
costs—pad and labor, stairs and tax,
his patient golden head bent over the numbers,
the muscles in his arms reflecting shadows
like water under summer clouds.
Each time he starts the motor on the forklift,

slowly pushing that long steel rod
into the center of a roll, then
lifting it out for me to see, Oh—
it's as if an inner sky were opening,
and all his hazy calculations
fall like stars into my heart.

————

GRIEF

Imagine that pure
melting of snow in Wisconsin
so that when it's gone, the earth
underneath is raw and damp,
needing sun, seed, any kind
of promise. But more snow comes
before the final thaw,
and this goes on, over and over,
so that in February, March,
you think the world may never
be green.
When you look out the picture window,
after your spirits have risen one last
slow time, old grass looks
as if it might leap to life.
Then you see those large flakes
floating down, and you weep,
past belief. It can happen
through April, hope going white
and silent again.

Lisel Mueller

THE ARTIST'S MODEL, CA. 1912

In 1886 I came apart—

I who had been Mme. Rivière,
whole under flowing silk,
had sat on the grass, naked,
my body an unbroken invitation—

splintered into thousands
of particles, a bright rock
blasted to smithereens,
even my orange skirt dissolved
into drops that were not orange.

Now they are stacking me like a child's
red and blue building blocks,
splitting me down the middle,
blackening half my face,

they tell me the world has changed,
haven't I heard, and give me
a third eye, a rooster's beak.

I ask for my singular name
back, but they say in the future
only my parts will be known,
a gigantic pair of lips,
a nipple, slick as candy,

and that even those will disappear,
white on white or black on black,
and you will look for me
in the air, in the absence of figure,
in space, inside your head,
where I started, your own work of art.

The Fall of the Muse

Her wings are sold for scrap,
her tiara goes to the museum.
She takes off her purple gown,
her long gloves.
In her underwear she is anyone.

Even when she is naked, they laugh.
It's not enough, they shout.
Take off your pubic hair,
mutilate your breasts,
cut off a finger,
put a patch on your left eye.

Now she is one of us.
She laughs the small laugh of the ordinary.
She gives us all equal kisses.
She counts her money at inaugural balls.
She is searched at airports.
She depends on sleeping pills.
She betrays art with life.
She lectures on the catharsis of drivel.
She learns about Mount Olympus from quiz shows.

She moves in a circle of victims;
they make her eat her heart in public.
She has been bled so many times
her blood has lost its color.
She comes on the stage on all fours
but insists that her teeth be straightened.

Democratic, she sits with us.
We share the flat bread of affluence,
the suicidal water;
we kill each other with jokes.
She wears false eyelashes
when she throws herself off the bridge.

FOR A THIRTEENTH BIRTHDAY

You have read *War and Peace*.
Now here is *Sister Carrie*,
not up to Tolstoy; still
it will second the real world:
predictable planes and levels,
pavement that holds you,
stairs that lift you,
ice that trips you,
nights that begin after sunset,
four lunar phases,
a finite house.

I give you Dreiser
although (or because)
I am no longer sure.
Lately I have been walking into glass doors.
Through the car windows, curbs disappear.
On the highway, wrong turnoffs become irresistible,
someone else is controlling the wheel.
Sleepless nights pile up like a police record;
all my friends are getting divorced.
Language, my old comrade, deserts me;
words are misused or forgotten,
consonants fight each other
between my upper and lower teeth.
I write "fiend" for "friend"
and "word" for "world",
remember comes out with an "m" missing.

I used to be able to find my way in the dark,
sure of the furniture,
but the town I lived in for years
has pulled up its streets in my absence,
disguised its buildings behind my back.

My neighbor at dinner glances
at his cuffs, his palms;
he has memorized certain phrases,
but does not speak my language.
Suddenly I am aware
no one at the table does.

And so I give you Dreiser,
his measure of certainty:
a table that's oak all the way through,
real and fragrant flowers,
skirts from sheep and silkworms,
no unknown fibers;
a language as plain as money,
a workable means of exchange;
a world whose very meanness is solid,
mud into mortar, and you are sure
of what will injure you.

I give you names like nails,
walls that withstand your pounding,
doors that are hard to open,
but once they are open, admit you
into rooms that breathe pure sun.
I give you trees that lose their leaves,
as you knew they would,
and then come green again.
I give you
fruit preceded by flowers,
Venus supreme in the sky,
the miracle of always
landing on your feet,
even though the earth
rotates on its axis.

Start out with that, at least.

173

Joyce Carol Oates

PARACHUTING

O our clothes buckle
crazily about our thighs
the wind screams bright and sharp
as castanets
or summer insects
everything flashes upward!
like roosters' feathers

together we fall down a highway
of steep air
the air is unbuttoning itself wildly
and love bursts

my love you are bursting
inside me   your atoms hot like coins
or cinders
why is the sky streaking upward?
why are we such heavy weights?

we are public here like roosters'
red fighting feathers
climbing the barnyard in fight
dirty and loving in air
scrambling red combs and toenails
their blood flecking happily outward
to arc upon the barnyard dust
of dots that dry shaped
like cindered stars

it is a scramble of lights and screams
like insects' deaths
two heavy weights falling amorous of earth
falling to flatten breasts and bellies
finally against the earth

Stanley Plumly

DRUNK

Once, in Canada, at dusk,
in the middle of a lake,
you stood up in the boat,
back to the sun,
a bottle of beer
in one hand,
your hat in the other,
and shouted at whatever rises,
whatever falls.

It was a poorman's summer.
I remember how
we rocked to the tune
of your voice on the water.
You wanted to dance,
you wanted to hug
your shadow.
In a cold country, nowhere,
you wanted to turn us over.

I was old enough to be afraid.
And some nights, still,
in the middle of sleep,
I hold my breath
as the bed drifts out
of its rocking dream:
I see you on the water,
nothing in your hands,
but dancing.

HERON

1

You still sometimes sleep
inside that great bird,
flopped out,
one wing tucked,
the other slightly broken over my back.
You still fall asleep before I do.
You still wake up
in tears.

You have what is called *thin skin:*
if I put my ear to it
I can hear the wingbeat in your heart.
I can only imagine
how far down those long flights go.

2

Last night in my dream
about the heron
I stood at the edge
of water with a handful
of stones.
I was twelve, I think.
The heron perfect, still, kneedeep,
looking at himself.

Once he lifted his wings
in a mockery of flight.
For a moment I was inside you:
I could hear the heart.
I had stones in my hands.

David R. Slavitt

Broads

1 *Diane*

If I were the kind of man I want
you to be, I'd be
beating the shit out of you
because I like toughs and
because I'm too sensitive/sensible
to put up with your double-
knit Orange County
leisure suits & your
hideous tan shoes.
But if you were the kind
of unkind man I want
you to be you'd
beat the shit out of me
or just beat it,
because of my stringy hair,
my tacky Goodwill/Illwill dress,
but most of all because of
my poems, poems like these
you'll never understand.

2 *Denise*

A dead bird
in a cage is not
depressing for I,
delicate, spooky
woman that I am,
can imagine songs
the bird ought to have sung,
had he been given
the gift—my gift.

I give it now,
transforming him perfectly.
I hope he knows now
why I had to wring
his inadequate neck.

3   *Maxine*

That everything moves its bowels and bleeds and then
dies and is buried or is eaten, or frequently both,
is pastoral and marvelous. O the country
is full of such wisdom: fields and stables are
abattoirs where the mallet of truth whomps
between my eyes. In the back of my pickup truck
is a dead horse, my birthday present, alive
with maggots and flies, busy as any city.
When I'm sad or out of sorts, I beat its bloat,
beat the dead horse, and the air hums, shines,
primitive, convincing, disgustingly real.

4   *Adrienne*

The griefs of women are quiet; rustle
like crinoline or whisper like
the tearing of old silk;

hum like appliances, give off the sharp sweet smell
of burnt-out motors; tap like typewriter keys.
The strengths of women are quiet
but hardy as the weed that finds its cranny
between the concrete block of the sidewalk
and the concrete slab of the wall, and grows there,
and blooms there.

Men are bums.
We're really better than they are.

ECZEMA

Tearing at my package like a child
eager for its present, I scratch my back
between the shoulder blades, my arms, my chest,
my face, and bloody myself, like one of those wild
self-flagellating enthusiasts. The attack
subsides eventually. Exhausted, I rest

but know another episode is waiting,
another battle in this civil war
my body wages with itself. My skin
erupts periodically; it's something hating
itself, the spirit revolting at the poor
flesh it must inhabit, is trapped within.

Doctors call it a psychogenic condition,
like asthma or colitis; it is an ill
in which the skin's itch is the soul's fret,
and scratching is the body's act of contrition.
I try to absolve with an antihistamine pill
and not to get excited, not to sweat,

but there is a rage inside me, a prophet's deep
revulsion at the flesh. When it gets bad,
I scratch as in a dream of purity,
of bare-boned whiteness, clean enough to keep
the soul that's mired there now, driving me mad,
desperate, righteous, clawing to be free.

Henry Taylor

ARTICHOKE

*If poetry did not exist, would you
have had the wit to invent it?*
— Howard Nemerov

He had studied in private years ago
the way to eat these things, and was prepared
when she set the clipped green globe before him.
He only wondered (as he always did
when he plucked from the base the first thick leaf,
dipped it into the sauce and caught her eye
as he deftly set the velvet curve against
the inside edges of his lower teeth
and drew the tender pulp toward his tongue
while she made some predictable remark
about the sensuality of this act
then sheared away the spines and ate the heart)
what mind, what hunger, first saw this as food.

AT THE SWINGS

    Midafternoon in Norfolk,
late July. I am taking our two sons for a walk
    away from their grandparents' house; we have
    directions to a miniature playground,
       and I have plans to wear them down
         toward a nap at five,

when my wife and I
will leave them awhile with her father. A few blocks
   south of here, my wife's mother drifts from us
   beneath hospital sheets, her small strength bent
      to the poisons and the rays they use
         against a spreading cancer.

      In their house now, deep love
is studying to live with deepening impatience
   as each day gives our hopes a different form
   and household tasks rise like a powdery mist
      of restless fatigue. Still, at five,
         my wife and I will dress

      and take the boulevard
across the river to a church where two dear friends
   will marry; rings will be blessed, promises kept
   and made, and while our sons lie down to sleep,
      the groom's niece, as the flower girl,
         will almost steal the show.

      But here the boys have made
an endless procession on the slides, shrieking down
   slick steel almost too hot to touch; and now
   they charge the swings. I push them from the front,
      one with each hand, until at last
         the rhythm, and the sunlight

      that splashes through live oak
and crape myrtle, dappling dead leaves on the ground,
   lull me away from this world toward a state
   still and remote as an old photograph
      in which I am standing somewhere
         I may have been before:

there was this air, this light,
a day of thorough and forgetful happiness;
    where was it, or how long ago? I try
    to place it, but it has gone for good,
        to leave me gazing at these swings,
            thinking of something else

        I may have recognized—
an irrecoverable certainty that now,
    and now, this perfect afternoon, while friends
    are struggling to put on their cutaways
        or bridal gowns, and my wife's mother,
            dearer still, is dozing

        after her medicine,
or turning a small thing in her mind, like someone
    worrying a ring of keys to make small sounds
    against great silence, and while these two boys
        swing back and forth against my hand,
            time's crosshairs quarter me

        no matter where I turn.
Now it is time to go. The boys are tired enough,
    and my wife and I must dress and go to church.
    Because I love our friends, and ceremony,
        the usual words will make me weep:
            hearing the human prayers

        for holy permanence
will remind me that a life is much to ask
    of anyone, yet not too much to give
    to love. And once or twice, as I stand there,
        that dappled moment at the swings
            will rise between the lines,

        when I beheld our sons
as, in the way of things, they will not be again,

though even years from now their hair may lift
a little in the breeze, as if they stood
    somewhere along their way from us,
        poised for a steep return.

Marilyn Nelson Waniek

———

EMILY DICKINSON'S DEFUNCT

She used to
pack poems
in her hip pocket.
Under all the
gray old lady
clothes she was
dressed for action.
She had hair,
imagine,
in certain places, and
believe me
she smelled human
on a hot summer day.
Stalking snakes
or counting
the thousand motes
in sunlight
she walked just
like an Indian.
She was New England's
favorite daughter,
she could pray
like the devil.
She was a
two-fisted woman,
this babe.

All the flies
just stood around
and buzzed
when she died.

WOMEN'S LOCKER ROOM

The splat of bare feet on wet tile
breaks the incredible luck
of my being alone in here.
I snatch a stingy towel
and sidle into the shower. I'm already soaped
by the time a white hand turns the neighboring knob.
I recognize the arm as one that flashed
for many rapid laps while I dogpaddled at the shallow end.
I dart an appraising glance: She arches down
to wash her lifted heel, and is beautiful.
As she straightens, I look into her eyes.

For an instant I remember human sacrifice:
The female explorer led skyward,
her blond tresses loose on her neck;
the drums of our pulses grew louder;
I raised the obsidian knife.
Violets bloomed in the clefts of the stairs.

I could freeze her name in an ice cube,
bottle the dirt from her footsteps
with potent graveyard dust.
I could gather the combings from her hairbrush
to burn with her fingernail clippings,
I could feed her Iago powder.
Childhood taunts, branded ears,
a thousand insults swirl through my memory
like headlines in a city vacant lot.

I jump, grimace, divide like an amoeba
into twin rages that stomp around
with their lips stuck out,
then come suddenly face to face.
They see each other and know that they
are mean mamas.
Then I bust out laughing
and let the woman live.

Miller Williams

———

A POEM FOR EMILY

Small fact and fingers and farthest one from me,
a hand's width and two generations away,
in this still present I am fifty-three.
You are not yet a full day.

When I am sixty-three, when you are ten,
and you are neither closer nor as far,
your arms will fill with what you know by then,
the arithmetic and love we do and are.

When I by blood and luck am eighty-six
and you are someplace else and thirty-three
believing in sex and god and politics
with children who look not at all like me,

sometime I know you will have read them this
so they will know I love them and say so
and love their mother. Child, whatever is
is always or never was. Long ago,

a day I watched awhile beside your bed,
I wrote this down, a thing that might be kept
awhile, to tell you what I would have said
when you were who knows what and I was dead
which is I stood and loved you while you slept.

———————

RUBY TELLS ALL

When I was told, as Delta children were,
that crops don't grow unless you sweat at night,
I thought that it was my own sweat they meant.
I have never felt as important again
as on those early mornings, waking up,
my body slick, the moon full on the fields.
That was before air conditioning.
Farm girls sleep cool now and wake up dry
but still the cotton overflows the fields.
We lose everything that's grand and foolish;
it all becomes something else. One by one,
butterflies turn into caterpillars
and we grow up, or more or less we do,
and, Lord, we do lie then. We lie so much
truth has a false ring and it's hard to tell.

I wouldn't take crap off anybody
if I just knew that I was getting crap
in time not to take it. I could have won
a small one now and then if I was smarter,
but I've poured coffee here too many years
for men who rolled in in Peterbilts,
and I have gotten into bed with some
if they could talk and seemed to be in pain.

I never asked for anything myself;
giving is more blessed and leaves you free.
There was a man, married and fond of whiskey.
Given the limitations of men, he loved me.

Lord, we laid concern upon our bodies
but then he left. Everything has its time.
We used to dance. He made me feel the way
a human wants to feel and fears to.
He was a slow man and didn't expect.
I would get off work and find him waiting.
We'd have a drink or two and kiss awhile.
Then a bird-loud morning late one April
we woke up naked. We had made a child.
She's grown up now and gone though God knows where.
She ought to write, for I do love her dearly
who raised her carefully and dressed her well.

Everything has its time. For thirty years
I never had a thought about time.
Now, turning through newspapers, I pause
to see if anyone who passed away
was younger than I am. If one was
I feel hollow for a little while
but then it passes. Nothing matters enough
to stay bent down about. You have to see
that some things matter slightly and some don't.
Dying matters a little. So does pain.
So does being old. Men do not.
Men live by negatives, like don't give up,
don't be a coward, don't call me a liar,
don't ever tell me don't. If I could live
two hundred years and had to be a man
I'd take my grave. What's a man but a match,
a little stick to start a fire with?

My daughter knows this, if she's alive.
What could I tell her now, to bring her close,
something she doesn't know, if we met somewhere?
Maybe that I think about her father,
maybe that my fingers hurt at night,
maybe that against appearances
there is love, constancy, and kindness,
that I have dresses I have never worn.

WHY GOD PERMITS EVIL:
FOR ANSWER TO THIS QUESTION
OF INTEREST TO MANY
WRITE BIBLE ANSWERS DEPT. E–7

       —ad on a matchbook cover

Of interest to John Calvin and Thomas Aquinas
for instance and Job for instance who never got

one straight answer but only his cattle back.
With interest, which is something, but certainly not

any kind of answer unless you ask
God if God can demonstrate God's power

and God's glory, which is not a question.
You should all be living at this hour.

You had Servetus to burn, the elect to count,
bad eyes and the Institutes to write;

you had the exercises and had Latin,
the hard bunk and the solitary night;

you had the neighbors to listen to and your woman
yelling at you to curse God and die.

Some of this to be on the right side;
some of it to ask in passing, Why?

Why badness makes its way in a world He made?
How come he looked for twelve and got eleven?

You had the faith and looked for love, stood pain,
learned patience and little else. We have E–7.

Churches may be shut down everywhere,
half-written philosophy books be tossed away.

Some place on the south side of Chicago
a lady with wrinkled hose and a small gray

bun of hair sits straight with her knees together
behind a teacher's desk on the third floor

of an old shirt factory, bankrupt and abandoned
except for this just cause, and on the door:

Dept. E–7. She opens the letters
asking why God permits it and sends a brown

plain envelope to each return address.
But she is not alone. All up and down

the thin and creaking corridors are doors
and desks behind them: E–6, E–5, 4, 3.

A desk for every question, for how we rise
blown up and burned, for how the will is free,

for when is Armageddon, for whether dogs
have souls or not and on and on. On

beyond the alphabet and possible numbers
where cross-legged, naked and alone,

there sits a pale, tall and long-haired woman
upon a cushion of fleece and eiderdown

holding in one hand a hand-written answer,
holding in the other hand a brown

plain envelope. On either side, cobwebbed
and empty baskets sitting on the floor

say *in* and *out*. There is no sound in the room.
There is no knob on the door. Or there is no door.

Al Young

W. H. AUDEN & MANTAN MORELAND

*in memory of the Anglo-American poet & the Afro-American comic actor
(famed for his role as Birmingham Brown, chauffeur in those ancient Charlie
Chan movies) who died on the same day in 1973*

Consider them both in paradise,
discussing one another—
the one a poet, the other an actor;
interchangeable performers
who finally slipped backstage
of a play whose cast favored lovers.

"You executed some brilliant lines,
Mr. Auden, & doubtless engaged our
innermost emotions & informed imagination,
for I pondered your *Age of Anxiety*
diligently over a juicy order of ribs."

"No shit!" groans Auden, mopping his brow.
"I checked out all your Charlie Chan
flicks & flipped when you turned up again
in *Watermelon Man* & that gas commercial
over TV. Like, where was you all that
time in between? I thought you'd done
died & gone back to England or somethin."

"Wystan, pray tell, why did you ever eliminate
that final line from 'September 1, 1939'?—
We must all love one another or die."

"That was easy. We gon die anyway no matter
how much we love, but the best thing I like
that you done was the way you buck them eyes
& make out like you runnin sked all the time.
Now, that's the bottom line of the black
experience where you be in charge of the scene.
For the same reason you probly stopped shufflin."

The University of Massachusetts Press

The University of Massachusetts Press was founded in 1964 and published a book of poetry in 1965. It has continued to publish one or two poetry volumes per year in a print run of 750 hardcover and 1,000 paper. In 1975 the Press established the Juniper Prize, named in honor of Robert Francis, who for many years has lived at Fort Juniper in Amherst. The $1,000 Juniper Prize is awarded annually to the winning poetry manuscript submitted in an open national competition. Books are selected by the Press staff in conjunction with an anonymous poetry board. As of 1987, the Juniper Prize is awarded in alternate years to first and subsequent books.

James Haug, *The Stolen Car,* 1989
Nell Altizer, *The Man Who Died En Route,* 1988
Robert Bagg, *Body Blows: Poems New and Selected,* 1988
Robert B. Shaw, *The Wonder of Seeing Double,* 1988
Walter McDonald, *After the Noise of Saigon,* 1987
Linda Hull, *Ghost Money,* 1986
Linda Hogan, *Seeing Through the Sun,* 1985
Jonathan Holden, *The Names of the Rapids,* 1985
Michael Blumenthal, *Laps: A Poem,* 1984
Marc Hudson, *Afterlight,* 1983
Jane Flanders, *The Students of Snow,* 1982
James Tate, *Hints to Pilgrims,* 1982
David Brendan Hopes, *The Glacier's Daughters,* 1981
Lucille Clifton, *Two-headed Woman,* 1980
Patricia Goedicke, *Crossing the Same River,* 1980
Frederic Will, *Our Thousand Year Old Bodies: Selected Poems, 1956–1976,* 1980
Anne Halley, *The Bearded Mother,* 1979
Eleanor Wilner, *Maya,* 1979

William Dickey, *The Rainbow Grocery*, 1978
Alexander Hutchison, *Deep-tap Tree*, 1978
Donald Junkins, *Crossing By Ferry*, 1978
Jane Shore, *Eye Level*, 1977
Robert Francis, *Collected Poems, 1936–1976*, 1976
David Dwyer, *Ariana Olisvos: Her Last Works and Days*, 1976
Alvin Greenberg, *Metaform*, 1975
Eleanor Lerman, *Come the Sweet By and By*, 1975
Ann Deagon, *Carbon 14*, 1974
Stephen Dunn, *Looking for Holes in the Ceiling*, 1974
Robert Francis, *Like Ghosts of Eagles: Poems, 1966–1974*, 1974
Laurence Lerner, *A.R.T.H.U.R.: The Life and Opinions of a Digital Computer*, 1974
Ellen Bass, *I'm Not Your Laughing Daughter*, 1974
Grandin Conover, *Ten Years*, 1972
Bill Tremblay, *Crying in the Cheap Seats*, 1971
Rosellen Brown, *Some Deaths in the Delta and Other Poems*, 1970
Donald Junkins, *And Sandpipers She Said*, 1970
Stanley Koehler, *The Fact of Fall*, 1969
Robert Francis, *Come Out into the Sun*, 1965

Lucille Clifton

FORGIVING MY FATHER

it is friday. we have come
to the paying of the bills.
all week you have stood in my dreams
like a ghost, asking for more time
but today is payday, payday old man;
my mother's hand opens in her early grave
and i hold it out like a good daughter.

there is no more time for you. there will
never be time enough daddy daddy old lecher
old liar. i wish you were rich so i could take it all
and give the lady what she was due
but you were the son of a needy father,
the father of a needy son;
you gave her all you had
which was nothing. you have already given her
all you had.

you are the pocket that was going to open
and come up empty any friday.
you were each other's bad bargain, not mine.
daddy old pauper   old prisoner,   old dead man
what am i doing here collecting?
you lie side by side in debtors' boxes
and no accounting will open them up.

these hips are big hips.
they need space to
move around in.
they don't fit into little
petty places. these hips
are free hips.
they don't like to be held back.
these hips have never been enslaved,
they go where they want to go
they do what they want to do.
these hips are mighty hips.
these hips are magic hips.
i have known them
to put a spell on a man and
spin him like a top!

William Dickey

FACE-PAINTINGS OF THE CADUVEO INDIANS

The face-paintings of the Caduveo, says Levi-Strauss,
reflect a society they have forgotten:
like heraldry, he says, like playing cards.

It is like that. Even my mother, now,
turning the pages of the photograph album,
forgets the older faces. She insists she remembers,
but what she remembers is a style of face,
a way she can remember people looking.

I saw you at the Greek Orthodox church on Sunday.
You had lost weight. I was drinking sweetened coffee.
We were no longer a society.

I saw you as a stranger might, with interest.
You had drawn back behind the surface of your face.

In the last days, having nothing in common, we played cards,
and the cards became their own society,
playing themselves, not responsible to the players.
Your face was new, as if it had not been used.

I do not know what became of the Caduveo.
The face-paintings are in a museum, with the relics
of other societies that forgot themselves,
that became too few to be able to remember.

It is like that: a lessening of chances,
the thought that I will never again be in love
but will sit foolishly waiting for what is in the cards
while your face becomes a photograph, becomes
only a way I remember people looking.

––––––––

THE FOOD OF LOVE

I could never sing. In the grade-school operetta
I sat dark offstage and clattered coconut shells.
I was the cavalry coming, unmusical, lonely.

For five years I played the piano and metronome.
I read *Deerslayer* in small print while I waited for my lesson,
and threw up after the recital at the Leopold Hotel.

I went to a liberal college, but I never learned
how to sit on the floor or help the sweet folk song forward.
My partridge had lice, and its pear-tree had cut-worm blight.

Yet this song is for you. In your childhood a clear falsetto,
now you sing along in the bars, naming old songs for me.
Even drunk, you chirrup; birds branch in your every voice.

It's for you, what I never sing. So I hope if ever
you reach, in the night, for a music that is not there
because you need food, or philosophy, or bail,

you'll remember to hear the noise that a man might make
if he were an amateur, clattering coconut shells,
if he were the cavalry, tone-deaf but on its way.

HAPPINESS

I sent you this bluebird of the name of Joe
with "Happiness" tattooed onto his left bicep.
(For a bluebird, he was a damn good size.)
And all you can say is you think your cat has got him?

I tell you the messages aren't getting through.
The Golden Gate Bridge is up past its ass in traffic;
tankers colliding, singing telegrams out on strike.
The machineries of the world are raised in anger.

So I am sending this snail of the name of Fred
in a small tricolor sash, so the cat will know him.
He will scrawl out "Happiness" in his own slow way.
I won't ever stop until the word gets to you.

Stephen Dunn

AT EVERY GAS STATION THERE ARE MECHANICS

Around them my cleanliness stinks.
I smell it. And so do they.
I always want to tell them I used to box,
and change tires, and eat heroes.

It is my hands hanging out
of my sleeves like white gloves.
It is what I've not done, and do not know.
If they mention the differential
I pay whatever price. When
they tell me what's wrong beneath my hood
I nod, and become meek.
If they were to say I could not
have my car back, that it was theirs,
I would say thank you, you must be right.
And then I would walk home,
and create an accident.

———————

DAY AND NIGHT HANDBALL

I think of corner shots, the ball
hitting and dying like a butterfly
on a windshield, shots so fine
and perverse they begin to live

alongside weekends of sex
in your memory. I think of serves
delivered deep to the left hand,
the ball sliding off the side wall

into the blindnesses of one's body,
and diving returns that are impossible
except on days when your body is all
rubber bands and dreams

unfulfilled since childhood.
I think of a hand slicing the face
of a ball, so much english
that it comes back drunk

to your opponent who doesn't have
enough hands to hit it,
who hits it anyway, who makes you think
of "God!" and "Goddamn!", the pleasure

of falling to your knees
for what is superb, better than you.
But it's position I think of most,
the easy slam and victory

because you have a sense of yourself
and the court, the sense that old men
gone in the knees have,
one step in place of five,

finesse in place of power,
and all the time
the four walls around you
creating the hardship, the infinite variety.

Jane Flanders

HEAVENLY BODIES

It is always night in the outhouse
and smells like a pig sty.
I unbutton my sunsuit, pull it down
and perch, feet dangling, on the rim of
the abyss beside a prewar Sears catalogue.
The seat is silky from the buttocks of my
aunt and uncle and grown-up cousin.
I imagine them grunting away
year after year, in all weathers,
emptying themselves into this bowl
of sticky soup the flies
love so much. Sighing,

I let my urine float downward, outward
through space, marking this spot as mine
too, knowing myself related to the universe
in yet another unspeakable way.

Patricia Goedicke
————

Like Animals

Over her like a dog
Muscular, tricky, neat

And she under, oh under
Nuzzling the nipple of the prick,
The shaggy brush of the balls

In the depths of summer
In the heat
In the red shadows of the bedroom

His belly like the ceiling
Arms and legs like doorposts

And she brown as the floorboards
Beneath him, jiggling like a pup

In the muddle of their bodies
Grappling for each other's souls

They are feeding on each other so fiercely
They are barely able to speak:

Locked in the cave of the self
They are all alone, they are lonely

Loneliness spreads like a hole in their chests
Wheezing for breath, in darkness

Like a bone stuck in a beast's craw
In the kitchen it is a brown shadow,
A whiff of sad air . . .

Nevertheless, between them
Every once in a while there is a quick flashing,
A sort of gurgling song:

With the bloated golden guts
Of turtle, snake, swan

With fine, spirited fingers
And nimble, intelligent feet

In a whir of mischievous wings
They cling to each other like animals

And oh it is sweet, it is sweet.

Linda Hogan
———

THE TRUTH IS

In my left pocket a Chickasaw hand
rests on the bone of the pelvis.
In my right pocket
a white hand. Don't worry. It's mine
and not some thief's.
It belongs to a woman who sleeps in a twin bed
even though she falls in love too easily,
and walks along with hands
in her own empty pockets
even though she has put them in others
for love not money.

About the hands, I'd like to say
I am a tree, grafted branches
bearing two kinds of fruit,
apricots maybe and pit cherries.
It's not that way. The truth is
we are crowded together
and knock against each other at night.
We want amnesty.

Linda, girl, I keep telling you
this is nonsense
about who loved who
and who killed who.

Here I am, taped together
like some old Civilian Conservation Corps
passed by from the Great Depression
and my pockets are empty.
It's just as well since they are masks
for the soul, and since coins and keys
both have the sharp teeth of property.

Girl, I say,
it is dangerous to be a woman of two countries.
You've got your hands in the dark
of two empty pockets. Even though
you walk and whistle like you aren't afraid
you know which pocket the enemy lives in
and you remember how to fight
so you better keep right on walking.
And you remember who killed who.
For this you want amnesty,
and there's that knocking on the door
in the middle of the night.

Relax, there are other things to think about.
Shoes for instance.

Now those are the true masks of the soul.
The left shoe
and the right one with its white foot.

Jonathan Holden
————

CASINO

Under this oppressive slippery sky
of mirrors, where the promise of cash
is a fragrance, voluptuous,
you could forget the ways of the gods.
One pull on a handle, *bells! lights!* the world
could go all to pieces, be turning
itself inside out as if in love
with you. A slot machine spits
me a coin. I'm unmoved by gifts.
Luck, you can see, was never anything
less obvious than a lady slipping
her slightly fat shoulders from her robe
as she picks some victim out
to throw herself at.
And winning, though it's the perversion
hardest to resist,
may be more dangerous than losing.
A man thirty years married once told me
how most of one wonderfully mild,
wronged Tuesday morning, after drying
the breakfast dishes, he lounged upstairs
in his marital bed,
committing deliberate adultery
with a family friend,
how the pale light of her body,
filling the room, contradicted
the worn shag rug, the famous old crack
in the bedroom ceiling.

The perversity of it awed him—
his shockingly clear sense of detail,
that this beautiful head, eyes half
closed, her hair slicked hard
around her temples,
could replace his wife's bruised face,
as we'd say, *in the flesh,* could be this
literal. He could no more stop
than could any of these broken people
release the handles that keep pulling
them, though they know as well as we do
that the next jackpot will drive them crazy,
how luck and adultery
are only two of the many low religions,
each waving its claim to make a word flesh,
and the gods remain abstract
as money, as love, as they ever were.

"THE SWING," BY HONORÉ FRAGONARD

*From this painting alone . . . one could have predicted the entire
French Revolution*
—Gerhardt Weis

Her pink chubby fingers trusting
the rope, one slipper flying
off one toy foot, a toy

herself, a girl is sailing through
the silly leaves. She hasn't heard
of the guillotine, she is plummeting,

rising into and out
of the pitfalls of pleasure,
her petticoats like a parasol blooming

over her Baron de Saint Julien
fainting in the bushes with desire
as she leaves him again to go high

into a leafy canopy that seems
to be connected to nothing—
How can it hang on any longer?

But she isn't thinking,
she's breathless, in a flutter,
a swoon as when, shopping, the mind

stops—We think, *This can be mine*—
and we give ourselves away just
as easily as this ignorant girl

secure on her plump velvet cushion
starting back down through the silly leaves
while the rope groans and holds,

now owning, now thoroughly
owned by the rush of the foliage,
by gravity.

Walter McDonald

THE FOOD PICKERS OF SAIGON

Rubbish like compost heaps burned every hour
of my days and nights at Tan Son Nhut.
Ragpickers scoured the edges of our junk,
risking the flames, bent over,
searching for food. A ton of tin cans

piled up each month, sharp-edged, unlabeled.
Those tiny anonymous people could stick
their hands inside and claw out whatever
remained, scooping it into jars, into their
mouths. No one went hungry. At a distance,

the dump was like a coal mine fire burning
out of control, or Moses' holy bush
which was not consumed. Watching them labor
in the field north of my barracks, trying
to think of something good to write my wife,

I often thought of bears in Yellowstone
our first good summer in a tent. I wrote
about the bears, helping us both focus
on how they waddled to the road and begged,
and came some nights into the campground

so long ago and took all food they found.
We sat helplessly naive outside our tent
and watched them, and one night rolled
inside laughing when one great bear
turned and shoulder-swayed his way toward us.

Through the zipped mosquito netting
we watched him watching us. Slack-jawed,
he seemed to grin, to thank us for all
he was about to receive from our table.
We thought how lovely, how much fun

to be this close to danger. No campers
had died in that Disneyland national park
for years. Now, when my children
eat their meat and bread and leave
good broccoli or green beans

on their plates, I call them back
and growl, I can't help it. It's like hearing
my father's voice again. I never tell them
why they have to eat it. I never say
they're like two beautiful children

I found staring at me one night
through the screen of my window,
at Tan Son Nhut, bone-faced. Or that
when I crawled out of my stifling monsoon
dream to feed them, they were gone.

Jane Shore

LOT'S WIFE

God evicts his tenants
on such short notice
who knew
what to take?
My husband, my daughters
loaded down
with things, things, only I
lagged behind.

Old men used to come to me
to pray and weep
and pull their long white beards
and the fringe
on their prayer shawls
as if I were the Wailing Wall.

If only I were the Wailing Wall
with a tenement of weeds
in my wrinkles.

Salt.
Magic in the lunchrooms
of public schools! Tricks!
A child balancing
a salt shaker
on one salt crystal.
I'm now that small.
Smaller than that.

I saw the dark rushing overhead
and the brimstone
flipping through the air
like fistfuls of coins.
They bounced on the ground.
They rolled on their edges.

If I said *manna*
it would be a lie.
All that shining!
I only wanted
to stuff my dress
with souvenirs. Evidence
I'd been there.

The University of Missouri Press

The University of Missouri Press's Breakthrough Books series was established in 1969 as a vehicle for poets and short-fiction writers who had not yet published in book form. When the series first began, the competition was conducted annually and was judged by faculty members at the University of Missouri and by Press staff. A Devins Award winner was selected by the Jewish Community Center's Prize Committee which sponsored a series of readings.

In the early 1970s the entire selection process was taken over by the Press, with the substantial involvement of William Peden and Thomas McAfee. In 1979 the Press shifted the competition to odd-numbered years only, appointing outside judges from different parts of the country for each judging cycle (Hollis Summers in 1979, Robert Boyers in 1981, David Wagoner in 1983, and George Garrett in 1985). All submitted manuscripts are read by the judge who selects approximately three manuscripts for publication in the two-year period. Breakthrough Books are published in editions of 1,000 paperback copies.

Penelope Austin, *Waiting for a Hero,* 1988
Richard Lyons, *These Modern Nights,* 1988
Nancy Schoenberger, *Girl on a White Porch,* 1987
Shirley Bowers Anders, *The Bus Home,* 1986
R. S. Gwynn, *The Drive-In,* 1986
Jane O. Wayne, *Looking Both Ways,* 1986
Robert Gibb, *The Winter House,* 1984
Wesley McNair, *The Faces of Americans in 1853,* 1984
Richard Robbins, *The Invisible Wedding,* 1984
Cathryn Hankla, *Phemomena,* 1983
Harry Humes, *Winter Weeds,* 1983
Mary Kinzie, *The Threshold of the Year,* 1982
Ronald Wallace, *Plums, Stones, Kisses & Hooks,* 1981

Frank Manley, *Resultances,* 1980
Molly Peacock, *And Live Apart,* 1980
G. E. Murray, *Repairs,* 1979
Janet N. Beeler, *Dowry,* 1978
Jonathan Aldrich, *Croquet Lover at the Dinner Table,* 1977
C. G. Hanzlicek, *Stars,* 1977
Willis Barnstone, *China Dolls,* 1976
Diana O'Hehir, *Summoned,* 1976
Daniel J. Langton, *Querencia,* 1976
Joseph di Prisco, *Wit's End,* 1976
Peter Cooley, *The Company of Strangers,* 1975
R. K. Meiners, *Journeying Back to the World,* 1975
James J. McAuley, *After the Blizzard,* 1975
Gerald Costanzo, *In the Aviary,* 1974
Annie Dillard, *Tickets for a Prayer Wheel,* 1974
Darcy Gottlieb, *No Witness But Ourselves,* 1973
Ed Ochester, *Dancing on the Edges of Knives,* 1973
Jonathan Holden, *Design for a House,* 1972
Henry Carlile, *The Rough-Hewn Table,* 1971
Dorothy Hughes, *The Great Victory Mosaic,* 1971
John Bennett, *The Struck Leviathan: Poems on "Moby Dick,"* 1970
R. P. Dickey, *Acting Immortal,* 1970
John Calvin Rezmerski, *Held for Questioning,* 1969

Gerald Costanzo

At Irony's Picnic

Silence is sight-reading
Swahili. Sin lumbers by on

stilts. Where did he get
that Hawaiian shirt? those

rose-colored glasses? Down
by the lake Desire is fondling

Regret's mother. Jealousy
and Happiness dance the mazurka.

Justice, wearing the same
old swimsuit, is cutting the

ballyhoo. Irony himself
isn't even here.

Vigilantes

There was a time in
their country when they
patrolled the streets
of villages on horseback,
lynching murderers and
thieves at gatherings
so formal they called them
neck-tie parties.

They wore sure thin smiles
as they yoked violence
from shadows to the
light.

When law broke down in
their towns they bent over it
and looked with pity deep into
its giant eyes. They offered
it smelling salts and soothed its
wounds. They stroked it,
they picked it up, they took it
into their own hands.

Annie Dillard

THE MAN WHO WISHES TO FEED ON MAHOGANY

*Chesterton tells us that if someone wished to feed exclusively on mahogany, po-
etry would not be able to express this. Instead, if a man happens to love and not
be loved in return, or if he mourns the absence or loss of someone, then poetry
is able to express these feelings precisely because they are commonplace.*
                    —Borges, interview in *Encounter,* April 1969

Not the man who wishes to feed on mahogany
and who happens to love and not be loved in return;
not mourning in autumn the absence or loss of someone,
remembering how, in a yellow dress, she leaned
light-shouldered, lanky, over a platter of pears—
no; no tricks. Just the man and his wish, alone.

That there should be mahogany, real, in the world,
instead of no mahogany, rings in his mind
like a gong—that in humid Haitian forests are trees,
hard trees, not holes in air, not nothing, no Haiti,
no zone for trees nor time for wood to grow:
reality rounds his mind like rings in a tree.

Love is the factor, love is the type, and the poem.
Is love a trick, to make him commonplace?

He wishes, cool in his windy rooms. He thinks:
of all earth's shapes, her coils, rays and nets,
mahogany I love, this sunburnt red,
this close-grained, scented slab, my fellow creature.

He knows he can't feed on the wood he loves, and he won't.
But desire walks on lean legs down halls of his sleep,
desire to drink and sup at mahogany's mass.
His wishes weight his belly. Love holds him here,
love nails him to the world, this windy wood,
as to a cross. Oh, this lanky, sunburnt cross!

Is he sympathetic? Do you care?
And you, sir: perhaps you wish to feed
on your bright-eyed daughter, on your baseball glove,
on your outboard motor's pattern in the water.
Some love weights your walking in the world;
some love molds you heavier than air.

Look at the world, where vegetation spreads
and peoples air with weights of green desire.
Crosses grow as trees and grasses everywhere,
writing in wood and leaf and flower and spore,
marking the map, "Some man loved here;
and one loved something here; and here; and here."

Cathryn Hankla

———

THE NIGHT-FATHER WAS FOUND ALIVE

Of sense and outward things,
Fallings from us, vanishings
                —Wordsworth

1.
The child lay freezing in snow
not feeling the cold
or the hollow of ice
she formed lying in darkness
behind the house.
She heard her parents' voices call
the name they'd given
and saw the headlights of their car
pass in the air between her and the stars.

As heat dissolved, her body
sank. She could no longer lift
her arms above her head
to wave them into wings.

2.
The night the father took a kitchen knife
to reason with the mother,
the child sat in a pink chair crowded with ballerinas
and screamed until she could not speak
or hear. The father whispered
he wouldn't hurt her, winked,
letting the blade glint with the little light
he stood to hide in the door.
The mother packed her clothes and cried,
"Hush, I'll take you with me, hush now."
The father said they'd never leave alive,
and they didn't.

That was when she killed him.
The child learned to keep silent, still,
and watch him like a movie screen
from which she could not look away.

3.
But in the field years later, numb,
when the voices stopped calling
her home, and windows in the house she'd left
disappeared one by one,
when the child was left alone—
into the clearness of the night,
she shouted to the little lights so far away
how much she hated her father.
Three times she chanted, in a hoarse whisper first.
The voice filled her throat and ached
for the words to be spoken.

A flashlight found her
staring toward blank sky—
the father finding her at last
in the last place he thought to look
before he closed his eyes.
He took the child up on his back, carried her
and sat before a fire,
rubbing her blue feet between his hands
until she could feel his touch again.

Harry Humes

THE MAN WHO CARVES WHALES

All summer long out of pine
and birch the great whales flow
from my knife, blue and finback,
sperm whale, right, and sei
with flukes easy as smooth runs
of deep water. I work hours
on the strange heads, the mouths
full of baleen plates or ivory teeth.

Other days when my knife
goes dull or quiet with loss,
I read of their convoluted brains
and half-ton hearts, the songs
deep in latitudes
of scrimshaw and krill.

I keep them close to my hands,
polish them, and all around me
the season moves toward Scammon Lagoon,
the Chuckchi and Bering Seas.
I think of them there
running out of breath, drowning
with the New World, with cities and faces
that have no need for the breach of mystery.

When I open my knife again
I see in the wood a moment,
the end of shapes I must carve my way into
over and over.

THE NEW SITE OF THE CALVARY TEMPLE

A year ago, cornfields; in winter
a snowy owl; older now, the season's
finished in stucco, the interstate
sparks and rattles with trucks. O God,
more parking, more bright vestibules
to crack against our cracks.
In the chilly rooms, wives and children
huddle in exact rows. What I breathe tonight
hurts beyond the church, the choir,
the remembered handshake. I think of everything
inside like a zigzag of trotlines
hooking the dead with the dead.
What place is better, hotter than the owl's kill?
What darkness preyed on more gracefully?

Ed Ochester

JAMES WRIGHT WALKS INTO A SUMAC PATCH NEAR ALIQUIPPA, PENNSYLVANIA

Just off the highway to Aliquippa, Pennsylvania,
smog billows forth on the grass.
And the eyes of two puppies
moisten with kindness.
They stumble out of the sumac,
where they have been playing alone, all day.
They quiver expectantly; they can hardly contain
    their happiness
that we are coming.
They jump shyly as little girls. They love each other.
There is no loneliness like theirs.
I would like to hold the big fellow in my arms,

for he has walked over to me
and nuzzled my left
hand.
He is black and white.
The skin inside his thigh
is delicate as the skin behind a girl's
thorax.
Suddenly I realize
that if I stepped out of my body, I would melt
into puddles.

Molly Peacock

THE LIFE OF LEON BONVIN

Leon Bonvin was a painter,
a watercolorist, in France
in the last century. He lived
in the country, a second son.
His father kept the inn, BONVIN.

Elder brother lived in Paris,
where he fed, sketched, bought oils, canvas,
and sundry extraordinary
horsehair brushes and quills. Bonvin
stayed home, although he was allowed

a short study in the city.
Goodwine: fine wines. There is nothing
against a man who wants a good name
kept above his tavern doors
and keeps his son at home

drawing water, asking the girls
politely to clear the tables,

watching the growing pile of stained
linens. At dusk or at dawn when
the suspenders of his father

dangle from a brass hook inside
the bedroom door, the painter paints.
There will be hours of men against
the tavern walls, and an hour
of sleep for Bonvin, drying hours

for the tints. Only at dawn and
only at dusk, in the barest
sufficiency of natural light
and in the barest absence of
père's powdery wheezes, "Son! Son!"

and when the brunette tendrils of
his young wife's hair are curled in sweat
above the bread oven—early,
when the inn is empty, or late,
when maids agree to serve alone

the ox-driving customers till
supper—Bonvin, a man of good
name, but always in haste, gathers
his paints to confront the light death
of sunset, or the death of dawn.

Extraordinary roses, dried
in layers of black beneath red,
the green vase, green as in bottles
of Beaujolais, the uneasy
gray light beneath fog ascending

out the open windows. There are
no figures in this work. Still life.
The continuing absence of sun.

In the blackened landscapes of dusk,
the bits of rouged spots, are they blooms?

It is difficult to see, it
is impossible to see—what
is that in the undergrowth, there:
Couldn't he have imagined light?
But they are beautiful. The fury

they breed. Did they bring him to speech
in the ill-lit tavern by day,
by morning his vista in fog,
by evening almost in final,
almost in ludicrous darkness?

Leon Bonvin, with two pails on
his shoulders, followed by his small
rambunctious sons upstairs to all
the rooms lined every other one
like headstones. "These times of day

are minor times!" The heart wants
midnight, or it wants noon . . . .
                                    After
1864 and '65,
the most frantic years, the years
in which flowers looked like crepe, skies

like the linen of the moon's hood,
where the number of paintings done
times the number of wheezing calls
of père Bonvin, blurred by welcomes,
thank-yous, and francs on the tables,

caused the damnation of his lids
drooping by a line from his brows,
caused the growth of an astounding
unlaundered pile of aprons fouled
with rosé, red wine, white, sweat, and

clogged brushes, Bonvin painted less
and less, then took his own life.
The artists of his time, who were
unknown to the artist alive,
auctioned his finished work abroad

on behalf of elder brother,
for the maintenance of the inn—

the sign of the tavern BONVIN
hung in the morning in fog—for
the burial of fils Bonvin,

for the food, rooms,
and well-being
of his widow,
and the schooling
of her two sons.

Janet Beeler Shaw

BURIAL DAY

on the way home
we stop at her picking garden
gone wild since July

tomato vines exploding fruit like nebulae
red suns, green moons

furry leaves parting
handfulls of little gold tomatoes
double handfulls of beefsteak tomatoes

her whole field for our feasting
spouts of hot juice in our mouths
juice on our chins
seeds and juice on our clothes

eating her tomatoes the way she liked to
warm in the field
without washing

without salt

————

Missouri Bottomland

I'll be the girl in her daddy's shirt
and her brother's Levi's,
riding in your pickup truck
with the six-pack between my knees,
waiting for the summer day to shut down.

You be the boy in wash pants and white bucks,
smelling of soap and Coke,
driving with one hand.

I've got the army blanket, honey,
you've got the church key,
and after dark the riverbank is blind.

I'll be the girl in the weeds and honeysuckle,
with cool hands and red lollipops,
and a slick, flat belly.

You be the boy who rolls me off the blanket.

I'll be the girl with sand on her bare ass
who makes the stars disappear
with her mouth.

Ronald Wallace

Oranges

This morning I eat an orange.
It is sour and juicy. My mouth
will tingle all day.
Outside, it is cold. The trees
do not anticipate their leaves.
When I breathe into my hand I smell
oranges.

I walk across the lake.
Ice fishermen twitch their poles until
perch flicker the surface, quick
and bright as orange slices.
The sun ripens in the sky.
The wind turns thin and citrus,
the day precise, fragile.

My mustache and eyelashes freeze.
When I arrive at your house
you are friendly as a fruitseller.
We peel off our clothes, slice through
that wordy rind.
When I lift my fingers to your lips:
oranges.

The University of North Carolina Press

Although the University of North Carolina Press had published poetry sporadically from its inception in 1922, it wasn't until 1961 that a consistent series was established. At that time Howard Webber, a young poet and editor at the Press, proposed the series to Lambert Davis, a press director who had spent ten years in commercial publishing where he "formed very firm conclusions about the extent to which commercial publishers were taking care of publishing fiction and poetry." Davis approved the series, and Webber edited it until 1971 when the Board of Governors of the University of North Carolina Press established a policy prohibiting the publication of poetry and fiction.

R. H. W. Dillard, *News of the Nile,* 1971
Jean Farley, *Figure and Field,* 1970
Christopher Brookhouse, *Scattered Light,* 1969
David R. Slavitt, *Day Sailing,* 1969
Jonathan Williams, *An Ear in Bartram's Tree,* 1969
Juan Ruiz, *The Book of Good Love,* 1968
Elizabeth Sewell, *Signs and Cities,* 1968
Charles David Wright, *Early Rising,* 1968
Edwin Godsey, *Cabin Fever,* 1967
Kenneth Pitchford, *A Suite of Angels and Other Poems,* 1967
Jack Matthews, *An Almanac for Twilight,* 1966
Phillis Wheatley, *The Poems of Phillis Wheatley,* 1966
Lisel Mueller, *Dependencies,* 1965
Julia Randall, *The Puritan Carpenter,* 1965
David R. Slavitt, *The Carnivore,* 1965
Mona Van Duyn, *A Time of Bees,* 1964
Martin Halpern, *Two Sides of an Island and Other Poems,* 1963
Arnold Kenseth, *The Holy Merriment,* 1963
Elizabeth Sewell, *Poems,* 1962

George Garrett, *Abraham's Knife,* 1961
Thomas Vance, *Skeleton of Light,* 1961
Charles Edward Eaton, *The Bright Plain,* 1942
R. H. W. Dillard, *The Day I Stopped Dreaming About Barbara Steele,* 1940
J. Saunders Redding, *To Make a Poet Black,* 1939
Philip Graham, *The Life and Poems of Mirabeau B. Lamar,* 1938
Victor S. Starbuck, *Saul, King of Israel,* 1938
John Charles McNeil, *Songs Merry and Sad,* 1932
Louise Crenshaw Ray, *Color of Steel,* 1932
Anne Blackwell Payne, *Released,* 1930
John Charles McNeil, *Lyrics from Cotton Land,* 1922

Mona Van Duyn

THE GARDENER TO HIS GOD

*"Amazing research proves simple prayer makes flowers grow many times faster,
stronger, larger."*

Advertisement in The Flower Grower

I pray that the great world's flowering stay as it is,
that larkspur and snapdragon keep to their ordinary size,
and bleedingheart hang in its old way, and Judas tree
stand well below oak, and old oaks color the fall sky.
For the myrtle to keep underfoot, and no rose
to send up a swollen face, I pray simply.

There is no disorder but the heart's. But if love goes leaking
outward, if shrubs take up its monstrous stalking,
all greenery is spurred, the snapping lips are overgrown,
and over oaks red hearts hang like the sun.
Deliver us from its giant gardening, from walking
all over the earth with no rest from its disproportion.

Let all flowers turn to stone before ever they begin to share
love's spaciousness, and faster, stronger, larger
grow from a sweet thought, before any daisy
turns, under love's gibberellic wish, to the day's eye.
Let all blooms take shape from cold laws, down from a cold air
let come their small grace or measurable majesty.

For in every place but love the imagination lies
in its limits. Even poems draw back from images
of that one country, on top of whose lunatic stemming
whoever finds himself there must sway and cling
until the high cold God takes pity, and it all dies
down, down into the great world's flowering.

1. *The Dormitory*

In Mexico the little mixed herds come home in the evening,
slow through that hard-colored landscape, all driven together—
the hens, a few pigs, a burro, two cows, and the thin
perro that is everywhere. It is the same scene here.

The nurses herd us. In our snouts and feathers
we move through the rigid cactus shapes of chairs
colored to lie, belie terror and worse.
Assorted and unlikely as the lives we bear,

we go together to bed, one dozen of us.
It was a hard day's grazing, we fed on spines of courtesy
and scratched up a few dry bugs of kindness.
But we deserved less than that generosity.

Our teats of giving hang dry. Our poor peons are bewildered
and poorer still, the whole landscape is impoverished
by the unnatural economy of this group's greed,
whose bark is bitter, who are swaybacked, fruitless, unfleshed.

The pen echoes to a meaningless moo, "I want to go home,"
one cackles over sins, one yaps in rhythmic complaining,
but those shapes under the sheets are not like mine.
We are locked in unlove. I am sick of my own braying.

The metaphor shakes like my hand. Come, Prince of Pills,
electric kiss, undo us, and we will appear
wearing each other's pain like silk, the awful
richness of feeling we blame, but barely remember.

II. *The Doctors*

Those who come from outside are truly foreign.
How are we to believe in the clear-eyed and clean-shaven?

The jungle I crawl through on my hands and knees,
the whole monstrous ferny land of my own nerves,
hisses and quakes at these upright missionaries
wearing immaculate coats, and will not open.
Mine is waiting outside like a mild boy.
He is unarmed, he will never make it to this anarchy.
Somewhere down his civil streams, through his system,
a survivor came babbling, half-wild from stink and sun,
and news leaked out about our savage customs.
I bit my bloody heart again today.

At night I dream of tables and chairs, beds,
hospitals. I wake. I am up to my waist in mud.
Everything shrieks, cloudbursts of confusion are beating
on my head as I twist and grab for vines, sweating
to make a raft, to tie something together. He is waiting.
I want his words after all, those cheap beads.

Stranger, forgive me, I have clawed as close as I can.
Your trinkets clink to the ground, it is all dark
on the other side of my impenetrable network.
I will wallow and gnaw—but wait, you are coming back,
and at touch, flamethrower, underbrush goes down.
Now I can stand by you, fellow-citizen.

III. A Memory

"Write a letter to Grandpa," my mother said, but he smelled old.
"He'll give you something nice," she said, but I was afraid.
He never looked at me, he muttered to himself, and he hid
bad things to drink all over his house, and Grandma cried.
A gray stranger with a yellowed mustache, why should I have mailed
my very first message to him? Well, consider the innocent need
that harries us all: "Your Aunt Callie thinks she's smart, but *her* kid
never sent her first letter to Pa." (To hold her I had to be good.)
"You've learned to write. Write Grandpa!" she said, so I did.

It was hard work. "Dear Grandpa, How are you, I am fine,"
but I couldn't come to the end of a word when I came to the
	margin,
and the lines weren't straight on the page. I erased that paper so thin
you could almost see through it in spots. I couldn't seem to learn
to look ahead. (Mother, remember we both had to win.)
"We are coming to visit you next Sunday if it does not rain.
Yours truly, your loving granddaughter, Mona Van Duyn."
That Sunday he took me aside and gave me the biggest coin
I ever had, and I ran away from the old man.

"Look, Mother, what Grandpa gave me. And as soon as I get back
	home
I'll write him again for another half dollar." But Mother said
	"Shame!"
and so I was ashamed. But I think at that stage of the game,
or any stage of the game, things are almost what they seem
and the exchange was fair. Later in the afternoon I caught him.
"Medicine," he said, but he must have known his chances were slim.
People don't hide behind the big fern, I wasn't dumb,
and I was Grandma's girl. "So, *Liebling,* don't tell them,"
he said, but that sneaky smile called me by my real name.

Complicity I understood. What human twig isn't bent
by the hidden weight of its wish for some strict covenant?
"Are you going to tell?" he wanted to know, and I said, "No, I won't."
He looked right at me and straightened his mouth and said, "So, *Kind,*
we fool them yet," and it seemed to me I knew what he meant.
Then he reached in his pocket and pulled out two candies covered
	with lint,
and we stood there and each sucked one. "*Ja,* us two, we know what
	we want."
When he leaned down to chuck my chin I caught my first Grandpa-
	scent.
Oh, it was a sweet seduction on pillows of peppermint!

And now, in the middle of life, I'd like to learn how to forgive
the heart's grandpa, mother and kid, the hard ways we have to love.

Northeastern University Press

The Northeastern University English department initiated the Samuel French Morse Poetry Prize in 1984 to honor Samuel Morse. The annual prize-winning manuscript is published by Northeastern University Press in an edition of 1,000 copies. Guy Rotella, and other members of the English department, screen the submissions to approximately five or ten, which are sent to an outside judge. Anthony Hecht, Maxine Kumin, X. J. Kennedy, and Donald Hall have served in that capacity.

Nell Altizer, *The Man Who Died En Route,* 1988
Yvonne Sapia, *Valentino's Hair,* 1987
Sue Ellen Thompson, *This Body of Silk,* 1986
William Carpenter, *Rain,* 1985
Susan Donnelly, *Eve Names the Animals,* 1984

William Carpenter

FIRE

This morning, on the opposite shore of the river,
I watch a man burning his own house.
It is a cold day, and the man wears thick gloves
and a fur hat that gives him a Russian look.
I envy his energy, since I'm still on the sunporch
in my robe, with morning coffee, my day not
even begun, while my neighbor has already piled
spruce boughs against his house and poured
flammable liquids over them to send a ribbon
of black smoke into the air, a column surrounded
by herring gulls, who think he's having a barbecue
or has founded a new dump. I hadn't known what labor
it took to burn something. Now the man's working
at such speed, he's like the criminal in a silent
movie, as if he had a deadline, as if he had
to get his house burned by a certain time, or it
would be all over. I see his kids helping, bringing
him matches and kindling, and I'd like to help out
myself, I'd like to bring him coffee and a bagel,
but the Penobscot River separates us, icebergs
the size of small ships drifting down the tide.
Moreover, why should I help him when I have a house
myself, which needs burning as much as anyone's?
It has begun to leak. I think it has carpenter ants.
I hear them making sounds at night like writing, only
they aren't writing, they are building small tubular
cities inside the walls. I start burning in the study,
working from within so it will go faster, so I can
catch up, and soon there's a smoke column on either
side, like a couple of Algonquins having a dialogue
on how much harder it is to destroy than to create.

I shovel books and poems into the growing fire. If
I burn everything, I can start over, with a future
like a white rectangle of paper. Then I notice
my neighbor has a hose, that he's spraying his house
with water, the coward, he has bailed out, but I
keep throwing things into the fire: my stamps,
my Berlioz collection, my photos of nude people,
my correspondence dating back to grade school.
Over there, the fire engines are reaching his home.
His wife is crying with relief, his fire's extinguished.
He has walked down to the shore to see the ruins
of the house across the river, the open cellar,
the charred timbers, the man laughing and singing
in the snow, who has been finally freed from his
possessions, who has no clothes, no library, who has
gone back to the beginning, when we lived in nature:
no refuge from the elements, no fixed address.

————

SOMETHING IS ADRIFT IN THE WATER

A man skis to a remote log cabin
in the White Mountains. He is not
young, so it takes an entire day
to get there, to unpack and build
his fire. There is some old whiskey
in the cabin, and, as he drinks it,
he remembers having seen a movie
where a woman is found floating
in a river, and the astonished hunter
takes her home, feeds her and falls
in love, so that his wife leaves him
and his life is ruined. The skier
watches the fire and tries to remember
the title or director or even the country
in Eastern Europe where the film was made,

but he can't recall them, and in the cabin
there is no phone to call someone who
would know, so he starts thinking maybe
it was not a movie but just something
he imagined, or even that the story was
his own life, that he was the hunter
or fisherman who broke through ice
in the Czech forest and saw the breasts,
the black hair, that it was he who brought
a body home that came to life, it was
his wife who left, taking his own children
in the Volvo, so that the house seemed
empty, even though a girl stood naked
at the stove, cooking this delicious
Slavic soup, that he began to ski,
as the hunter in the film had skied,
to a remote cabin with no electricity,
no running water. Now he remembers
that the Czech hunter died, and he
orders his own heart to stop, because
it made a terrible mistake, only this is
Franconia, New Hampshire, and the heart
keeps going, the man finally remembers
the director's name, his own name, he eats
two snowballs soaked in bourbon so that
he'll stop thinking of a body just beneath
the surface, of hands reaching up for air.

Susan Donnelly

EVE NAMES THE ANIMALS

To me, *lion* was sun on a wing
over the garden. *Dove,*
a burrowing, blind creature.

I swear that man
never knew animals. Words
he lined up according to size,

while elephants slipped flat-eyed
through water

and trout
hurtled from the underbrush, tusked
and ready for battle.

The name he gave me stuck
me to him. He did it to comfort me,
for not being first.

Mornings, while he slept,
I got away. Pickerel
hopped on the branches above me.
Only spider accompanied me,

nosing everywhere,
running up to lick my hand.

Poor finch. I suppose I was
woe to him—

the way he'd come looking for me,
not wanting either of us
to be ever alone.

But to myself I was
palomino
      raven
           fox . . .

I strung words
by their stems and wore them
as garlands on my long walks.

The next day
I'd find them withered.

I liked change.

Ohio State University Press

Ohio State University Press was incorporated in 1957 and began publishing an average of one poetry book per year in 1962. A poetry reading committee, composed of English department faculty members, read all submitted manuscripts. In 1986, Peter Givler, who helped found the University of Wisconsin Press poetry series before moving on to become director of Ohio State University Press, appointed David Citino editor of a new series which considers manuscripts in an annual competition cosponsored by the Press and *The Ohio Journal: The Literary Magazine of the Ohio State University.* The Press publishes one book per year from this competition, and occasionally another book from outside the competition. *The Ohio Journal* award in poetry includes a $750 cash prize from the Helen Hooven Santmyer Fund.

Sue Owen, *The Book of Winter,* 1989
Robert Cording, *Life-List,* 1988
Walter McDonald, *The Flying Dutchman,* 1988
David Weiss, *The Fourth Part of the World,* 1986
David Bergman, *Cracking the Code,* 1985
Richard Hague, *Ripening,* 1984
B. Wongar, *Bilma,* 1984
Patrick Todd, *A Fire by the Tracks,* 1983
Tom Absher, *Forms of Praise,* 1982
David Citino, *Last Rites and Other Poems,* 1981
Michael J. Zimroth, *Giselle Considers Her Future,* 1980
Gordon Grigsby, *Tornado Watch,* 1978
John Perlman, *Kachina,* 1978
Bill McLaughlin, *Conspiracies of Love and Death,* 1973
Sonya Dorman, *Poems,* 1970
Robert Canzoneri, *Watch Us Pass,* 1970

Mac Hammond, *The Horse Opera and Other Poems,* 1968
A. R. Ammons, *Expressions at Sea Level,* 1964
William Dickey, *Interpreter's House,* 1963
Milton Kessler, *A Road Came Once,* 1962

David Citino

GRYNSZPAN, 1938

November in Paris:
a teenage Jew who loved the sound he made
when he prayed his name
and wanted all the world to be moved
by such fine singing
waltzed into the German Embassy,
a pistol sweating in his fist,
and spun around in a shower
of paperwork and spectacles
a small envoy of the Reich who hated
his father but bowed one time too many.
Just seventeen years from silence, eyes
crystal, teeth clenched tight, tendon and sinew
twitching in rigid columns,
he sang his Polish curses as the trigger
snapped back away from him and flesh
collapsed around the dark and dark
around the flesh.

In Germany two nights later, Dr. Goebbels
smiles beneath a twisted cross
at the cadenced schemes his fingernails drum out
along the tabletop, rattles his broken foot
to all the discord that has been and will be,
twenty thousand city souls danced into forest,
burghers prancing in the street below
to the lumbering polka of stone
and tears and shattered glass.

MARY'S SECOND CHILD

Then Joseph . . . took unto him his wife: and knew her not till she had brought forth her first born son.

—Matthew

It's no miracle I'm what I am, believe me.
I was the harvest of a sweaty, human planting,
never far enough from the whine of father's saw.
No credulous beasts, no Eastern mystics
tired of gold or human boys heard my birth;
and where was I to find a winged heaven
to trumpet my entrance? I had no connections.

Mother worked to give me light,
her first curse my first lullaby.
If there was in her groaning a measure
of disappointment—even outrage—who could blame her?
The only men she knew before me or her husband
were angelic, everlasting and painless,
their bodies light as cloud.

Joseph grasped at what he couldn't comprehend,
shook his dusty hands at the sky, his lust
fed by the jeers of every young fool in town.
On the night he first touched her,
as much in anger as need, he told me later,
she lay looking at him as if she were
queen of heaven, and he grew soft as cloth.

But after what she'd been through
the first time, she was ready to see
in every pail of water drawn from the well
a shining dove hovering near her reflection,
in each wine cup or scrap of fish
an alien son, arrogant and cold.
Love held no more surprises for her.

When she died gray and confused
just before learning to fly
she looked at me, the image of her two lovers,
and called me "Jesus"—she's up there now
singing at him, most likely, beaming.
When you're conceived to walk with angels
can children of earth and flesh move you?

Walter McDonald

HAULING OVER WOLF CREEK PASS IN WINTER

If I make it over the pass
I park the rig, crawl back to the bunk
and try to sleep, the pigs swaying
like a steep grade, like the last curve
Johnson took too fast and burned.
But that was summer. His fire
spread to the next county.

It doesn't worry me.
I take the east climb no sweat
and the rest is a long coasting
down to the pens in Pagosa Springs.
It's the wolves I wait for.
We never see them any other way,
not in this business.
Sometimes five, six hauls before
propped on one arm, smoking,
I see them slink from the dark pines
toward the truck. They drive the pigs
crazy, squealing
as if a legion of demons had them.
Later, when I start up and go,
the pigs keep plunging,
trying to drive us over the cliff.

I let them squeal, their pig hearts
exploding like grenades.
The wolves are dark and silent.
Kneeling, I watch them split up
like sappers, some in the tree lines,
some gliding from shadow to shadow,
red eyes flashing in moonlight,
some farther off, guarding the flanks.
Each time, they know they have me.

I take my time, knowing I can crawl
over the seat, light up,
sip from the steaming thermos.
I crank the diesel,
release the air brakes
like a rocket launcher.
Wolves run in circles. I hit the lights.
Wolves plunge through deep snow
to the trees, the whole pack starving.
Revving up, the truck rolls down the highway
faster, the last flight out of Da Nang.
I shove into third gear, fourth,
the herd of pigs screaming, the load
lurching and banging on every turn,
almost delivered, almost airborne.

Ohio University Press

From 1965 to 1980 Ohio University Press published new poetry annually. In 1980, because of poor sales of poetry in particular and overall financial difficulties, the Press began to publish only new work by those poets who had previously published with Ohio, and that policy continues today. In addition, from 1980 to 1987 the Press copublished the International Poetry Series edited by Samuel Hazo, and from 1979 to the present the Press has published poetry for Swallow Press. Books are printed in editions of 600–700 copies.

Hollis Summers, *Other Concerns & Brother Clark*, 1988
William Meissner, *The Sleepwalker's Son*, 1987
James Schevill, *Ambiguous Dancers of Fame*, 1987
John Matthias, *Northern Summer, New and Selected Poems
1963–83*, 1984
Lucien Stryk, *Collected Poems*, 1984
Charles Doria, *The Game of Europe: A Comedy of High Gothic
Romance, Frankly Rendered Out of the Senseless*, 1983
James Erwin Schevill, *American Fantasies*, 1983
Raphael Rudnik, *Frank 207: Poems*, 1982
Anthony Sobin, *The Sunday Naturalist*, 1982
Alan Archer Stephens, *In Plain Air: Poems 1958–1980*, 1982
Carolyn Stoloff, *Swiftly Now*, 1982
Elizabeth Bartlett, *Memory is No Stranger*, 1981
Carl Bode, *Practical Magic*, 1981
Albert Spaulding Cook, *Adapt the Living*, 1981
Gene Frumkin, *Clouds and Red Earth*, 1981
Janet Lewis, *Poems Old and New, 1918–78*, 1981
E. L. Mayo, *Collected Poems*, 1981
Mark Perlberg, *The Feel of the Sun*, 1981
Natalie S. Robins, *Eclipse*, 1981

Lucien Stryk, *Encounter with Zen*, 1981
Chad Walsh, *Hang Me up My Begging Bowl*, 1981
Robert Dana, *In a Fugitive Season*, 1980
Thomas McGrath, *The Movie at the End of the World*, 1980
John Matthias, *Crossing*, 1979
William Meissner, *Learning to Breathe Underwater*, 1979
Michael Sheridan, *The Fifth Season*, 1978
Yvor Winters, *The Collected Poems of Yvor Winters*, 1978
Colette Inez, *Alive and Taking Names*, 1977
Beth Bentley, *Country of Resemblances*, 1976
Peter Dale, *Mortal Fire*, 1976
Sonya Dorman, *Stretching Fence*, 1976
David Evans, *Train Windows*, 1976
Alan Archer Stephens, *White River Poems*, 1976
Samuel Hazo, *Inscripts*, 1975
Lloyd Frankenberg, *The Stain of Circumstances*, 1974
Conrad Hilberry, *Rust*, 1974
Dave Smith, *The Fisherman's Whore*, 1974
Victor Depta, *The Creek*, 1973
James Schevill, *Buddhist Car and Other Characters*, 1973
Lucien Stryk, *Awakening*, 1973
Eugene Wildman, *Nuclear Love*, 1972
J. V. Cunningham, *The Collected Poems and Epigrams of
   J. V. Cunningham*, 1971
John Montague, *Tides*, 1971
Beth Bentley, *Phone Calls from the Dead*, 1970
Robert Dana, *Power of the Visible*, 1971
Richard Frost, *Getting Drunk with the Birds*, 1970
Hugh MacDiarmid, *More Collected Poems*, 1970
Thomas McGrath, *Letter to an Imaginary Friend, Pts. I & II*, 1970
Alan Archer Stephens, *Tree Meditation, and Others*, 1970
Eugene Wildman, *Montezuma's Ball*, 1970
James Schevill, *Violence and Glory*, 1969
Chad Walsh, *The End of Nature: Poems*, 1969
Conrad Hilberry, *Encounter on Burrows Hill*, 1968
Jerome Mazzaro, *Changing the Windows*, 1966

Josephine Jacobsen, *The Animal Inside,* 1966
T. Carmi, *The Brass Serpent,* 1965
Richard Frost, *The Circus Villains,* 1965
Anaïs Nin, *House of Incest,* 1958
Alan Archer Stephens, *The Sum: Poems,* 1958

Beth Bentley

THE POET AT SEVEN

She watched her hand flicker, flash out,
recoil, whiter than lightning,
thin as a snake's tongue, tensile;

and then the stain spreading
on the other child's cheek, a live thing
that transferred itself to her, her face.

Can the body have a life its own,
apart from the mind? Does it work
that way, swiftly, without intention?

Anger. Anger like her mother's. But
she felt no anger, seeing her friend's
red face, only wonder at what she'd done.

And wonder as she learned her mind
was a hidden place, deep as grass,
thick as the scent of peach-blossom,

quieter than sky seen through branches;
a quiet into which she moved, swimming
down, down, down through dark waters

toward trees, beasts, changing weather:
the place her self lived. It waited for her,
the country of resemblances.

Conrad Hilberry

HARRY HOUDINI
THE HIPPODROME, NEW YORK, JANUARY 7, 1918

Jennie clomped on stage,
Ten thousand pounds they say
And you can well believe it,
Lumpy elephant standing
In those four wash buckets
Of feet. They opened
The cabinet, front and back,
And turned it to show us:
Empty right through.
Jennie walked around, then in.
Houdini raised his arms
Like a preacher
And fired his pistol.
When they drew the curtain,
Nothing. Ten thousand pounds
Vanished. Blue ribbon around her neck,
Alarm-clock wrist watch
On her left hind leg,
Gone.

I felt the Lord moving in me
The way He moved in Jennie,
His hand on my shoulder.
I shouted, "Praise God.
He is taking off my flesh.
I am like to fly. Praise the Lord."
My body vanishing, the flesh melting
Upward into the air.

But Houdini stopped it. "Go back
To your body," he said. "It is not yet
Judgment Day. Go back to your body,
Madame." And fired the foolish pistol again.

He couldn't stand a real miracle.
So I went back. Flesh in its sack of skin
Slung from my shoulders. Jennie was gone,
Ten thousand pounds, but he wouldn't let me
Shed my sackful.

                  The room went heavy.
Arms, buttocks, breasts hung
Fat as sausages across the chairs.

––––––––

POET

"If the poet is tone-deaf as to sounds, it is best to rely upon the phonetic symbols above each group of rhyming words in the rhyming dictionary that terminates this book, or upon dictionary markings. Many people can not distinguish the obvious difference in sounds between this pair of words, which do not rhyme:
NORTH, FORTH.
Take away the TH *sound, and many people still hear no difference between this pair of words, which do not rhyme:*
NOR, FORE.
Take away the R *sound, and some people still hear no difference between this pair of words, which do not rhyme:*
GNAW, FOE.
GNAW *plus* R *plus* TH *can not rhyme with* FOE *plus* R *plus* TH."
  —Clement Wood, *The Complete Rhyming Dictionary and Poet's Craft Book*

O, lucky poet tone-deaf
As to something else than sounds!
(Tone-deaf to the turning leaf?
Tone-deaf to autumn wounds?)

He walks in step with what he hears,
Keeps both beat and pitch;
Without a circumflex he fares
Foe plus *r* plus *th*.

This striding, compass-perfect poet
Never strays to *know-earth*.
Impeccably he sounds the note
And sets his foot to *gnaw-earth*.

Colette Inez

NICOLETTE

Nicolette, my little carrot,
I pull you out of the dark ground
of Pennsylvania
where they blasted my thighs
and scraped your seed away.

You are twelve, my counterpart child
breathlessly running into rooms
with acorns and leaves
you want to arrange
for the most senseless beauty.

I have married your father.
We are reconciled to minus signs.

The moist kiss you give me
comes from the forest
of a dark time;

anthracite in the earth,
old signals from the stars
when I walked away from the kill,
blood on my legs, a phrase to caulk
the falling walls in a universe
moving light years away
from our promises.

Nicolette, we will meet
in my poem and when the light
calls your name
you will rise like a fern
to live all summer long,
a green integer
in a pure equation of song.

The University of Pittsburgh Press

The University of Pittsburgh Press Poetry Series was conceived in 1967 when Paul Zimmer, its first editor, was hired as sales and promotion manager of the Press. Planning to publish one younger poet per year, Frederick Hetzel, director of the Press, and Samuel Hazo, director of Pittsburgh's International Poetry Forum which partially funded the competition, announced the United States Award of the International Poetry Forum. Zimmer and Hazo served as screening judges, and James Dickey, Abbie Houston Evans, and William Meredith served as final judges. Because so many of the 1200 submitted manuscripts were good, the Press decided to publish four, expanding to an average of six today.

Although the United States Award was discontinued in 1977, the tradition of the first-book prize continues in the Agnes Lynch Starrett Poetry Prize (named after a retired director of the Press), which consists of a cash award of $2,000 and publication in the series.

In 1978 Paul Zimmer left Pittsburgh to become director of the University of Georgia Press, and Ed Ochester took over as editor of the Pitt series. Ochester reduced the number of first books published annually to one or two, and increased the number of veteran poets to four or five, including one or two who had not previously published with Pittsburgh. Although Pittsburgh uses screening readers from the area, Ochester makes the final decisions himself. Pitt publishes six books per year in editions of 500 hardback and 1500 paperback.

Bill Knott, *Selected Poems 1963–1988,* 1989
Carol Muske, *Applause,* 1989
Irene McKinney, *Six O'clock Mine Report,* 1989
Maxine Scates, *Toluca Street,* 1989
Claribel Alegria, *Woman of the River,* 1988
Kate Daniels, *The Niobe Poems,* 1988
Jane Flanders, *Timepiece,* 1988

Lawrence Joseph, *Curriculum Vitae,* 1988
David Rivard, *Torque,* 1988
Peggy Shumaker, *The Circle of Totems,* 1988
Phyllis Janowitz, *Temporary Dwellings,* 1987
Leslie Ullman, *Dreams by No One's Daughter,* 1987
Peter Meinke, *Night Watch on the Chesapeake,* 1987
Ronald Wallace, *People and Dog in the Sun,* 1987
Robley Wilson, Jr., *Kingdoms of the Ordinary,* 1987
David Wojahn, *Glassworks,* 1987
Maggie Anderson, *Cold Comfort,* 1986
Barbara Helfgott Hyett, *In Evidence: Poems of the Liberation of Nazi
   Concentration Camps,* 1986
Etheridge Knight, *The Essential Etheridge Knight,* 1986
Alicia Ostriker, *The Imaginary Lover,* 1986
William Pitt Root, *Faultdancing,* 1986
Liz Rosenberg, *The Fire Music,* 1986
Chase Twichell, *The Odds,* 1986
Ted Kooser, *One World at a Time,* 1985
Larry Levis, *Winter Stars,* 1985
Carol Muske, *Wyndmere,* 1985
Leonard Nathan, *Carrying On,* 1985
Arthur Smith, *Elegy on Independence Day,* 1985
Gary Soto, *Black Hair,* 1985
Siv Cedering, *Letters from the Floating World,* 1984
Kate Daniels, *The White Wave,* 1984
Gary Gildner, *Blue Like the Heavens,* 1984
Greg Pape, *Black Branches,* 1984
Lawrence Joseph, *Shouting at No One,* 1983
Robert Louthan, *Living in Code,* 1983
James Reiss, *Express,* 1983
Constance Urdang, *Only the World,* 1983
Ronald Wallace, *Tunes For Bears to Dance To,* 1983
Paul Zimmer, *Family Reunion,* 1983
Kathy Callaway, *Heart of the Garfish,* 1982
Bruce Guernsey, *January Thaw,* 1982
Leonard Nathan, *Holding Patterns,* 1982

Richard Shelton, *Selected Poems 1969–81*, 1982
Michael Burkard, *Ruby for Grief*, 1981
Peter Meinke, *Trying to Surprise God*, 1981
Judith Minty, *In the Presence of Mothers*, 1981
Kathleen Norris, *The Middle of the World*, 1981
Gary Soto, *Where Sparrows Work Hard*, 1981
Chase Twichell, *Northern Spy*, 1981
Michael Benedikt, *The Badminton at Great Barrington; Or, Gustave Mahler & The Chattanooga Choo-Choo*, 1980
Ted Kooser, *Sure Signs*, 1980
Leonard Nathan, *Dear Blood*, 1980
Sharon Olds, *Satan Says*, 1980
Constance Urdang, *The Lone Woman and Others*, 1980
Cary Waterman, *The Salamander Migration and Other Poems*, 1980
Stuart Dybek, *Brass Knuckles*, 1979
Gwen Head, *The Ten Thousandth Night*, 1979
David Huddle, *Paper Boy*, 1979
Shirley Kaufman, *From One Life to Another*, 1979
David Young, *The Names of a Hare in English*, 1979
Bruce Weigl, *A Romance*, 1979
Robert Coles, *A Festering Sweetness: Poems of American People*, 1978
Gary Gildner, *The Runner*, 1978
Patricia Hampl, *Woman Before an Aquarium*, 1978
John Hart, *The Climbers*, 1978
Greg Pape, *Border Crossings*, 1978
Richard Shelton, *The Bus to Veracruz*, 1978
Gary Soto, *The Tale of Sunlight*, 1978
Dannie Abse, *Collected Poems*, 1977
Jack Anderson, *Towards the Liberation of the Left Hand*, 1977
John Engles, *Blood Mountain*, 1977
Brendan Galvin, *The Minutes No One Owns*, 1977
Peter Meinke, *The Night Train and the Golden Bird*, 1977
Gary Soto, *The Elements of San Joaquin*, 1977
Alberta T. Turner, *Lid and Spoon*, 1977
Mark Halperin, *Backroads*, 1976
Paul-Marie Lapointe, *First Selected Poems*, 1976

Jim Lindsey, *In Lieu of Mecca,* 1976
Ed Robertson, *Etai-Eken,* 1976
Norman Dubie, *In the Dead of the Night,* 1975
John Engels, *Signals from the Safety Coffin,* 1975
Gwen Head, *Special Effects,* 1975
Gary Gildner, *Nails,* 1975
Archibald MacLeish, *The Great American Fourth of July Parade,* 1975
James Moore, *The New Body,* 1975
Carol Muske, *Camouflage,* 1975
Richard Shelton, *You Can't Have Everything,* 1975
Thomas Rabbit, *Exile,* 1975
Jon Anderson, *In Sepia,* 1974
John Balaban, *After Our War,* 1974
Michael Culross, *The Lost Heroes,* 1974
Odysseus Elytis, *The Axion Esti,* 1974
Brendan Galvin, *No Time for Good Reasons,* 1974
Samuel Hazo, *Quartered,* 1974
Judith Minty, *Lake Songs and Other Fears,* 1974
Herbert Scott, *Disguises,* 1974
Alberta T. Turner, *Learning to Count,* 1974
Michael S. Harper, *Song: I Want a Witness,* 1973
Shirley Kaufman, *Gold Country,* 1973
Belle Randall, *101 Different Ways of Playing Solitaire and Other
    Poems,* 1973
Dennis Scott, *Uncle Time,* 1973
David Steingass, *American Handbook,* 1973
Marc Weber, *48 Small Poems,* 1973
Samuel Hazo, *Once for the Last Bandit,* 1972
Larry Levis, *Wrecking Crew,* 1972
Richard Shelton, *Of All the Dirty Words,* 1972
Thomas Transtromer, *Windows and Stones,* 1972
James Den Boer, *Trying to Come Apart,* 1971
Norman Dubie, *Alehouse Sonnets,* 1971
Gary Gildner, *Digging for Indians,* 1971
Richard Shelton, *The Tattooed Desert,* 1971
Jon Anderson, *Death and Friends,* 1970

Gerald W. Barrax, *Another Kind of Rain,* 1970
Abbie Huston Evans, *Collected Poems,* 1970
Michael S. Harper, *Dear John, Dear Coltrane,* 1970
Ed Robertson, *When thy King is a Boy,* 1970
Jack Anderson, *The Invention of New Jersey,* 1969
Gary Gildner, *First Practice,* 1969
Shirley Kaufman, *The Floor Keeps Turning,* 1969
David Steingass, *Body Compass,* 1969
David P. Young, *Sweating Out the Winter,* 1969
Jon Anderson, *Looking for Jonathan,* 1968
James Den Boer, *Learning the Way,* 1968
John Engels, *Homer Mitchell Place,* 1968
Samuel Hazo, *Blood Rights,* 1968

Jack Anderson

CALAMITOUS DREAMS

He dreamed the old woman he had jeered at in the street took off all his clothes and wrapped him in a squirrel skin. Then he was set among the other squirrels and guinea pigs who were very well mannered and waited on the old woman. First he learned to clean her walnut-shell shoes. Then he learned to catch little moths and grind them into flour, from which he baked a soft white bread. When he awoke, he discovered his nose had grown down to his chin, his hands were covered with warts, and though his belly was round as a barrel, he tottered about on matchstick legs. He was even uglier than the old woman herself. The squirrels and guinea pigs ran chittering after him.

He was dreaming about the cat he let starve. He dreamed his cat left town and lived beside the road. If anyone passed, it devoured him. If a cow went past, the cat devoured it. If a goat went past, the cat devoured it. Whoever went along the road, the cat devoured. When he awoke, he found himself in the cat's belly. He had been devoured by the cat while he slept. Then he was digested. And that was the end of him.

Ever since he could remember, there was a sword growing out of him. When he was a little boy, it was a little sword. As he grew older and bigger, the sword grew bigger, too. Now that he was grown up, it was very big. One night, he had a dream. He dreamed the sword was really a penis. But when he awoke, he discovered it was only a sword, after all.

He dreamed his country had been changed. Earth and water, trees and plants, birds and beasts, all looked the same as before, but what struck terror into his heart was the silence that reigned. Not a rustle could be heard. Birds sat on their branches with heads erect and swelling throats, but his ear caught nothing. Dogs opened their mouths as if to bark, the toiling oxen seemed about to bellow, but neither bark nor bellow reached him. When he came to the city, people were running through the streets, yet he heard no footfall, and other people stood at their windows, their mouths open as though screaming, yet there was no sound. When he awoke, the people were still at their windows and there was no sound for a long time. Then a voice in the street rang out, "This is what became of us while you slept on." And when he tried to answer, he felt his voice die in his throat.

————

THE INVENTION OF NEW JERSEY

Place a custard stand in a garden
or in place of a custard stand
    place a tumbled-down custard stand
in place of a tumbled-down custard stand
    place miniature golf in a garden
    and an advertisement for miniature golf
        shaped for no apparent reason
        like an old Dutch windmill
in place of a swamp
    place a swamp

            or a pizzeria called the Tower of Pizza
                sporting a scale model
                    of the Tower of Pisa
            or a water tower resembling
                a roll-on deodorant
            or a Dixie Cup factory
                with a giant metal Dixie Cup on the roof

In place of wolverines, rabbits, or melons
    place a vulcanizing plant
in place of a deer
    place an iron deer
    at a lawn furniture store
    selling iron deer
        Negro jockeys
        Bavarian gnomes
        and imitation grottoes
        with electric Infants of Prague
in place of phosphorescence
    of marshy ground at night
        place smears of rubbish fires
in place of brown water with minnows
    place brown water

            gigantic landlords
            in the doorways of apartment houses
            which look like auto showrooms
            auto showrooms which look like diners
            diners which look like motels
            motels which look like plastic chair covers
            plastic chair covers which look like
            plastic table covers which look like plastic bags

            the mad scientist of Secaucus
            invents a plastic cover
            to cover the lawn
            with millions of perforations
            for the grass to poke through

In place of the straight lines of grasses
    place the straight lines of gantries
in place of lights in the window
    place lighted refineries
in place of a river
    place the road like a slim pair of pants
        set to dry beside a neon frankfurter

in place of New Jersey
  place a plastic New Jersey

      on weekends a guy has nothing to do
      except drive around in a convertible
      counting the shoe stores
      and thinking of screwing
        his date beside him
        a faintly bilious look
        perpetually on her face

THE PRINTED PAGE

I am not now thinking about the tree struck by lightning.
It is you
Who are thinking about the tree, how
It was struck by lightning.

Siv Cedering

THE JUGGLER

I had practiced for years. Whenever I had a chance, I juggled with
oranges, plates, pine cones, pennies. My uncle encouraged me, though
my mother said: The boy should do something better. He should read.
He should learn to make a living. She said: If your father was alive, he
would show you. But I didn't stop. How could I stop? There was always
some space above my hands calling me. Behind a tree, behind a tent,
behind a truck, on the other side of the field, there was always this space
where I could be God throwing the planets, or the wind commanding the
leaves.

On the night of the first kiss, the air touched my hands in some new way. I juggled soft skin, Lena's lips, not quite open, her lapel, my own chin, the two pimples by my ear. My hands were clumsy. I almost dropped something, but caught it, just in time. I juggled No, Well, Maybe, Yes. The director saw me. The boy is not so bad, he said. Give him some time in the third ring. I juggled lights. I juggled time. I juggled sound.

On the night I first entered a woman, the lights danced out of my hands. I juggled hair and lips and breasts and vulvas. I juggled small wet spaces that could suck me into some sweet oblivion I mastered. I juggled a soft curtain, a blood stain, my own large penis swelling. The music lifted me. I juggled applause and more applause. I juggled a soft voice calling me.

On the night my son was born, there was nothing to throw. My hands were empty, waiting. There was a strange fear inside me. The music was building, the lights were on me, but nothing happened. Until out of all that waiting, something came. I could reach my hand up into that waiting space, and suddenly there was a small shape, settling to the shape of my hand. My hand fell, rose, lifted high, fell again, and all things in the world were attached to my hand, rising, falling, holding, protecting.

On the night the girl died, my hands were some independent objects moving without me. A broken leg, a cut thigh, some blood stained clothing, a sequined ribbon, all tore out of my hands, pulling at the skin, exposing the bone, catapulting with a small scream out of my hands, to fall back to the space of my palms with a moan. The lights were on me, but I didn't juggle them, they juggled me. In the dark space of the tent, I bounced up and down, while the music of my own voice came from some strange distance, a slow heartbeat of sound repeating. No. No. No. No.

Like a Woman in the Kitchen

You talk constantly
like a woman in the kitchen
at home with pots and pans
and stirring.

The words follow a natural motion:
a quick wrist whipping cream into froth,
the knife chopping
scallions.

It is the kind of talk
that knows that someone's listening:
   "Spread your legs.
   I have thought about your cunt
   all day. I like to feel it
   changing."

And like a girl coming home from school
I melt into the talking.
All instructions are as natural as
"dry those glasses, taste some frosting,
lick the spoon."

And as a woman lifts something
that has cooked all day—
a broth rich with roots:
carrots and potatoes,
parsnips, turnips, rutabaga,
you lift my hips, smell, taste,
start to eat.

Marrow
slips out of your bone.
I eat it warm.

Stuart Dybek

LITTLE OSCAR

was the midget in the 50s
who represented the Oscar Mayer Meat Co.
Maybe you remember him singing: *acquire*
the desire to buy Oscar Mayer . . .
He drove the Wiener Mobile—an enormous,
motorized hotdog, with a yellow band around it.
There were TV commercials of Little Oscar
emerging from the Wiener Mobile, surrounded
by cheering kids, and him
throwing the hotdogs. It wasn't just
something they filmed either, he actually
rode around in it. I know because
it was over at the A&P, just a few
blocks from my house, that the Wiener Mobile
ran over one of the kids ganged around it.
The boy was killed, but even as the ambulance
was pulling away, small snickering groups
were splitting from the crowd—a few
already laughing openly. The rest
stood staring at the blood, fists
clenched at their sides, muttering: "They
shouldn't let a fucken midget drive a thing like that,"
glancing sidelong at one another.

MAROON

for Anthony Dadaro, 1946–58

A boy is bouncing a ball off a brick wall after school. The bricks have
been painted maroon a long time ago. Steady as a heartbeat the ball
rebounds oblong, hums, sponges back round. A maroon Chevy goes by.
Nothing else. This street's deserted: a block-long abandoned factory,

glass from the busted windows on the sidewalk mixed with brown glass from beer bottles, whiskey pints. Sometimes the alkies drink here. Not today.

Only the ball flying between sunlit hands and shadowed bricks and sparrows brawling in the dusty gutters. The entire street turning maroon in the shadow of the wall, even the birds, even the hands.

He stands waiting under a streetlight that's trying to flicker on. Three guys he's never seen in the neighborhood before, coming down the street, carrying crowbars.

Gary Gildner
———

Burn-out

In the vacant lot
next to Eddie's Sundries, two young bruisers

forty feet apart, in heat,
burn a baseball back and forth.

Dry, I step inside
for beer.

The cooler's empty; Eddie's widow lifts her eyes
from Maeterlinck's *Life of the Bee*—

she knuckles the sweat on her lip
and calls the Hamm's man a son of a bitch.

I nod,
she lights a Kool

and sighing returns to her page.
I leave.

Outside, the boys have moved in
a dozen feet. The game is serious,

speechless, the ball lands with an oily *smack!*
It takes me back. I remember

how red my palm got
when I caught the ball too much

in the pocket
instead of the webbing—

and once so hard in the lower gut
I urinated pink for a week.

Suddenly one boy yells "You mother!"
and makes a wild heave over the other's

head. The ball hits and cracks
the plastic PEPSI sign sticking out of Eddie's.

They scram.
Eddie's widow's face

appears behind the screen
like an engraving. I can't tell how

she feels. Then
the Hamm's man

pulls his truck up, jumps down grinning.
Eddie's widow steps outside, she's wearing

yellow bedroom slippers sporting
dandelions. Shading

her tiny eyes
with the bee book, she blinks at the street,

then at the sky.
Several seasons go by.

The Hamm's man, loading his dolly,
throws her a wolfish whistle.

But she is still blinking—trying to make sure,
I think, the sky isn't kidding,

and that her eyes are in OK,
and that the voice saying

"Save it, lard ass"
really belongs to her,

and she to us, whoever we are,
before it's time to go in.

————

FIRST PRACTICE

After the doctor checked to see
we weren't ruptured,
the man with the short cigar took us
under the grade school,
where we went in case of attack
or storm, and said
he was Clifford Hill, he was
a man who believed dogs
ate dogs, he had once killed
for his country, and if
there were any girls present
for them to leave now.
                  No one
left. OK, he said, he said I take
that to mean you are hungry
men who hate to lose as much
as I do. OK. Then
he made two lines of us
facing each other,

and across the way, he said,
is the man you hate most
in the world,
and if we are to win
that title I want to see how.
But I don't want to see
any marks when you're dressed,
he said. He said, *Now.*

Patricia Hampl
———

Fire Engine

The women are singing.
At night the fireman lies awake sweating
with desire and terror.
The engines rise from the fog.
This is burning, this is drowning.
He makes a fist, promises something
to the white sheet.
The women are coming, riding
red horses, they swim in the air,
their drowning is for men,
their salt water comes in sharp flames.
He is no sword-swallower,
he drowns every night.
As they sing, the women's skirts flare with blood.
He is afraid of sirens, he says.
Women! he says, stuffing his ears with cotton.
See, it's a joke, he says.
He laughs,
but like a belly whose man has disappeared.

Michael S. Harper

We Assume: On the Death of our Son, Reuben Masai Harper

We assume
that in 28 hours,
lived in a collapsible isolette,
you learned to accept pure oxygen
as the natural sky;
the scant shallow breaths
that filled those hours
cannot, did not make you fly—
but dreams were there
like crooked palmprints on
the twin-thick windows of the nursery—
in the glands of your mother.

We assume
the sterile hands
drank chemicals in and out
from lungs opaque with mucus,
pumped your stomach,
eeked the bicarbonate in
crooked, green-winged veins,
out in a plastic mask;

A woman who'd lost her first son
consoled us with an angel gone ahead
to pray for our family—
gone into that sky
seeking oxygen,
gone into autopsy,
a fine brown powdered sugar,
a disposable cremation:

We assume
you did not know we loved you.

Etheridge Knight

DARK PROPHECY: I SING OF SHINE

And, yeah, brothers
while white / america sings about the unsink-
able molly brown
(who was hustling the titanic
when it went down)
I sing to thee of Shine
the stoker who was hip enough to flee the fucking ship
and let the white folks drown
with screams on their lips
(jumped his black ass into the dark sea, Shine did,
broke free from the straining steel).
Yeah, I sing to thee of Shine
and how the millionaire banker stood on the deck
and pulled from his pockets a million dollar check
saying Shine Shine save poor me
and I'll give you all the money a black boy needs—
how Shine looked at the money and then at the sea
and said jump in mothafucka and swim like me—
And Shine swam on—Shine swam on—
and how the banker's daughter ran naked on the deck
with her pink tits trembling and her pants roun her neck
screaming Shine Shine save poor me
and I'll give you all the pussy a black boy needs—
how shine said now pussy is good and that's no jive
but you got to swim not fuck to stay alive—
And Shine swam on Shine swam on—

How Shine swam past a preacher afloating on a board
crying save *me* nigger Shine in the name of the Lord—
and how the preacher grabbed Shine's arm and broke his stroke—
how Shine pulled his shank and cut the preacher's throat—
And Shine swam on—Shine swam on—
And when the news hit shore that the titanic had sunk
Shine was up in Harlem damn near drunk

Ted Kooser

At the Bait Stand

Part barn, part boxcar, part of a chicken shed,
part leaking water, something partly dead,
part pop machine, part gas pump, part a chair
leaned back against the wall, and sleeping there,
part-owner Herman Runner, mostly fat,
hip-waders, undershirt, tattoos and hat.

In an Old Apple Orchard

The wind's an old man
to this orchard; these trees
have been feeling
the soft tug of his gloves
for a hundred years.
Now it's April again,
and again that old fool
thinks he's young.
He's combed the dead leaves
out of his beard; he's put on
perfume. He's gone off
late in the day
toward the town, and come back
slow in the morning,
reeling with bees.
As late as noon, if you look
in the long grass,
you can see him
still rolling about in his sleep.

So This Is Nebraska

The gravel road rides with a slow gallop
over the fields, the telephone lines
streaming behind, its billow of dust
full of the sparks of redwing blackbirds.

On either side, those dear old ladies,
the loosening barns, their little windows
dulled by cataracts of hay and cobwebs
hide broken tractors under their skirts.

So this is Nebraska. A Sunday
afternoon; July. Driving along
with your hand out squeezing the air,
a meadowlark waiting on every post.

Behind a shelterbelt of cedars,
top-deep in hollyhocks, pollen and bees,
a pickup kicks its fenders off
and settles back to read the clouds.

You feel like that; you feel like letting
your tires go flat, like letting the mice
build a nest in your muffler, like being
no more than a truck in the weeds,

clucking with chickens or sticky with honey
or holding a skinny old man in your lap
while he watches the road, waiting
for someone to wave to. You feel like

waving. You feel like stopping the car
and dancing around on the road. You wave
instead and leave your hand out gliding
larklike over the wheat, over the houses.

Larry Levis

WINTER STARS

My father once broke a man's hand
Over the exhaust pipe of a John Deere tractor. The man,
Rubén Vásquez, wanted to kill his own father
With a sharpened fruit knife, & he held
The curved tip of it, lightly, between his first
Two fingers, so it could slash
Horizontally, & with surprising grace,
Across a throat. It was like a glinting beak in a hand,
And, for a moment, the light held still
On those vines. When it was over,
My father simply went in & ate lunch, & then, as always,
Lay alone in the dark, listening to music.
He never mentioned it.

I never understood how anyone could risk his life,
Then listen to Vivaldi.

Sometimes, I go out into this yard at night,
And stare through the wet branches of an oak
In winter, & realize I am looking at the stars
Again. A thin haze of them, shining
And persisting.

It used to make me feel lighter, looking up at them.
In California, that light was closer.
In a California no one will ever see again,
My father is beginning to die. Something
Inside him is slowly taking back
Every word it ever gave him.
Now, if we try to talk, I watch my father
Search for a lost syllable as if it might
Solve everything, & though he can't remember, now,
The word for it, he is ashamed. . . .
If you can think of the mind as a place continually

Visited, a whole city placed behind
The eyes, & shining, I can imagine, now, its end—
As when the lights go off, one by one,
In a hotel at night, until at last
All of the travelers will be asleep, or until
Even the thin glow from the lobby is a kind
Of sleep; & while the woman behind the desk
Is applying more lacquer to her nails,
You can almost believe that the elevator,
As it ascends, must open upon starlight.

I stand out on the street, & do not go in.
That was our agreement, at my birth.

And for years I believed
That what went unsaid between us became empty,
And pure, like starlight, & that it persisted.

I got it all wrong.
I wound up believing in words the way a scientist
Believes in carbon, after death.

Tonight, I'm talking to you, father, although
It is quiet here in the Midwest, where a small wind,
The size of a wrist, wakes the cold again—
Which may be all that's left of you & me.

When I left home at seventeen, I left for good.

That pale haze of stars goes on & on,
Like laughter that has found a final, silent shape
On a black sky. It means everything
It cannot say. Look, it's empty out there, & cold.
Cold enough to reconcile
Even a father, even a son.

Peter Meinke

MISS ARBUCKLE

Miss Arbuckle taught seventh grade.
She hid her lips against her teeth:
her bottom like the ace of spades
was guarded by the virgin queen.

Miss Arbuckle wore thick-soled shoes,
blue dresses with white polka dots.
She followed and enforced the rules:
what she was paid to teach, she taught.

She said that Wordsworth liked the woods,
that Blake had never seen a tiger,
that Byron was not always good
but died in Greece, a freedom-fighter.

She gave her students rigid tests
and when the school let out in June,
she painted rings around her breasts
and danced by the light of the moon.

THE POET, TRYING TO SURPRISE GOD

The poet, trying to surprise his God
composed new forms from secret harmonies,
tore from his fiery vision galaxies
of unrelated shapes, both even & odd.
But God just smiled, and gave His know-all nod
saying, "There's no surprising One who sees
the acorn, root, and branch of centuries;
I swallow all things up, like Aaron's rod.

So hold this thought beneath your poet-bonnet:
no matter how free-seeming flows your sample
God is by definition the Unsurprised."
"Then I'll return," the poet sighed, "to sonnets
of which this is a rather pale example."

"Is that right?" said God. "I hadn't realized. . . ."

————

RECIPE

Let us say you want to write a poem
yes?
a good poem, maybe not The Second Coming but
your hair is getting thin already and
where's your Dover Beach?

Everything seems somehow out of reach
no?
all of a sudden everyone's walking faster than you and
you catch yourself sometimes staring not at girls

You live in at least two worlds
yes?
one fuzzy one where you always push
the doors that say pull and
one clear cold one where you live alone

This is the one where your poem is
yes?
no.
It's in the other one
tear your anthologies into small pieces
use them as mulch for your begonias and
begin with your hands

Carol Muske

CHINA WHITE

—M. S. H.

Lately your eyes watch me
out of animal eyes,
out of the sad clerk's eyes
at the makeup counter.
She didn't have the right shade
of shadow, but I charged to my account
the kind of green I chide myself with.

I kept thinking—
Why did you take so long to cry?
You were just fifteen
when it happened.
Still, you insisted on indifference,
like the Stoics, you said.

Next day, in class, leaves fell
from your Latin book.
He had gloves on, you said later,
when I held you, in that strange room
where you finally wept.
There were leaves beneath,
I couldn't breathe.

As usual, I got you laughing—
we made up our eyes,
you disembodied your gaze
with China White, and gray.
You didn't cry again.
That night you sang the Magnificat
for Glee. It wasn't in your voice
to rephrase the Virgin's words
but there's a part where she accepts it,
accepts the miracle they want her body for

and your eyes came looking for mine
as you sang, moving slowly at first,
then faster: face to face to face.

———————

SURPRISE

The mind dislikes surprise.
Witness the nurse of good syntax,
how she pushes her drugged charges
across the courtyard below
to the Center for Impaired Speech.

Witness the doorman hesitating
before ringing your bell to tell you
someone's on the way up.

It's why you're getting up slowly
this morning, why you don't look too closely
at the mirror, nor the coffee table
offering its testimony: the matches

crippled in their books, crushed by
the insistent pressure of thumb and forefinger,
the empty fifth, the Zig Zag litter,
the pages of unclothed women, legs apart,

smiling out as if there were no danger
in this world, even from those you love.
And from those who love you in ways you have
not yet imagined—and which might surprise you,

like a style of perverse instruction
say, teaching the blind pornography,
their trained fingers hesitating above
the machined welts of braille.

It is possible to teach someone that love
is pain—by taking a fistful of hair, pulling
it up from the skull and back, till the neck
locks in place, as if breaking, till the lover

stops thinking about politics, or the five days
of fine weather—and begins to cooperate
with this gesture, applied one night
in passion, the next in pure rage.

Still, the mind is stubborn, resists
the unexpected—shuttling back and forth,
as it was taught, between similar forms—refusing
in the only way it knows how, to make sense.

So you sit this morning, while the mail comes,
and the *Times*, the phone rings and you can touch
your hair, your face, rethinking it all—

        but recall your horror once
opening the front door, on your birthday, on seeing the faces
of your friends disfigured by the weight of occasion.
You thought the ones who liked you least screamed loudest:
Surprise!

Sharon Olds

——————

THE LANGUAGE OF THE BRAG

I have wanted excellence in the knife-throw,
I have wanted to use my exceptionally strong and accurate arms
and my straight posture and quick electric muscles
to achieve something at the center of a crowd,
the blade piercing the bark deep,
the haft slowly and heavily vibrating like the cock.

I have wanted some epic use for my excellent body,
some heroism, some American achievement
beyond the ordinary for my extraordinary self,
magnetic and tensile, I have stood by the sandlot
and watched the boys play.

I have wanted courage, I have thought about fire
and the crossing of waterfalls, I have dragged around

my belly big with cowardice and safety,
my stool black with iron pills,
my huge breasts oozing mucus,
my legs swelling, my hands swelling,
my face swelling and darkening, my hair
falling out, my inner sex
stabbed again and again with terrible pain like a knife.
I have lain down.

I have lain down and sweated and shaken
and passed blood and feces and water and
slowly alone in the center of a circle I have
passed the new person out
and they have lifted the new person free of the act
and wiped the new person free of that
language of blood like praise all over the body.

I have done what you wanted to do, Walt Whitman,
Allen Ginsberg, I have done this thing,
I and the other women this exceptional
act with the exceptional heroic body,
this giving birth, this glistening verb,
and I am putting my proud American boast
right here with the others.

Satan Says

I am locked in a little cedar box
with a picture of shepherds pasted onto
the central panel between carvings.
The box stands on curved legs.
It has a gold, heart-shaped lock
and no key. I am trying to write my
way out of the closed box
redolent of cedar. Satan
comes to me in the locked box
and says, *I'll get you out. Say*
My father is a shit. I say
my father is a shit and Satan
laughs and says, *It's opening.*
Say your mother is a pimp.
My mother is a pimp. Something
opens and breaks when I say that.
My spine uncurls in the cedar box
like the pink back of the ballerina pin
with a ruby eye, resting beside me on
satin in the cedar box.
Say shit, say death, say fuck the father,
Satan says, down my ear.
The pain of the locked past buzzes
in the child's box on her bureau, under
the terrible round pond eye
etched around with roses, where
self-loathing gazed at sorrow.
Shit. Death. Fuck the father.
Something opens. Satan says
Don't you feel a lot better?
Light seems to break on the delicate
edelweiss pin, carved in two
colors of wood. I love him too,

you know, I say to Satan dark
in the locked box. I love them but
I'm trying to say what happened to us
in the lost past. *Of course,* he says
and smiles, *of course. Now say: torture.*
I see, through blackness soaked in cedar,
the edge of a large hinge open.
*Say: the father's cock, the mother's
cunt,* says Satan, *I'll get you out.*
The angle of the hinge widens
until I see the outlines of
the time before I was, when they were
locked in the bed. When I say
the magic words, Cock, Cunt,
Satan softly says, *Come out.*
But the air around the opening
is heavy and thick as hot smoke.
Come in, he says, and I feel his voice
breathing from the opening.
The exit is through Satan's mouth.
Come in my mouth, he says, *you're there
already,* and the huge hinge
begins to close. Oh no, I loved
them, too, I brace
my body tight
in the cedar house.
Satan sucks himself out the keyhole.
I'm left locked in the box, he seals
the heart-shaped lock with the wax of his tongue.
It's your coffin now, Satan says.
I hardly hear;
I am warming my cold
hands at the dancer's
ruby eye—
the fire, the suddenly discovered knowledge of love.

TRICKS

My mother
the magician
can make eggs
appear in her hand.
My ovaries
appear in her hand, black as figs
and wrinkled as fingers on washday.

She closes her hand,
and when she opens it
nothing.

She pulls silk scarves out of her ears
in all colors, jewels from her mouth,
milk from her nipples. My mother the naked
magician stands on the white stage
and pulls her tricks.

She takes out her eyes.
The holes of her sockets
fill with oil, it seeps up,
with bourbon and feces.
Out of her nostrils
she pulls scrolls
and they take fire.

In the grand finale
she draws my father
slowly out of her cunt and puts him
in a tall silk hat
and he disappears.

I say she can turn anything
into nothing, she's a hole in space,

she's the tops, the best
magician. All this

I have pulled out of my mouth right
before your eyes.

James Reiss
————

BY THE STEPS OF THE METROPOLITAN MUSEUM OF ART

for Thomas Lux

Choking with silent laughter, the chalk-faced mime
jousts with the crowd, grabs a smiling sailor,
and sets him on his knees before a schoolgirl posed with a rose in her teeth.
The crowd explodes, and the air
is charged with the jingle of loose change.

A driver waiting for the light to change
pulls to the curb and tosses the mime
a silver coin that glitters in midair
before dropping at the feet of the sailor,
making him smile more widely and show his teeth
like a politician visiting a high school.

I drift and think of a dancing school
I drove my daughters to. I watched them change
into shy swans, gifted to the teeth
with graceful napes and wrists—just as the mime
is graceful in his placement of the sailor
whose smile unwinds in the afternoon air

when all at once an air-
raid siren I haven't heard since public school
starts shrieking from some roof. The sailor
takes off with the pigeons, unsmiling for a change.
The schoolgirl puts fingers in her ears. The mime
pretends he's screaming, gritting his teeth.

It is like fingernails down chalkboards setting teeth
on edge, this siren slicing the air.
People scatter. Even the mime
slinks uptown, and the school-
girl disappears without her rose—as if she could change
my image of her with the sailor

at her feet, that skittery peacoated sailor,
both blushing red as the rose in her teeth,
posed statuelike without change. . . .
I leave the museum to escape the air-
raid siren. Up the street school
buses idle, double-parked, and I notice the mime,

the chalk-faced mime, outside my daughter's school
in the three-o'clock air. He lists like a sailor,
whistles through his teeth, and begs for change.

William Pitt Root
———

As If

We speak of dying as if we will live forever
to speak of it at all
in this bare forest of lies
words are, each illusion
a luminous fear
only language can secure.

Of all noise-making creatures
only we
believe this wilderness
we dare not leave and cannot harvest,
although we thresh and refine
syllables and ciphers
as if they were grain. As if.

INFERENCE FROM THE EYES OF A HAWK

Before the tender glaring of these eyes
the world brightens. Must brighten.
Glows with the light of being seen.
Glows with the sheen of an immanence
        delicate as golden powder.
Air among his feathers whispers.
Blood within his veins.
For whomsoever he chooses, the air bursts red.

Liz Rosenberg

THE CHRISTMAS CACTUS

All during the Christmas rush
I waited for the thing to come alive.
Eyed it while I gift wrapped scarves,
withered it with scorn as I threw
the green and silver bundles under the tree.
By New Year's
I vowed to be happy
living with just stems.

Then one day in February—
the worst month of the year,

making up in misery what it lacks in length—
the blooms shot out,
three ragged cerise bells that rang
their tardy Hallelujahs on the sill.
Late bloomers,
like the girls that shine
and shine at long last
at the spring dance
from their corner of the gym.

———

MARRIED LOVE

The trees are uncurling their first
green messages: Spring, and some man
lets his arm brush my arm in a darkened
theater. Faint-headed, I fight the throb.
Later I dream
the gas attendant puts a cool hand
on my breast, asking a question.
Slowly I rise through the surface of the dream,
brushing his hand and my own heat away.

Young, I burned to marry. Married,
the smoulder goes on underground,
clutching at weeds, writhing everywhere.
I'm trying to talk to a friend on burning
issues, flaming from the feet up,
drinking in his breath, touching his wrist.
I want to grab the pretty woman
on the street, seize the falcon
by its neck, beat my way into whistling steam.

I turn to you in the dark, oh husband,
watching your lit breath circle the pillow.

Then you turn to me, throwing first one limb
and then another over me, in the easy brotherly
lust of marriage. I cling to you
as if I were a burning ship and you
could save me, as if I won't go sliding down
beneath you soon; as if our lives are made of rise
and fall, and we could ride this out forever,
with longing's thunder rolling heavy in our arms.

Richard Shelton
————

A KIND OF GLORY

years after the neighbors
started using machines
Grandpa still did the milking
with his small-boned
delicate hands
but his cows gave better milk
than any herd in the valley

at night he danced the schottische
with Grandma and always
put his little foot right there
more gracefully than she could manage

he smelled of cow manure
and Prince Albert pipe tobacco
women found him irresistible

we knew we would never be famous
or anything out of the ordinary
but for awhile after Grandpa
dropped his flashlight
into the outhouse hole we had
a kind of glory

it continued to shine
straight up from down there
and our most private moments
were illuminated

———

LETTER TO A DEAD FATHER

Five years since you died and I am
better than I was when you were living.
The years have not been wasted.
I have heard the harsh voices
of desert birds who cannot sing.
Sometimes I touched the membrane
between violence and desire
and watched it vibrate.
I learned that a man
who travels in circles
never arrives at exactly the same place.

If you could see me now
side-stepping triumph and disaster,
still waiting for you to say *my son*
my beloved son. If you could only see
me now, you would know I am stronger.

Death was the poorest subterfuge
you ever managed, but it was permanent.
Do you see now that fathers
who cannot love their sons
have sons who cannot love?
It was not your fault
and it was not mine. I needed
your love but I recovered without it.
Now I no longer need anything.

THE NEW ROAD

Tonight at the end of a long
scar in the desert a bulldozer
sleeps with its mouth open
like a great yellow beast.

A coyote sits down to watch it
from a safe distance. An owl
questions again and again.
No answer. Someone is building

a new road, a fine road, wide
and smooth. The huge saguaros
in its path have stood here
two hundred years looking up

at the sky. This will be their
last chance to see the moon.
In the morning the yellow beast
will wake up and move toward them.

We believe in movement. We live
in the sanctity of mobile homes.
We are children of those
who created the portable Indian

and moved him from place to place.
Ours is a republic of cylinders
and pistons, a republic of wheels.
Progress moves before us over

the hill and we pursue it as fast
as we can. With our horses
in trailers, our politicians
in limousines, and all our angels

on motorcycles, we pursue it.
The world rolls on and these gods
of the desert cannot get out
of its way. They are no use to us.

I have stroked them until my hands
are bloody, but what comfort
can I offer? They are doomed
and I am tired of being human,

tired of being mad in a mad world.
Now I lay me down in the new road
but to whom can I pray? The owl
has stopped calling. The coyote

gets up and fades away. I will
look at the moon as long as I can.
Then I will sleep in the desert,
helpless in the path of progress,
waiting for the sound of wheels.

David Steingass

MIDWEST U.F.O.

She tosses, one midnight so close
The melons perspire on their loam,
And pitches stark awake in silence,
For no reason. The clock's luminous
Fingers point to a sprattled *Reader's
Digest* on the bed table, the county
Paper, her son's last letter
From the seminary in Wichita.

She touches it, her hands so white
From milkhouse disinfectant, they look
Sandblasted. She feels there is little
Time, and throws on the print, feed bag
Robe that was so pretty new,
Hurries past the lumped husband
To an apple grove behind the house,
Where she has come before.

It is not lonely, she thinks, breaking off
A twig, but only that the pastor
Comes each third Thursday for dinner.
An Ozark flight ponders overhead
Toward Pueblo. She knows the schedules.
There is not a light to see at night
And not another house by day.
She has memorized the Grange calendar.
Never on an airplane, she faces
With a shudder, never left the state.
The twig snaps in her hand, the leaves
Twist and crush. It takes a plane
Four hours all the way across.
On tiptoe, breathing all she can hold,
Stretching three thousand miles,
Good gray strands of hair over her nose,
She pulls her hands down her face.
The twigs catch in her hair.

A light like Christmas bulbs
Flickers inches from her nose.
The wind rises, blowing her hair
Right, catching her robe, writhing.
She runs at last, as she has not run
Ever, and the light twinkles
In conversation, friendly, warm.

It is saying something she can hear
Almost, beyond the farm and darkness,
Beyond anything, beyond New York,

And only to herself. Perhaps to land
Another night and speak, to look
At her as human,
To hear her explanation first:
They know where things are friendly.

Constance Urdang

MINIMALISTS

In the old days they ate buffalo; now they eat radishes.

These days take the wish for the deed, as certain painters,
Disdaining brush and palette, dictate a landscape
In one or two shorthand sentences, or describe
A masterpiece, ideal because unrealized on canvas,
In lieu of what was called art. The mundane part,
The skill, the doing, the craft, is scorned
In times like ours, so why not eliminate
What really happened, and replace it with
What one might have preferred, the daring deeds
Undone, races unwon, adventures not attempted?
Not a new trick; Vespucci, even,
They say, left two sets of letters, "both purporting
To describe his expeditions, but full
Of inexplicable contradictions," until
There is no way of knowing which is history,
Or if he ever touched the fabulous shores
Named for him, the Americas; and Frederick Cook
Laid claim to the North Pole, but none was there
To see him—and what charms us, is the doubt.
There's a perverseness in our times, that relishes
These tantalizing ambivalences, delighting
In the question more than the answer, the telling
More than the truth. It maddened Crowhurst,

Who knew himself unfit to be a hero
But schemed to seem one, calculating how
To show by logbooks he had sailed nonstop
Around the world, to win the glorious race;
Instead, the perfect hero for our time,
Minimalist of adventure, he left only
An empty craft with but one mizzen sail
Ghosting along in the Sargasso Sea.

———

The World Is Full of Poets

On days like this I see that the world is full of poets,
Some are lying under a tree, others on a piazza,
Some are riding the subways or streetcars, some
Far away from home, perhaps,
Look for a letter in an empty box.
They are everywhere! No boundaries contain them!
When the laurel wreaths are distributed
They will stand in a jostling procession,
Elbowing one another.
When the medals and lovingcups are given out
The line of poets will stretch from here to Brooklyn!
On days like this all the poets of the world
Might soar to the skies, arm in arm with one another
Like glorious brothers and sisters, to astonish
The world, with a single enormous hosanna.

Ronald Wallace

THE FACTS OF LIFE

She wonders how people get babies.
Suddenly vague and distracted,
we talk about "making love."
She's six and unsatisfied, finds
our limp answers unpersuasive.
Embarrassed, we stiffen, and try again,
this time exposing the stark naked words:
penis, vagina, sperm, womb, and egg.
She thinks we're pulling her leg.
We decide that it's time
to get passionate and insist.
But she's angry, disgusted.
Why do we always make fun of her?
Why do we lie?
We sigh, try cabbages, storks.
She smiles. That's more like it.
We talk on into the night, trying
magic seeds, good fairies, God. . . .

GROUND ZERO

"I felt a great shriek in nature"
　　　　—Edvard Munch

He knew how everything, at extremes, is the same:
how heat freezes, joy pains;
how the most unbearable sound is silence;
how a scream turns even the firm world liquid,
a sea beyond human keening;

how the bell of the skull starts vibrating out
into the great heart of the sky;
how the dull hands are clapped
like dogs' ears to the head;
how we'd pull that head off, if only
the lake weren't its mouth,
the sky its skinned eyelids,
the night oozing in oily and woozy.

Why was it given him to hear this?
This scream of the possum-faced preener,
the simian seductress,
the sweetheart that turns all men green;
this scream of the papery matron
draped in a greatcoat of syphilis,
her raw hands mittened in flesh,
basting her naked child;
this scream of the white house drowning
in bloodfire, the gray face rolling off
of the terrified canvas,
the long tongue of the road
breaking up in intemperate paint;
this scream of lopped limbs and two-headed men
in all their ludicrous, formal dress,
as if no one must ever lose face,
as if no one were incomplete;
this scream of the murderer's
thick hands and wrists, as he twists
slightly sideways, and toward us.

Ground zero. Hairless and legless. The scream
of this whole goddamned universe squirms into us.
While somewhere above us,
safe on their bridge into space,
two blue friends walk off the deaf canvas,
as if at a certain distance,
as if in an obdurate silence,
as if toward some not unimaginable bright town.

David Young

Tool Talk

Put tip of pot through loop. Pull tight.
Call this position B. File flash and sand.
Use adze to strike off wobbly-pump
of Handley-Page or Spad. Dry roller stocks,
make notch in carrick bits with extra pick
and fit in spindle bush. Dash for the churn,
dash for the peak. Lakes equal paddles, bridles
are for camels, skies, a harness punch will fix
my son's new watch or fill that ladle in the stable.
Fit pitching chisel into granite crotch: release.
If cannon diagram does not apply, destroy.
Let sun god slide through threading lathe. Tie
lightning rod with thong. Work cork in slots of loom.
Rewind. Let sonnet slide from side to side.

Paul Zimmer

The Ancient Wars

Dear Imbellis:

When I think of the old days
I start to bleed again,
Recalling my terrified exits;
The alleys and swamps I hid in;
Your fists exploding in my face
And the light fog of concussions.
I wonder, old bull, old turk,
Old hammer, if we passed
Each other on the street,
Would your anger spill out
Again over your eye rims?

Would your ears redden
Like a rooster's wattle,
Would you knock my bridge
Back down my throat and beat
My glasses back into my dim eyes?
I like to think that
By now you have relented,
That some woman or work
Has doused your fires,
That if we met again we would
Slap each other on the back
And laugh about the ancient wars.
Imbellis, old bravo, super pug,
Could we be friends now?
Would you let me forgive you?

                    Peace,
                    Zimmer

Dear Zimmer,

Remember how you loved the Friday Night Fights?
That was always you and me in the ring,
Circling, jabbing, throwing classy combinations
Until the abrupt explosion, my fists crashing
Down like boulders, your body suddenly limp;
You collapsing as a hammered cow into
Your own spit and blood as the crowd
Came to its feet growling and hooting;
You on the canvas flapping and quaking,
You crawling up the ropes to your feet
And me sledging you down again
And you screaming at the television,
"Stop it! Stop it!" Remember?

Zimmer, start sweating again.
I am waiting for you still,

Maybe around the next corner.
One day you'll come
Blundering into my sights again;
When you do I'll clean your clock
But good, shred your cheeks,
Roll your bloody teeth,
Crunch your jewels and punch
Your dim lights out forever.

Yours,
Imbellis

———

ONE FOR THE LADIES AT THE TROY LAUNDRY WHO COOLED THEMSELVES FOR ZIMMER

The ladies at the Troy Laundry pressed
And pressed in the warm fog of their labor.
They cooled themselves at the windows,
The steam rising from their gibbous skins
As I dawdled home from school.
In warmer weather they wore no blouses
And if I fought the crumbling coke pile
To the top, they laughed and waved
At me, billowy from their irons.

Oh man, the ladies at the Troy Laundry
Smelled like cod fish out of water
And yet the very fur within their armpits
Made me rise wondering and small.

What Zimmer Would Be

When asked, I used to say,
"I want to be a doctor."
Which is the same thing
As a child saying,
"I want to be a priest,"
Or
"I want to be a magician,"
Which is the laying
Of hands, the vibrations,
The rabbit in the hat,
Or the body in the cup,
The curing of the sick
And the raising of the dead.

"Fix and fix, you're all better,"
I would say
To the neighborhood wounded
As we fought the world war
Through the vacant lots of Ohio.
"Fix and fix, you're all better,"
And they would rise
To fight again.

      But then
I saw my aunt die slowly of cancer
And a man struck down by a car.

All along I had really
Wanted to be a poet,
Which is, you see, almost
The same thing as saying,
"I want to be a doctor,"
"I want to be a priest,"

Or
"I want to be a magician."
All along, without realizing it,
I had wanted to be a poet.

Fix and fix, you're all better.

Princeton University Press

Although Princeton University Press considered publishing poetry as long ago as the late 1950s because of a perception that commercial presses were unwilling to take a chance on new poets, the Princeton Series of Contemporary Poets was not instituted until 1975. The inaugural program was under the advisorship of Theodore Weiss, editor of the *Quarterly Review of Literature* and a professor at Princeton. In 1978 Weiss was succeeded as advisor by David Wagoner, and the Press adopted a plan of appointing series advisors on a three-year renewable-term basis. Since 1981 there have been three anonymous advisors who have made final selections in consultation with a Press editor who screens all manuscripts submitted in an open competition. Although Princeton considers all submitted manuscripts, the series is "devoted to publishing first works of promising poets or providing a hearing for fine poets whose work may not otherwise find the audience it deserves." Princeton publishes an average of three books of poetry per year.

James Applewhite, *River Writing: An Eno Journal*, 1988
John Burt, *The Way Down*, 1988
Rachel Hadas, *Pass It On*, 1988
Emily Grosholz, *Shores and Headlands*, 1988
David Mus, *Wall to Wall Speaks*, 1988
Harry Mathews, *The Armenian Papers*, 1987
Jay Wright, *Selected Poems*, 1987
Debora Greger, *And*, 1986
A. F. Moritz, *The Tradition*, 1986
Ann Lauterbach, *Before Recollection*, 1986
David Lehman, *An Alternative to Speech*, 1986
Christopher Jane Corkery, *Blessing*, 1985
Frederick Turner, *The New World*, 1985
John Koethe, *The Late Wisconsin Spring*, 1984

Judith Moffett, *Whinny Moor Crossing,* 1984
Michael Rosen, *A Drink at the Mirage,* 1984
Jorie Graham, *Erosion,* 1983
Vicki Hearne, *In the Absence of Horses,* 1983
Gary Miranda, *Grace Period,* 1983
Phyllis Janowitz, *Visiting Rites,* 1982
Alicia Ostriker, *A Woman Under the Surface,* 1982
Jordan Smith, *An Apology for Loving the Old Hymns,* 1982
Pattiann Rogers, *The Expectations of Light,* 1981
Susan Stewart, *Yellow Stars and Ice,* 1981
Jorie Graham, *Hybrids of Plants and of Ghosts,* 1980
Debora Greger, *Movable Islands,* 1980
John Allman, *Walking Four Ways in the Wind,* 1979
Carl Dennis, *Signs and Wonders,* 1979
Diana O'Hehir, *The Power to Change Geography,* 1979
Robert Pinsky, *An Explanation of America,* 1979
Gary Miranda, *Listeners at the Breathing Place,* 1978
Ben Belitt, *The Double Witness,* 1977
Richard Pevear, *Night Talk and Other Poems,* 1977
James Richardson, *Reservations,* 1977
Grace Schulman, *Burn Down the Icons,* 1976
Leonard Nathan, *Returning Your Call,* 1975
Robert Pinsky, *Sadness and Happiness,* 1975

Carl Dennis

GRANDMOTHER AND I

Grandmother sits on the couch in our tiny apartment
Over the drugstore, leafing through the news.
She's larger than my parents and knows all things.
It's turning out just as she expected.
The same hoodlums are climbing on the trains
And buying up all the seats.
"You don't have to read the paper to learn this,"
She mutters to herself, and nods.

When I come to the couch and ask for a story
She bends down and whispers, slightly deaf,
"Obey your father." Her voice is warm.
Such phrases in her Russian accent often mean, "Young man,
How are you today, whoever you are?
Where are you going in your cowboy suit?"

We don't expect her to remember all our names.
By middle age she'd outlived five presidents
And the sons of two czars.
Napoleon himself, it's rumored, as he neared the border,
Stopped at Grandmother's for advice.
"You'll be sorry, Napoleon," she said;
"Go home and stay warm."
It's hard to convince an emperor.

Many have grown small with the years,
But every year Grandmother grows larger,
Like a tree by clear water.
The whole family sleeps without fear
In the widening circle of her shade.

At night in my bed,
Groping my way in dream through cloudy streets,
I hear from her branches far above
Birds that sing of the workshop of my father,
Boris the long-lost tailor, still alive,
Waiting in the story I've always loved.

Jorie Graham

I WATCHED A SNAKE

hard at work in the dry grass
        behind the house
catching flies. It kept on
        disappearing.
And though I know this has
        something to do

with lust, today it seemed
        to have to do
with work. It took it almost half
        an hour to thread
roughly ten feet of lawn,
        so slow

between the blades you couldn't see
        it move. I'd watch
its path of body in the grass go
        suddenly invisible
only to reappear a little
        further on

black knothead up, eyes on
        a butterfly.

This must be perfect progress where
       movement appears
to be a vanishing, a mending
       of the visible

by the invisible—just as we
       stitch the earth,
it seems to me, each time
       we die, going
back under, coming back up. . . .
       It is the simplest

stitch, this going where we must,
       leaving a not
unpretty pattern by default. But going
       out of hunger
for small things—flies, words—going
       because one's body

goes. And in this disconcerting creature
       a tiny hunger,
one that won't even press
       the dandelions down,
retrieves the necessary blue-
       black dragonfly

that has just landed on a pod . . .
       all this to say
I'm not afraid of them
       today, or anymore
I think. We are not, were not, ever
       wrong. Desire

is the honest work of the body,
       its engine, its wind.

It too must have its sails—wings
          in this tiny mouth, valves
in the human heart, meanings like sailboats
          setting out

over the mind. Passion is work
          that retrieves us,
lost stitches. It makes a pattern of us,
          it fastens us
to sturdier stuff
          no doubt.

———

KIMONO

The woman on the other side
          of the evergreens
a small boy is hidden in,
          I'm wearing
valleys, clear skies,
          thawing banks

narcissus and hollow reeds
          break through.
It means the world to him, this flat
          archaic fabric
no weather worries.
          Each time I bend,

brushing my hair, a bird
          has just dipped
through its sky out of
          sight. He thinks
I don't see him, my little man
          no more than seven

catching his lost stitch of breath.
         What he sees,
in my garden, is the style
         of the world
as she brushes her hair
         eternally beyond

the casual crumbling forms
         of boughs. I bend
and reeds are suddenly
         ravines. . . . How soothing
it is, this enchanted gap, this tiny
         eternal

delay which is our knowing,
         our flesh.
How late it is, I think,
         bending,
in this world we have mis-
         taken, late

for the green scrim to be
         such an open
door. And yet, even now, a small
         spirit accurate
as new ice is climbing
         into the gentle limbs

of an evergreen, the scent rubbing off
         on his elbows
and knees, his eyes a sacred store
         of dares,
to watch, as on the other side,
         just past

the abstract branches, something
         most whole
loosens her stays
         pretending she's alone.

Debora Greger

The Armorer's Daughter

My father is a hard man.
When my mother couldn't give him a son,
he made the best of it, that is
he made me into what was missing.
So I polish a breastplate until
my smudged face is reflected blue-black
and my arm is stiff as a gauntlet.

I have my father's stubborn jaw
they tell me, those boys from the village
who tease, envious of my lot.
The roughened men who come for a mending,
who bring their smooth sons to be measured,
say I have his hands, too wide for a woman.
Then I think of the beetle on the stoop
whose shell shamed the finest armor.
It scuttled away when I reached down.
With his hand.
                          I am and am not him.
Give me the dusty wings of the moths
that dared spend the night on his workbench
and I would fly—where?
Out to the hill with the shepherd?
To the mill where the miller's son
is clouded in the finest-ground flour?
This wool-gathering angers my father.
He pounds music from metal,
a chorus of glow and chill, bend and stay.
I drop a helmet with a carelessness
I barely recognize and run into the yard,
into the road, tripping on my skirts.

Late afternoon, after a rain, already
the sun's low flame lights the edges
of everything. This world shines,
rings and shines, like his dream of heaven.

John Koethe

IN THE PARK

This is the life I wanted, and could never see.
For almost twenty years I thought that it was enough:
That real happiness was either unreal, or lost, or endless,
And that remembrance was as close to it as I could ever come.
And I believed that deep in the past, buried in my heart
Beyond the depth of sight, there was a kingdom of peace.
And so I never imagined that when peace would finally come
It would be on a summer evening, a few blocks away from home
In a small suburban park, with some children playing aimlessly
In an endless light, and a lake shining in the distance.

Eventually, sometime around the middle of your life,
There's a moment when the first imagination begins to wane.
The future that had always seemed so limitless dissolves,
And the dreams that used to seem so real float up and fade.
The years accumulate; but they start to take on a mild,
Human tone beyond imagination, like the sound the heart makes
Pouring into the past its hymns of adoration and regret.
And then gradually the moments quicken into life,
Vibrant with possibility, sovereign, dense, serene;
And then the park is empty and the years are still.

I think the saddest memory is of a certain kind of light,
A kind of twilight, that seemed to permeate the air
For a few years after I'd grown up and gone away from home.

It was limitless and free. And of course I was going to change,
But freedom means that only aspects ever really change,
And that as the past recedes and the future floats away
You turn into what you are. And so I stayed basically the same
As what I'd always been, while the blond light in the trees
Became part of my memory, and my voice took on the accents
Of a mind infatuated with the rhetoric of farewell.

And now that disembodied grief has gone away.
It was a flickering, literary kind of sadness,
The suspension of a life between two other lives
Of continual remembrance, between two worlds
In which there's too much solitude, too much disdain.
But the sadness that I felt was real sadness,
And this elation now a real tremor as the deepening
Shadows lengthen upon the lake. This calm is real,
But how much of the real past can it absorb?
How far into the future can this peace extend?

I love the way the light falls over the suburbs
Late on these summer evenings, as the buried minds
Stir in their graves, the hearts swell in the warm earth
And the soul settles from the air into its human home.
This is where the prodigal began, and now his day is ending
In a great dream of contentment, where all night long
The children sleep within tomorrow's peaceful arms
And the past is still, and suddenly we turn around and smile
At the memory of a vast, inchoate dream of happiness,
Now that we know that none of it is ever going to be.

Don't you remember how free the future seemed
When it was all imagination? It was a beautiful park
Where the sky was a page of water, and when we looked up,
There were our own faces, shimmering in the clear air.
And I know that this life is the only real form of happiness,

But sometimes in its midst I can hear the dense, stifled sob
Of the unreal one we might have known, and when that ends
And my eyes are filled with tears, time seems to have stopped
And we are alone in the park where it is almost twenty years ago
And the future is still an immense, open dream.

Gary Miranda

MAGICIAN

What matters more than practice
is the fact that you, my audience,
are pulling for me, want me to pull
it off—this next sleight. Now
you see it. Something more than
whether I succeed's at stake.

This talk is called patter. This
is misdirection—how my left
hand shows you nothing's in it.
Nothing is. I count on your mistake
of caring. In my right hand your
undoing blooms like cancer.

But I've shown you that already—
empty. Most tricks are done
before you think they've started—you
who value space more than time.
The balls, the cards, the coins—they go
into the past, not into my pocket.

If I give you anything, be sure
it's not important. What I keep
keeps me alive—a truth on which
your interest hinges. We are like
lovers, if you will. Sometimes even
if you don't will. Now you don't.

A Marzipan for Einstein's Birthday

As rain sometimes against the rock
of a singular thought effects its own
undoing, turning from drop to plop
to wet, which, caught by the late-
arriving sun, shimmers in the after-
thought of easy money, so do the words
of the great dissolve in the mouths of fools.

In spite of this, the majesty of rain
is sheer largesse, if only by default—
that is, a code that can't be broken,
though the shapes of clouds are
corrigible enough, and lightning,
however oracular, is merely a glib
god's version of instant hype.

The space between the world and any word
is rife with political static, statistical
strife, and the census confirms not
every sail that swells with breeze
is big with child. In short, by the time
two people know a truth, it isn't
true. Given which, I side with those

conspiratorial spirits that arch, like
invisible rainbows, somewhere beyond our
repertoire of medicinal music. Big
with fable, they strike like constellations the mind's eye, a blight
on philosophies you or I might salvage
or savor, stranded, high and dry.

Leonard Nathan

GREAT

It's great to be miserable and know it—
Pascal. That's manhood: misery.
It's great. My dog Oliver
Is not great, nor the apple tree.

Pity them, lacking this aptitude
For being great like you and me,
Or my father who is even greater,
More prone to misery.

His ulcer tells him at three AM:
You are great, Jack, and his spine,
When he pulls on a sock, measures his greatness
In miles of glorifying pain.

Sometimes I catch in Oliver's eyes
A shade of something very like grief,
But no—my own reflection; and the apple?
How can it hurt to lose a leaf?

Let's get together and compare miseries;
It will be great, because whoever
Has most we'll give a prize—Pascal's
Jawbone or a day in the skull of Oliver.

THE PENANCE

This is the penance: a recurring dream,
This child running down the road, its mouth
A hole filled up with blackness, its little wings
Two flares of napalm and it runs toward you.

You can't yet hear its scream but know it's screaming,
Know if it can reach you, it will try to
Hug you and that napalm is contagious,
A deadly foreign plague for darker people.

Nothing can save you—voting, letters, marches—
So you close your eyes. A hundred years
It seems to take, the child getting nearer,
Bigger, maybe not so scared as furious.

Now you hear its scream—a supersonic
Jet-like whine that peels your skin off patch
By patch, and then the face is in your face,
Close as a lover's, eyes as bleak as bullets.

Then black-out till you wake forgetting all,
Forgetting him who felt the burning arms
Around him, but who can't, it seems, save any
Thing that matters though he knows what matters.

So this is the penance: a recurring dream
That you're awake and doing good, loving
The children, saving for their education
And your own retirement—till you close your eyes.

Diana O'Hehir

Illinois Central Hospital

For Seth

Everywhere I go I have the sense
Of two arms around my ribs, a head under my chin; it feels like
A frightened child or an animal.

And I think of you, crouched asleep on two chairs
In a green hospital waiting room;
The squeaky waxed floor, the whispers, your son in his nest of tubes.

And I keep wanting to send you a telegram, a passport to a new
     country
Cut out of the seam of my arm.

I carry and soothe my tenant, its hand at my rib, the thumb
Tight against serrated skin,
The palm no bigger than an oak leaf.

Is there a comfort in carrying something? Its with me in your
                              vinyl corridors; it's heavy
Like the last stages of doubt; it changes my shadow; it alters

The way I want for you, the way I walk.

Alicia Ostriker

The Exchange

I am watching a woman swim below the surface
Of the canal, her powerful body shimmering,
Opalescent, her black hair wavering
Like weeds. She does not need to breathe. She faces

Upward, keeping abreast of our rented canoe.
Sweet, thick, white, the blossoms of the locust trees
Cast their fragrance. A redwing blackbird flies
Across the sluggish water. My children paddle.

If I dive down, if she climbs into the boat,
Wet, wordless, she will strangle my children
And throw their limp bodies into the stream.
Skin dripping, she will take my car, drive home.

When my husband answers the doorbell and sees
This magnificent naked woman, bits of sunlight
Glittering on her pubic fur, her muscular
Arm will surround his neck, once for each insult

Endured. He will see the blackbird in her eye,
Her drying mouth incapable of speech,
And I, having exchanged with her, will swim
Away, in the cool water, out of reach.

Homecoming

We know that nothing
It says is true, necessarily. When the man
Returned, he was still attractive
And strong, after a decade of war and a decade
Of adventure, according to the story.

The wife, Penelope, was a good lay
Even as a young, slender girl, and
Was now a better one, richer, riper.
But he only found this out
After passing tests. First his dog recognized him,

Yap! Yap! then the stooped crone
Who had nursed him,
Then beautiful Penelope. He had to sneak
In, past a hundred swaggering
Male invaders.

Sullen they were, and arrogant, as snakes.
He frowned: rape artists.
Cold was his anger, and incredibly
Loosed was her burden of control at last.
From rock, she became water, and

In terror and tears,
Kill the sonofabitches! Kill them!
She said. And he did so,
He and the boy, together, in her honor,
Or the story says so.

A man is a fool who
Questions his weeping wife too curiously
(While the carcasses pile up) and a woman is a fool
Who thinks this life
Can ever offer safety,
My husband says that, and he happens to be
The man who wrote the brutal but idealistic
Iliad, while I am the woman who wrote
The romantic, domestic *Odyssey,* filled
With goddesses, mortal women, pigs, and homecoming.

THOSE WHO KNOW DO NOT SPEAK,
THOSE WHO SPEAK DO NOT KNOW

They split up after attending the excellent experimental film
Program, she wanting to attend a meeting which he did not
Wish to attend. The meeting, which was in a church, was almost
Over by the time she arrived. When she returned home, conditions
Were such that she believed a betrayal of synchronicity
And a lapse of energy and love had occurred, involving the fat
Young babysitter they felt sorry for. She
Immediately expressed her anger and disappointment about this, she
Thought, eloquently and artistically, twice hurling
A kitchen knife at the door where he stood on the stairs
From the kitchen. It was a white door and a medium
Sized wooden handled knife. She had never done this before,
Being a usually inhibited person.
                                    He responded to
This performance with loathing and sadness. He sat on the stairs
Behind the door she shut on him. He did feel like beating her up.
They had some further words, which were not important. He was tired.
He closed his mouth, his eyes, and his pores, like curtains.
Finally they went to bed, made medium sized love.
In the morning they had more words. She cried and felt confused.
He was kind, and told her while shaving there were three ways
Of interpreting her behavior: (a) as folly, (b) as a neutral blowing
Off of steam, or (c) as successful drama. He also pointed out that
Such acts on her part never did bring them together, but made her
Very unattractive to him. He suggested that personal anger was
Seldom valid. She sat on the tub and agreed.

                                    Then after a
Little while they got undressed and made fantastic love. They did
Something new, of which the particular shape and sensation
Was quite queer to her, but powerful, like caviar or mangoes. It was a
Warm beautiful spring day.

Robert Pinsky

A LOVE OF DEATH

from *An Explanation of America,*
Part Two: Its Great Emptiness

Imagine a child from Virginia or New Hampshire
Alone on the prairie eighty years ago
Or more, one afternoon—the shaggy pelt
Of grasses, for the first time in that child's life,
Flowing for miles. Imagine the moving shadow
Of a cloud far off across that shadeless ocean,
The obliterating strangeness like a tide
That pulls or empties the bubble of the child's
Imaginary heart. No hills, no trees.

The child's heart lightens, tending like a bubble
Towards the currents of the grass and sky,
The pure potential of the clear blank spaces.

Or, imagine the child in a draw that holds a garden
Cupped from the limitless motion of the prairie,
Head resting against a pumpkin, in evening sun.
Ground-cherry bushes grow along the furrows,
The fruit red under its papery, moth-shaped sheath.
Grasshoppers tumble among the vines, as large
As dragons in the crumbs of pale dry earth.
The ground is warm to the child's cheek, and the wind
Is a humming sound in the grass above the draw,
Rippling the shadows of the red-green blades.
The bubble of the child's heart melts a little,
Because the quiet of that air and earth
Is like the shadow of a peaceful death—
Limitless and potential, a kind of space
Where one dissolves to become a part of something
Entire . . . whether of sun and air, or goodness
And knowledge, it does not matter to the child.

Dissolved among the particles of the garden
Or into the motion of the grass and air,
Imagine the child happy to be a thing.

Imagine, then, that on that same wide prairie
Some people are threshing in the terrible heat
With horses and machines, cutting bands
And shoveling amid the clatter of the threshers,
The chaff in prickly clouds and the naked sun
Burning as if it could set the chaff on fire.
Imagine that the people are Swedes or Germans,
Some of them resting pressed against the strawstacks,
Trying to get the meager shade.
                                        A man,
A tramp, comes laboring across the stubble
Like a mirage against that blank horizon,
Laboring in his torn shoes toward the tall
Mirage-like images of the tilted threshers
Clattering in the heat. Because the Swedes
Or Germans have no beer, or else because
They cannot speak his language properly,
Or for some reason one cannot imagine,
The man climbs up on a thresher and cuts bands
A minute or two, then waves to one of the people,
A young girl or a child, and jumps head-first
Into the sucking mouth of the machine,
Where he is wedged and beat and cut to pieces—
While the people shout and run in the clouds of chaff,
Like lost mirages on the pelt of prairie.

The obliterating strangeness and the spaces
Are as hard to imagine as the love of death . . .
Which is the love of an entire strangeness,
The contagious blankness of a quiet plain.
Imagine that a man, who had seen a prairie,
Should write a poem about a Dark or Shadow
That seemed to be both his, and the prairie's—as if
The shadow proved that he was not a man,

But something that lived in quiet, like the grass.
Imagine that the man who writes that poem,
Stunned by the loneliness of that wide pelt,
Should prove to himself that he was like a shadow
Or like an animal living in the dark.
In the dark proof he finds in his poem, the man
Might come to think of himself as the very prairie,
The sod itself, not lonely, and immune to death.

None of this happens precisely as I try
To imagine that it does, in the empty plains,
And yet it happens in the imagination
Of part of the country: not in any place
More than another, on the map, but rather
Like a place, where you and I have never been
And need to try to imagine—place like a prairie
Where immigrants, in the obliterating strangeness,
Thirst for the wide contagion of the shadow
Or prairie—where you and I, with our other ways,
More like the cities or the hills or trees,
Less like the clear blank spaces with their potential,
Are like strangers in a place we must imagine.

Pattiann Rogers

How the Body in Motion Affects the Mind

Consider the mind
As it perceives the hands rising
To grasp the tree branch, each finger
Tightening on the limb and the effort
Of the arms pulling the body upward.
What pattern of interpretation synthesized
From that event
Must establish itself in the neocortex?

We know there are precise configurations
Forced on the brain by the phenomena
Of the hand clenched, by the tucking in
Of the thumb, by the sight of the foot
Flexed on the ground and pushing backward.
How do these configurations influence the study
Of duty or manipulate the definition
Of power? The mind, initiating the motion,
Must be altered itself
By the concepts contained in the accomplishment.

I could almost diagram on this paper
The structure of interactions implanted
In the neuronic fibers by the runner's
Leap across the dry gully. Who can say for certain
That structure has nothing to do
With the control of grief?
Think how the mind has no choice
But to accommodate itself to the restrained
Pressure of the fingertips tracing
The lover's spine. The subtlety
Of that motion must turn back
To modify the source of itself.

We are bound by the theorum of sockets and joints,
Totally united with contraction and release.
The idea of truth cannot be separated
From the action of the hand releasing
The stone at the precise apogee of the arm's motion
Or from the spine's flexibility easing
Through a wooden fence. The notion
Of the vast will not ignore the arm swinging
In motion from the shoulder or the fingers
Clasped together in alternation.

And when the infant, for the first time,
Turns his body over completely, think
What an enormous revelation in the brain
Must be forced, at that moment, to right itself.

PORTRAIT

This is a picture of you
Reading this poem. Concentrate
On the finite movement
Of your eyes as they travel
At this moment across
The page, your fingers
Maintaining the stability
Of the sheet. Focus on the particular
Fall of your hair, the scent
Of your hands, the placement of your
Feet now as they acknowledge
Their name.

Simultaneously with these words, be aware
Of your tongue against
Your teeth, the aura
Of heat at your neckline
And wrists, the sense
Of your breath inside its own hollows.

Imagine yourself
Ten feet away and look back
At your body positioned
Here with this book. Picture
The perspective, the attitude
Of your shoulders and hips,
The bend of your head as you
Read of yourself.

Watch how you turn back as you
Remember the sounds surrounding you now,
As you recall the odors
Of wood fibers in this place
Or the lack of them.

And take note of this part
Of your portrait—the actual
Mechanism by which you are perceiving
The picture, the fixed
Expression on your face as you
Arrange these words at this moment
Into their proper circles, as you
Straighten out the aspects
Of the page, the linguistics of the sight
And color of light on the paper.

This is the printed
Form of you watching
Yourself now as you consider
Your person. This portrait is
Finished when you raise
Your eyes.

Grace Schulman

BILL FLANAGAN AT MARYKNOLL

"I'm sure it is a drag if you don't believe,"
You say at last, staring at absolute air.
Now you must rise at three o'clock for prayer,
And I remember, as I turn to leave,
The night you challenged probability,
Sending a penny dancing from your hand.
Waking to laws that tranquilize the mind:
Eight hours, a hundred heads. No miracle.
Question all earthly currency. You are
Startled by all things palpable, familiar.
Love, love is a drag if you don't believe . . .
And now you stiffen as you pass the chapel
Trailing your silent wonder and afraid,
Eyes low, of seeing higher than your God.

Texas Tech Press

The Texas Tech Press Poetry Series was instituted in 1976 to broaden the scope of the Press's publishing ventures. In 1977 the Associated Writing Programs offered the Press the opportunity to select a manuscript from among the finalists in the annual AWP poetry competition. From 1977–1986 Walter McDonald, the series editor, selected seven AWP finalist volumes for publication. Starting in 1987 Texas Tech Press took over from the University Press of Virginia the responsibility of publishing the winning manuscript.

Christopher Davis, *The Tyrant of the Past and the Slave of the Future,* 1989
Robin Behn, *Paper Bird,* 1988
Judith Hemschemeyer, *The Ride Home,* 1987
Kathryn Stripling Byer, *The Girl in the Midst of the Harvest,* 1986
Linda McCarriston, *Talking Soft Dutch,* 1984
Joan Aleshire, *Cloud Train,* 1982
Lisa Zeidner, *Talking Cure,* 1982
Janet Kauffman, *The Weather Book,* 1981
Walter McDonald, *Burning the Fence,* 1981
Carole Oles, *The Loneliness Factor,* 1979
Gibbons Ruark, *Reeds,* 1978
Walter McDonald, *Caliban in Blue and Other Poems,* 1976

Kathryn Stripling Byer

SOLSTICE

for PCP

Riding home on the subway,
you tried not to look at the old woman
mumbling in Spanish, "Mi corazón,
mi corazón de soledad."

Longest dark. Hours after sunset
and no coffee left in the pot, you are saying
your rosary, each word a wing beat against
blackened window glass. (Mother of Letting Go,

Mother of Dust, Holy Mother of Mother's
Hearts) Outside, the lights of New York
gleam like candles, burning till dawn
for the souls of the lost.

"It is easy to pray to her,
she is so human," you told me last night,
though your voice on the long-distance line
stammered, trying to clarify something

you feared I'd dismiss as no more
than nostalgia, old charm
against darkness. I stared at the crèche
where a virgin in wooden robes knelt

while you spoke of her blood seeping
into the straw, how her hand,
holding close to the child's face
a guttering candle-stub, trembled.

Then silence. I thought the line
dead till I heard a match strike
for your cigarette. "Who knows,"
you sighed, watching smoke find

its way to the ceiling.
"Perhaps there is such a thing as grace,
the smallest twig kindling,
the empty hearth filling with light."

———————

WIDE OPEN, THESE GATES

Going down the road feeling good, I snap
my fingers. Hear, hear! At an auction my father
bid sixty-five dollars for a fat Hampshire pig
just by rubbing his nose. When my grandfather
scattered his seed to the four corners, corn stood up
tall as his hat brim. My grandmother's sheets
flapped like bells on the line. Crabbed youth,
crab apple, crepe myrtle, I mumble

as I shuffle downhill, my crabbed youth
behind me like gnats singing. I've come a long way
from what's been described as a mean and starved
corner of backwoods America. That has a ring
to it. Rhythm, like my grandmother's hands
in the bread dough. Her food made the boards creak,
my grandfather mellow. He had a wild temper
when he was a young man. Most folks talk too much,
he'd say, aiming slow spit at a dung beetle.
He never mumbled. Sometimes he talked nonsense

to roosters and fierce setting hens. My nonsense coos
like a dove. Goodbye swallowtails cruising
the pigpen. Goodbye apple dumplings. Goodbye
little turkeys my grandmother fed with her fingers.

Big Belle was a nanny goat. Holler "Halloo"
after sundown and all the cows come home. Some words
are gates swinging wide open, and I walk on through
one more summer that like this road's going
down easy. The gnats sing, and I'm going
to sing. One of these days I'll be gone.

Linda McCarriston

———

BARN FIRE

for Mike

When lightning hit, the whole barn
flashed blue; the edges of the metal roof
rose, or seemed to in that instant,
like the ribbed wings of some vast bird
struggling to lift away. And it did,
with its full cargo of hay, its stanchions,
buckets, barn rubbers, leads and halters:
generations of men and milkers
with their shapes in everything.

In sleep, the farmer starts his slow
goodbye, nightly entering the old barn
through a door of flame, and walking
among punky beams and boards into high summer
years ago: one good bull in a stall
deep with yellow straw, sleek heifers,
the first swallows diving in high rafters.

Every time I dream you, we are younger.
We sit at the table, and all the errors
fall away. Down the road, the neighbors
raise up another barn, and the old,

released into memory, reassembles itself
in a field of grasses sweet and still
and distant. O the fire was terrible,
and the cows came staggering up the hill at six
for milking, stunned and urgent.
I loved you. And we lived so long together.

———

TROUBLE

It should happen
the way a house burns down:
orange fire spouting out
as if from a hole in the earth,
timbers shimmering
by the hollows where walls were,
all around the chimney
sparks and spray—
and the people keening openly.

Not like this.
Not like a message
that might be wrong, a rumor,
or a dream half-true
on the lip of morning.

No.
Make it visible.
Give it heat.
Give me ashes to sweep
and a blackened face
white where tears ran.

Lisa Zeidner

Audience

We love a spectacle of loneliness.
The piano's stranded on the stage, the soloist
brave as Crusoe floating notes to us,
for of course the quadriplegic
lighting matches with his teeth
has no expertise until we are impressed—
how many times has he set fire to his lips
to make it look so easy now for us?
God wracked His brain inventing forests
so we could hear the lone tree falling there.

Yet in not falling, the soloist
threatens to forget his debt to us.
The weight of our attention
can't distract him long enough for one flat note,
and if it could, we might not notice,
for even this predictable sonata
has a life much greater than our concentration:
its tides reach us like a sprinkler
from a neighbor's lawn, still he plays on,
driven as the Channel swimmer—

why, it's disconcerting
that he's *happy* in his isolation tank
when only our accomplishment is having not
dozed off, not coughed or shuffled
our programs too loudly as we looked to see
if that was, indeed, Scarlatti
and if we would last until intermission
when we could go to the rest room to check
if our teeth have stained from the Burgundy,
for even we are on display;

the woman in the box across the way,
with the better view of the pianist's hands
and the *pizzicato* diamond, has more than once
provided a reminder that there is no "us":
our scores are discrete as Bach and Bartok.
I'm glad, for instance, that I'm not
that rude man clamoring from the center of a row—
he reaches the exit and keels over!
The usher shoves him through the door!
"Now it's the doctors' show," my companion warns,

to our percussive gasp, and sure enough,
the doctors' heads begin to surface
like Nessie's from her Loch, showily discreet.
Our hearts skip a beat of the encore
in wishes for the man's recovery.
The genius of merely living stays with me,
a melody quick as the ripple of foot on a pedal,
as we begin to give each other pleasure
with the dramatic development
of our virtuoso hands.

The University of Utah Press

The University of Utah Press Poetry Series was begun in 1970 to give attention to regional poetry of international importance. Until 1982, the University of Utah Press Faculty Editorial Advisory Committee and selected readers edited the poetry submissions. In 1983 Dave Smith was appointed poetry editor. The Press is partially subsidized by the University of Utah and the NEA, and publishes one volume of poetry each year.

Sidney Burris, *A Day at the Races,* 1989
Jeannine Savard, *Snow Water Cove,* 1988
James McKean, *Headlong,* 1987
Richard Cecil, *Einstein's Brain,* 1986
W. S. Di Piero, *Early Light,* 1985
Maura Stanton, *Cries of Swimmers,* 1984
Carole Oles, *Quarry,* 1983
R. H. W. Dillard, *The Greeting,* 1981
Brewster Ghiselin, *Windrose: Poems 1929–1979,* 1980
Adrien Stoutenberg, *Greenwich Mean Time,* 1979
Henry Taylor, *An Afternoon of Pocket Billiards,* 1975
Clarice Short, *The Old One and the Wind,* 1973
Brewster Ghiselin, *Country of the Minotaur,* 1970

Carole Oles

BETTER VISION

I'm not an unusual case. Even my joke
about my arms not being long enough
to hold out the news is old stuff to Doc.
Uncross your knees, he says, and moves close
the iron mask. The house lights go off
and on the far wall appear . . . letters, I suppose.
In another place I'd imagine
chromosomes or cells in mitosis.
Click click and before each eye the magician
produces, voilà, a *T*, an *F*, a diminutive *E*
and time hasn't entirely won
yet. I am told not to blink away
the cobalt light aiming a direct hit
(the blue named for goblins in Germany);
next I am placed in the glare of an oncoming freight,
tied to the tracks but saved when the room
snaps heroically back so Doctor can note
the shape, color, and size of my visual jetsam.
Then, *Uncross your knees* again, and darkness,
nothing between us but a cone of light on the stem
he holds. Every exam a woman has
by a man is gynecological. I think of an onion-
eating eye man who exhaled and touched my face,
kissed me goodbye when I couldn't see at 14.
A dentist who gave the most painless, suave
injections and claimed to be nicer outside his office.
But today it's all eyes. I'm either deranged or alive.
Or something between: the form in the chair, object
of his verb, patient, the one who must move
back to see. Who sheds yellow tears in his Kleenex.

Maura Stanton

CHILDHOOD

I used to lie on my back, imagining
A reverse house on the ceiling of my house
Where I could walk around in empty rooms
All by myself. There was no furniture
Up there, only a glass globe in the floor,
And knee-high barriers at every door.
The low silled windows opened on blue air.
Nothing hung in the closet; even the kitchen
Seemed immaculate, a place for thought.
I liked to walk across the swirling plaster
Into the parts of the house I couldn't see.
The hum from the other house, now my ceiling,
Reached me only faintly. I'd look up
To find my brothers watching old cartoons,
Or my mother vacuuming the ugly carpet.
I'd stare amazed at unmade beds, the clutter,
Shoes, half-dressed dolls, the telephone,
Then return dizzily to my perfect floorplan
Where I never spoke or listened to anyone.

I must have turned down the wrong hall,
Or opened a door that locked shut behind me,
For I live on the ceiling now, not the floor.
This is my house, room after empty room.
How do I ever get back to the real house
Where my sisters spill milk, my father calls,
And I am at the table, eating cereal?
I fill my white rooms with furniture,
Hang curtains over the piercing blue outside.
I lie on my back. I strive to look down.
This ceiling is higher than it used to be,
The floor so far away I can't determine
Which room I'm in, which year, which life.

Adrien Stoutenberg

HYPOCHONDRIA

There is always dread that the disease,
    unnamed as yet,
will escape our vigil. The twitch in the night—
    a fork turning—
the tug in the cave of the heart,
    the giddiness without reason,
the sense of falling and failing,
    even the exhilaration
just before the plumb-weight of fatigue
    hauls down, and breath dangles
at the edge of the edge—
    all the blue meadows of the past
running off with their live shadows,
    birds broken,
winds bruised beyond recognition,
    mementos (whole albums of flowers, soft hair,
and the light on faces)
    tossed out with leaves
for the annual burning.

Morning rituals are required:
    investigation of the sudden blemish;
a cyst, unwarranted, beside an ear;
    a knot in heel or groin,
an itch, a pang,
    a narrow drumbeat in the bone
where deep beyond the X-ray hides
    an unoriginal but nervous sin.

There is always dread that the disease,
    if left unmonitored,
might turn into some common thing—
    a simple wart, heat rash, a fading bruise—

and leave us unprepared to bear
    the knife within
that like a red key turns
    to expose the inner void,
inoperable as love,
    and as deadly as despair.

Henry Taylor

BERNARD AND SARAH

"Hang them where they'll do some good," my grandfather
said, as he placed the dusty photograph
in my father's hands. My father and I stared
at two old people posed stiffly side by side—
my great-great-great-grandparents, in the days
when photography was young, and they were not.
My father thought it out as we drove home.

Deciding that they might do the most good
somewhere out of sight, my father drove
a nail into the back wall of his closet;
they have hung there ever since, brought out
only on such occasions as the marriage
of one of his own children. "I think you ought
to know the stock you're joining with," he says.

Then back they go to the closet, where they hang
keeping their counsel until is it called for.
Yet, through walls, over miles of fields and woods
that flourish still around the farm they cleared,
their eyes light up the closet of my brain
to draw me toward the place I started from,
and when I have come home, they take me in.

The University Press of Virginia

From 1976–1986 the University Press of Virginia published the winning manuscript in the annual Associated Writing Programs Award Series in Poetry, an open national competition. Established in 1974 in a cooperative arrangement between Virginia Commonwealth University and the University Press of Virginia, the award carried a $1,000 honorarium (named the Edith Shiffert Prize in Poetry in 1984 in honor of its endower). Walton Beacham served as series editor until 1979. Manuscripts are screened by established poets around the country, and final decisions are made by a distinguished judge. Final judges for the series have included Richard Eberhart, Elizabeth Bishop, Robert Penn Warren, Donald Justice, Maxine Kumin, and William Meredith. Texas Tech Press now publishes the winning manuscript.

Sandra Alcosser, *A Fish To Feed All Hunger,* 1986
Lisa Ress, *Flight Patterns,* 1985
Jonathan Holden, *Leverage,* 1983
Paul Nelson, *Days Off,* 1982
William Carpenter, *The Hours of Morning,* 1981
James Applewhite, *Following Gravity,* 1980
Jeanne Larsen, *James Cook in Search of Terra Incognita,* 1979
Phyllis Janowitz, *Rites of Strangers,* 1978
Robert Huff, *The Ventriloquist,* 1977
David Walker, *Moving Out,* 1976

William Carpenter

CALIFORNIA

I think of the California poets,
how easy it is for them.
They have vast open spaces,
they drive jeeps and live nowhere,
they drift from cabin to cabin
on mountains with beautiful Spanish names
and there are girls in the cabins
who love poetry and sleep with the poets freely,
for in California there is no guilt nor shame
nor hunger, life is as a dream,
lobsters crawl up on the shore to be caught,
they shoot seabirds and fry them in butter on the beach.

There are no seasons in California.
You make your own, you move from
places where the sun shines all the time
to places where it rains or snows forever.
If you want June or October or some cross-country skiing,
you go to that place in your jeep
and the season is there always.

It is a good climate for poetry, since it is full
of images. You pluck them from the trees like breadfruit
with your feet or knock them down like coconuts.
It is good also for religion, as the Three Winds
bring secret doctrines from the East,
sensual and voluptuous names for the emotions,
creeds that make holy your underground desires,
your daily habits and the parts of your body.

In New England we scratch in the soil with sticks,
find scarce turnips among the rocks,
have no religion at all, fence out our neighbors,

wear clothes, work hard, abstain from sex
and write poems, when we do, on the way to the madhouse.

I spent some time in the Midwest, where they
were neither wholly free nor wholly tragic.
They lived, screwed, married, divorced, and died
like regular folk. They grew corn and fed it to
their pigs, then shipped them east and west
for slaughter. It made sense.
When I am finished with this rocky ground,
wet weather and neurotic ocean,
I will become a Baptist in Des Moines,
rise early and drive over to the river
to watch the fall migrations.
I will take photographs and keep
a family album, write no poems, for poems,
Maine or California, drive you crazy.

Jonathan Holden

FATE

I could picture it as a jagged edge.
Each time our month-old son
made another lunge to breathe
it tripped him up, his breath
would catch, stagger into coughs.
I guess we were possessive, we thought
that by themselves our arms ought
to be enough to insulate him. Stubborn,
I'd stamp outdoors into the snow for wood.
It was ten below, the air a bramble patch.
I resented it, I wanted to trample
its stalks, crush it underfoot.
But it was too green to break.

It merely bent, sprang back behind me,
stung again. The toughened snow
winced beneath my boots.
Finally, to mute that edge,
we fortified him by the humidifier.
That didn't work. White mold flourished
on the windows, new shoots slipped
through the cracks. I'd whet the fire.
But the minute we rested
in the clearing it cut
its blades would rust, we could feel
the silence outside growing fat.

There is a common little word. Fate.
I hadn't cared before what it meant.
It's not a euphemism, it means
that anger is a pathetic religion,
almost a faith. And that we're ignorant.
When at last we relented, left him
with his apricot-colored haze of hair
packaged in the cellophane wrapper
of the oxygen tent,
I knew we'd relinquished him to Fate.
That night, alone, as never before
I could appreciate how indifferently
moonlight always did assail the snow.
Sometimes we're too late to feel.
The facts we face are odds.
Totally exposed, you simply wait, calm,
as I did at the window, fascinated
with some funny twist of matter,
watching a cloud adjacent to the moon,
eccentric, wrinkled like my palm,
watching its edge drift, find its direction:
grief. Or faith, that other accident.

Phyllis Janowitz

A Family Portrait

This is a house the wind blows through

And this is a child
who doesn't speak
as he rocks in a chair
with a wicker seat
but who grunts or shrieks
and can't be reached
who will need years
of costly care
who never leaves
a three-story house
the house the wind blows through

And this is the red
eye of the mother
blurred with love
and rage as she
watches the child
who never speaks
but rocks back
and forth like
a pendulum
or bangs his head
in a rhythmic beat

Here is the father
with bitter mouth
who loves the mother
with reddened eyes
and fears the child
who costs so much
in the house the wind
blows through

This is the drafty heart of the house:
an unspeakable room
the child in a chair
rocking and rocking

away from the man
with blood in his eyes
the woman with bitter-
sweet mouth
not knowing
how far their child
will rock or why

as they love and rage
faster and harder
each day they find less
to say to each other

in the house the wind blows through

———

VEAL

I love to watch the butcher
wipe the sharp
blade on his
apron stained
with fresh blood. I'm
going to marry him.

WHAM

the side of beef split open
he tenderly spreads
it like a woman's legs

between smeared fingers
stroking the cold smoothness

from his fingertips
                    bloody red
drops on the floor spotting the sawdust there
fluffs of fat lie covered decently
the meat is red and lean

He is huge with the scissors and knives of love
and I so refined so shrinking violet
am in love in love
and bite the inside of my mouth
to taste the hot spurts
of blood
swallowing
the sudden salt

WHAM

                    the chopper
right through   the bone
the knife   cleaving clean

        any thickness desired

as beautiful as birth
as normal
as bloody

Again he wipes the knife
on his apron
thin thin slices scooped

with swollen hands onto pieces of
white paper
weighs them

no fat   no fat

arms thick as a roast
he lets my mother
keep the bills
for a year
like love letters
on a spike in the kitchen

Jeanne Larsen
———

A NATURAL HISTORY OF PITTSBURGH

    1.

The duck falcon hunts Fifth Street.
Over flat, pebbled roofs
where the nighthawk's eggs lie,
chimney swifts mount up,
chittering in the Pittsburgh dawn.

    2.

This play of color in the skin
may continue for several hours
after the death of the cephalopod.
    —*B. H. McConnaughey,* Introduction to Marine Biology

What rare shades!
Mount Washington is a nautilus.
The city, a squid,
secretive, benthic,
distracting predators, prey,
with its sepia ink.

3.

The Golden Triangle
is not what you think it is.

4.

Walk quietly through the streets of suburban Pittsburgh.
It is so late
that only the bathrooms are awake.

5.

1770: Twenty cabins surround the trading post.
Brown leaves on the hillsides
glow in the long sun.
Ore bewitches the compass.
Monongahela, Allegheny, Ohio,
the rivers fork like a dowsing rod.

6.

In winter it appears to be
a daguerreotype of itself.

7.

The life of the glacier is one eternal grind.
—Encyclopedia Americana
The people of Pittsburgh rarely consider this.

8.

Around her neck,
like a saint's medal, Pittsburgh
wears the lava of her mills.

9.

The young queen ant,
royally fed,
is led to the surface and flies.
Come down from the bright air,
she pulls off her wings,
leaves them near the small males,
and goes to begin
a new city, underground, in the dark.

Wesleyan University Press

The Wesleyan University Press Poetry Series was instituted in 1958 at the suggestion of Richard Wilbur, then a member of Wesleyan's English department. Three advisors were appointed—William Meredith, Donald Hall, and Norman Holmes Pearson—and the first four books were published in 1959. Over the years many distinguished poets have served on the poetry board, including Howard Nemerov, A. R. Ammons, Denise Levertov, Louise Gluck, Charles Simic, William Matthews, and Charles Wright.

First books are considered by a three-member New Poets Board, and subsequent books are considered by outside readers drawn from a pool of poetry consultants. Up to twelve books are published annually, in editions of 500–800 for new poets and 500–1,000 for established poets.

With nearly 200 books on its list, Wesleyan has published more poetry than any other university press.

Ellery Akers, *Knocking on the Earth,* 1989
Marianne Boruch, *Descendant,* 1989
Lisa Bernstein, *Transparent Body,* 1989
David Ray, *The Maharani's New Wall,* 1989
Alane Rollings, *In Your Own Sweet Time,* 1989
Sherod Santos, *Southern Reaches,* 1989
Judith Baumel, *The Weight of Numbers,* 1988
Bruce Beasley, *Spirituals,* 1988
Karen Brennan, *Here on Earth,* 1988
Glover Davis, *Legend,* 1988
James Baker Hall, *Stopping on the Edge to Wave,* 1988
Jane Hirschfield, *Of Gravity & Angels,* 1988
Mark Irwin, *Against the Meanwhile,* 1988
Heather McHugh, *Shades,* 1988
Lynne McMahon, *Faith,* 1988

Harvey Shapiro, *National Cold Storage Company*, 1988
Jordan Smith, *Lucky Seven*, 1988
David Young, *Earthshine*, 1988
Dean Young, *Design with X*, 1988
Shahid Ali Agha, *The Half-inch Himalayas*, 1987
Sharon Bryan, *Objects of Affection*, 1987
Rachel Hadas, *A Son from Sleep*, 1987
Mary Karr, *Abacus*, 1987
Colleen McElroy, *Bone Flames*, 1987
Robert Mezey, *Evening Wind*, 1987
Barbara Molloy-Olund, *In Favor of Lightning*, 1987
Heather McHugh, *To the Quick*, 1987
Robert Morgan, *At the Edge of Orchard Country*, 1987
Gregory Orr, *New and Selected Poems*, 1987
David Ray, *Sam's Book*, 1987
A. E. Stringer, *Channel Markers*, 1987
Ralph Angel, *Anxious Latitudes*, 1986
Don Bogen, *After the Splendid Display*, 1986
Michael Collier, *The Clasp and Other Poems*, 1986
David Ignatow, *New and Collected Poems 1970–1986*, 1986
Richard Katrovas, *Snug Harbor*, 1986
Yusef Komunyakaa, *I Apologize for the Eyes in My Head*, 1986
Maureen Mulhern, *Parallax*, 1986
Gregory Orr, *We Must Make a Kingdom of It*, 1986
Pattiann Rogers, *The Tattooed Lady in the Garden*, 1986
James Tate, *Reckoner*, 1986
David Young, *Foraging*, 1986
Marianne Boruch, *View from the Gazebo*, 1985
Olga Broumas and Jane Miller, *Black Holes/Black Stockings*, 1985
Thulani Davis, *Playing the Changes*, 1985
Russell Edson, *The Wounded Breakfast*, 1985
William Harmon, *Mutatis Mutandis: 27 Invoices*, 1985
Brenda Hillman, *White Dress*, 1985
Janet Sylvester, *That Mulberry Wine*, 1985
Paul Zweig, *Eternity's Woods*, 1985

Julia Budenz, *From the Gardens of Flora Baum*, 1984
Ernesto Cardenal, *With Walker in Nicaragua*, 1984
Gloria Fuertes, *Off the Map*, 1984
Elton Glaser, *Relics*, 1984
Marea Gordett, *Freeze Tag*, 1984
Richard Howard, *Quantities/Damages*, 1984
Yusef Komunyakaa, *Copacetic*, 1984
Colleen McElroy, *Queen of the Ebony Isles*, 1984
James Richardson, *Second Guesses*, 1984
Harvey Shapiro, *The Light Holds*, 1984
Jeffrey Skinner, *Late Stars*, 1984
Richard Tillinghast, *Our Flag Was Still There*, 1984
Sharon Bryan, *Salt Air*, 1983
John Cage, *X: Writings 79–82*, 1983
James Dickey, *The Central Motion*, 1983
Rachel Hadas, *Slow Transparency*, 1983
Dennis Hinrichsen, *The Attraction of Heavenly Bodies*, 1983
Richard Katrovas, *Green Dragons*, 1983
Susan Mitchell, *The Water Inside the Water*, 1983
Richard Tillinghast, *Sleep Watch*, 1983
Robert Farnsworth, *Three or Four Hills and a Cloud*, 1982
John Haines, *News from the Glacier*, 1982
Garrett Hongo, *Yellow Light*, 1982
Thomas Luhrmann, *The Objects in the Garden*, 1982
John Pijewski, *Dinner with Uncle Jozef*, 1982
Norman Shapiro, *Fables from Old French: Aesop's Beasts and Bumpkins*, 1982
Charles Wright, *Country Music*, 1982
William Clipman, *Dog Light*, 1981
James Dickey, *The Early Motion*, 1981
James Dickey, *Falling, May Day Sermon, and Other Poems*, 1981
Lloyd Schwartz, *These People*, 1981
Elizabeth Spires, *Globe*, 1981
Lawrence Kearney, *Kingdom Come*, 1980
James Nolan, *What Moves Is Not the Wind*, 1980

Richard Tillinghast, *The Knife,* 1980
Ricardo Alonso, *Cimarron,* 1979
Frederick Buell, *Full Summer,* 1979
John Cage, *Empty Words,* 1979
Mike Lowery, *Masks of the Dreamer,* 1979
Al Zolynas, *The New Physics,* 1979
Anne Hussey, *Baddeck & Other Poems,* 1978
Adam LeFevre, *Everything All at Once,* 1978
Steve Orlen, *Permission to Speak,* 1978
Vern Rutsala, *Paragraphs,* 1978
John Witte, *Loving the Days,* 1978
Russell Edson, *The Reason Why the Closet-Man is Never Sad,* 1977
Cynthia Genser, *Taking On the Local Color,* 1977
John Haines, *Cicada,* 1977
Barbara Howes, *A Private Signal,* 1977
Robert Shaw, *Comforting the Wilderness,* 1977
Charles Wright, *China Trace,* 1977
Michael Benedikt, *Night Cries,* 1976
William Robert Moses, *Passage,* 1976
James Tate, *Viper Jazz,* 1976
Ellen Voigt, *Claiming Kin,* 1976
Judith Hemschemeyer, *Very Close and Very Slow,* 1975
David Ignatow, *Selected Poems,* 1975
Stephen Tapscott, *Mesopotamia,* 1975
Sherley Williams, *The Peacock Poems,* 1975
Charles Wright, *Bloodlines,* 1975
D. J. Enright, *The Terrible Shears: Scenes from a Twenties'
Childhood,* 1974
Calvin Forbes, *Blue Monday,* 1974
Barbara Greenberg, *The Spoils of August,* 1974
James Nolan, *Why I Live in the Forest,* 1974
David Ray, *Gathering Firewood,* 1974
James Seay, *Water Tables,* 1974
Anne Stevenson, *Correspondences: A Family History in Letters,* 1974
John Cage, *M: Writings 67–72,* 1973

John Cage, *Silence*, 1973
Russell Edson, *The Clam Theatre*, 1973
Kenneth Hanson, *The Uncorrected World*, 1973
William Harmon, *Legion: Civic Choruses*, 1973
Judith Hemschemeyer, *I Remember the Room Was Filled with Light*, 1973
Eleanor Lerman, *Armed Love*, 1973
Charles Wright, *Hard Freight*, 1973
Evan Chigounis, *Secret Lives*, 1972
Barbara Howes, *The Blue Garden*, 1972
Dave Kelly, *Instructions for Viewing a Solar Eclipse*, 1972
Frederick Turner, *Between Two Lives*, 1972
Michael Benedikt, *Mole Notes*, 1971
William Dickey, *More Under Saturn*, 1971
Dugan Gilman, *Upstate*, 1971
John Haines, *The Stone Harp*, 1971
Harvey Shapiro, *This World*, 1971
Jon Silkin, *Amana Grass*, 1971
James Wright, *Collected Poems*, 1971
Michael Benedikt, *Sky*, 1970
William Harmon, *Treasury Holiday*, 1970
David Ignatow, *Poems 1934–1969*, 1970
Charles Levendosky, *Perimeters*, 1970
Clarence Major, *Swallow the Lake*, 1970
James Seay, *Let Not Your Hart*, 1970
Charles Wright, *The Grave of the Right Hand*, 1970
Gray Burr, *A Choice of Attitudes*, 1969
Leonard Nathan, *The Day the Perfect Speakers Left*, 1969
Marge Piercy, *Hard Loving*, 1969
Anne Stevenson, *Reversals*, 1969
Michael Benedikt, *The Body*, 1968
Edwin Honig, *Spring Journal*, 1968
David Ignatow, *Rescue the Dead*, 1968
Philip Levine, *Not This Pig*, 1968
Vassar Miller, *Onions and Roses*, 1968

Marge Piercy, *Breaking Camp*, 1968
James Wright, *Shall We Gather At the River*, 1968
John Cage, *A Year from Monday*, 1967
James Dickey, *Poems 1957–1967*, 1967
Richard Howard, *The Damages*, 1967
Donald Justice, *Night Light*, 1967
Lou Lipsitz, *Cold Water*, 1967
Josephine Miles, *Kinds of Affection*, 1967
Philip Murray, *Poems After Martial*, 1967
Turner Cassity, *Watchboy, What of the Night?* 1966
John Haines, *Winter News*, 1966
Harvey Shapiro, *Battle Report*, 1966
Jon Silkin, *Poems: New and Selected*, 1966
Tram Combs, *Saint Thomas*, 1965
Donald Davie, *Events and Wisdoms*, 1965
W. H. Davies, *The Complete Poems of W. H. Davies*, 1965
James Dickey, *Buckdancer's Choice*, 1965
William Robert Moses, *Identities*, 1965
James Wright, *The Branch Will Not Break*, 1965
James Dickey, *Helmets*, 1964
David Ignatow, *Figures of the Human*, 1964
Donald Peterson, *The Spectral Boy*, 1964
Vern Rutsala, *The Window*, 1964
Chester Kallman, *Absent and Present*, 1963
Vassar Miller, *My Bones Being Wiser*, 1963
Louis Simpson, *At the End of the Open Road*, 1963
John Ashbery, *The Tennis Court Oath*, 1962
Robert Bly, *Silence in the Snowy Fields*, 1962
James Dickey, *Drowning With Others*, 1962
Richard Howard, *Quantities*, 1962
Alan Ansen, *Disorderly Houses*, 1961
Robert Bagg, *Madonna of the Cello*, 1961
Donald Davie, *New and Selected Poems*, 1961
David Ignatow, *Say Pardon*, 1961
David Ferry, *On the Way to the Island*, 1960
Robert Francis, *The Orb Weaver*, 1960

Donald Justice, *The Summer Anniversaries*, 1960
Vassar Miller, *Wage War on Silence*, 1960
Barbara Howes, *Light and Dark*, 1959
Hyam Plutzik, *Apples from Shinar*, 1959
Louis Simpson, *A Dream of Governors*, 1959
James Wright, *Saint Judas*, 1959

John Ashbery

Faust

If only the phantom would stop reappearing!
Business, if you wanted to know, was punk at the opera.
The heroine no longer appeared in *Faust*.
The crowds strolled sadly away. The phantom
Watched them from the roof, not guessing the hungers
That must be stirred before disappointment can begin.

One day as morning was about to begin
A man in brown with a white shirt reappearing
At the bottom of his yellow vest, was talking hungers
With the silver-haired director of the opera.
On the green-carpeted floor no phantom
Appeared, except yellow squares of sunlight, like those in *Faust*.

That night as the musicians for *Faust*
Were about to go on strike, lest darkness begin
In the corridors, and through them the phantom
Glide unobstructed, the vision reappearing
Of blonde Marguerite practicing a new opera
At her window awoke terrible new hungers

In the already starving tenor. But hungers
Are just another topic, like the new Faust
Drifting through the tunnels of the opera
(In search of lost old age? For they begin
To notice a twinkle in his eye. It is cold daylight reappearing
At the window behind him, itself a phantom

Window, painted by the phantom
Scene painters, sick of not getting paid, of hungers
For a scene below of tiny, reappearing
Dancers, with a sandbag falling like a note in *Faust*,
Through purple air. And the spectators begin
To understand the bleeding tenor star of the opera.)

That night the opera
Was crowded to the rafters. The phantom
Took twenty-nine curtain calls. "Begin!
Begin!" In the wings the tenor hungers
For the heroine's convulsive kiss, and Faust
Moves forward, no longer young, reappearing

And reappearing for the last time. The opera
Faust would no longer need its phantom.
On the bare, sunlit stage the hungers could begin.

Michael Benedikt

Fred, the Neat Pig

(1) Fred was certainly one of the neatest persons you would ever want to meet, and also one of the most polite. In order to keep neat, and not burden you with the sight of any homely or unseemly personal details, he used to put parts of his body that had fallen off back on those portions of his body. For example, whenever a hair fell off his head, he'd pick it up and drop it back on his scalp. If even so much as a beard-strand or an eyelash dislodged, he'd stick it back. If he happened to spit by mistake in the cleanliness of some public place, such as the subway, he'd bend right over and cup it up and put it right back where it belonged. . . . On hot days he'd wrap himself up especially neatly, to prevent the escape of sweat! Fred would glue scabs back on; reattach warts and corns; if he felt something had fallen from his nose during the course of the day, he'd retrace his steps all night in hopes of being able to restore it. Fred's mornings in the bathroom were the most extraordinary of all! (2) He even saved his ear-wax, in order to make candles, so you could see him at all times and admire his neatness better. Yes, when you saw old Fred coming toward you with his flaming candles, his eye-lashes matted, staggering under the weight of warts, his shoetops not too dim despite the deposit of skin products, his clothes all spotted and stained, with piss and shit all over his tunic, the first thing you'd comment on was Fred's neatness. (3) All those people running off when Fred appeared any place would upset any young man, whose virtues were identical with those of tidiness;

and so it upset Fred, too. Particularly since his neatness had originally been intended to increase not decrease his circle of friends! Finally, poor Fred tried to solve his sadness at the way others avoided him by carrying around a funnel for use in pouring the tears back down the ducts.

Robert Bly

Poem Against the Rich

Each day I live, each day the sea of light
Rises, I seem to see
The tear inside the stone
As if my eyes were gazing beneath the earth.
The rich man in his red hat
Cannot hear
The weeping in the pueblos of the lily,
Or the dark tears in the shacks of the corn.
Each day the sea of light rises
I hear the sad rustle of the darkened armies,
Where each man weeps, and the plaintive
Orisons of the stones.
The stones bow as the saddened armies pass.

Poem in Three Parts

I
Oh, on an early morning I think I shall live forever!
I am wrapped in my joyful flesh,
As the grass is wrapped in its clouds of green.

II
Rising from a bed, where I dreamt
Of long rides past castles and hot coals,

The sun lies happily on my knees;
I have suffered and survived the night
Bathed in dark water, like any blade of grass.

III

The strong leaves of the box-elder tree,
Plunging in the wind, call us to disappear
Into the wilds of the universe,
Where we shall sit at the foot of a plant,
And live forever, like the dust.

THREE KINDS OF PLEASURES

I

Sometimes, riding in a car, in Wisconsin
Or Illinois, you notice those dark telephone poles
One by one lift themselves out of the fence line
And slowly leap on the gray sky—
And past them, the snowy fields.

II

The darkness drifts down like snow on the picked cornfields
In Wisconsin: and on these black trees
Scattered, one by one,
Through the winter fields—
We see stiff weeds and brownish stubble,
And white snow left now only in the wheeltracks of the combine.

III

It is a pleasure, also, to be driving
Toward Chicago, near dark,
And see the lights in the barns.
The bare trees more dignified than ever,
Like a fierce man on his deathbed,
And the ditches along the road half full of a private snow.

Sharon Bryan

HOLLANDAISE

The sauce thickens. I add more butter,
slowly. Sometimes we drank the best wine
while we cooked for friends,
knowing nothing could go wrong,
the soufflé would rise, the custard set,
the cheese be ripe. We imagined
we were reckless but we were just happy,
and good at our work. The cookbook is firm:
It is safer not to go over two ounces
of butter for each egg yolk. I try to describe
to myself how we could have been safer,
what we exceeded. If the sauce "turns"
there are things to be done, steps
to be taken that are not miraculous,
that assume the failed ingredients,
that assume a willing suspension of despair.

Thulani Davis

POTHOLES

love for you decays
like new york streets
falls short
like heat inspectors
and water supplies
the longer i stay here
the less i even like you
my ceiling gives out
a little each night
and i think of you

little crashes
like birds with bad wings
wake me up
to a certain bitter desire
for radio, credit or a car
i could get out of new york
with the proper attitude
you're not that cute
and crying may be good
for the complexion
but so is oatmeal
i'm not that good at it
your love is crooked
running all in my way
leaning, falling
looking for a place to lay
new york is a hard rock
for that sort of thing
people will just turn
and walk away saying
i really don't need this
i was going uptown

James Dickey
———

DROWNING WITH OTHERS

There are moments a man turns from us
Whom we have all known until now.
Upgathered, we watch him grow,
Unshipping his shoulder-bones

Like human, everyday wings
That he has not ever used,
Releasing his hair from his brain,
A kingfisher's crest, confused

By the God-tilted light of Heaven.
His deep, window-watching smile
Comes closely upon us in waves,
And spreads, and now we are

At last within it, dancing.
Slowly we turn and shine
Upon what is holding us,
As under our feet he soars,

Struck dumb as the angel of Eden,
In wide, eye-opening rings.
Yet the hand on my shoulder fears
To feel my own wingblades spring,

To feel me sink slowly away
In my hair turned loose like a thought
Of a fisherbird dying in flight.
If I opened my arms, I could hear

Every shell in the sea find the word
It has tried to put into my mouth.
Broad flight would become of my dancing,
And I would obsess the whole sea,

But I keep rising and singing
With my last breath. Upon my back,
With his hand on my unborn wing,
A man rests easy as sunlight

Who has kept himself free of the forms
Of the deaf, down-soaring dead,
And me laid out and alive
For nothing at all, in his arms.

GAMECOCK

Fear, jealousy and murder are the same
When they put on their long reddish feathers,
Their shawl neck and moccasin head
In a tree bearing levels of women.
There is yet no thread

Of light, and his scabbed feet tighten,
Holding sleep as though it were lockjaw,
His feathers damp, his eyes crazed
And cracked like the eyes
Of a chicken head cut off or wrung-necked

While he waits for the sun's only cry
All night building up in his throat
To leap out and turn the day red,
To tumble his hens from the pine tree,
And then will go down, his hackles

Up, looking everywhere for the other
Cock who could not be there,
Head ruffed and sullenly stepping
As upon his best human-curved steel:
He is like any fierce

Old man in a terminal ward:
There is the same look of waiting
That the sun prepares itself for;
The enraged, surviving-
another-day blood,

And from him at dawn comes the same
Cry that the world cannot stop.
In all the great building's blue windows
The sun gains strength; on all floors, women
Awaken—wives, nurses, sisters and daughters—

And he lies back, his eyes filmed, unappeased,
As all of them, clucking, pillow-patting,
Come to help his best savagery blaze, doomed, dead-
game, demanding, unreasonably
Battling to the death for what is his.

―――――

The Heaven of Animals

Here they are. The soft eyes open.
If they have lived in a wood
It is a wood.
If they have lived on plains
It is grass rolling
Under their feet forever.

Having no souls, they have come,
Anyway, beyond their knowing.
Their instincts wholly bloom
And they rise.
The soft eyes open.

To match them, the landscape flowers,
Outdoing, desperately
Outdoing what is required:
The richest wood,
The deepest field.

For some of these,
It could not be the place
It is, without blood.
These hunt, as they have done,
But with claws and teeth grown perfect,

More deadly than they can believe.
They stalk more silently,
And crouch on the limbs of trees,

And their descent
Upon the bright backs of their prey

May take years
In a sovereign floating of joy.
And those that are hunted
Know this as their life,
Their reward: to walk

Under such trees in full knowledge
Of what is in glory above them,
And to feel no fear,
But acceptance, compliance.
Fulfilling themselves without pain

At the cycle's center,
They tremble, they walk
Under the tree,
They fall, they are torn,
They rise, they walk again.

Russell Edson

AN HISTORICAL BREAKFAST

A man is bringing a cup of coffee to his face, tilting it to his mouth. It's historical, he thinks. He scratches his head: another historical event. He really ought to rest, he's making an awful lot of history this morning.

Oh my, now he's buttering toast, another piece of history is being made.

He wonders why it should have fallen on him to be so historical. Others probably just don't have it, he thinks, it is, after all, a talent.

He thinks one of his shoelaces needs tying. Oh well, another important historical event is about to take place. He just can't help it. Perhaps he's taking up too large an area of history? But he has to live, hasn't he? Toast needs buttering and he can't go around with one of his shoelaces needing to be tied, can he?

Certainly it's true, when the 20th century gets written in full it will be mainly about him. That's the way the cooky crumbles—ah, there's a phrase that'll be quoted for centuries to come.

Self-conscious? A little; how can one help it with all those yet-to-be-born eyes of the future watching him?

Uh oh, he feels another historical event coming . . . Ah, there it is, a cup of coffee approaching his face at the end of his arm. If only they could catch it on film, how much it would mean to the future.

Oops, spilled it all over his lap. One of those historical accidents that will influence the next thousand years; unpredictable, and really rather uncomfortable . . . But history is never easy, he thinks . . .

––––––

My Uncle in the Distance

My uncle had a mustache made of spinach. It was green and full of sand. It was lovely in the distance when one had lost sight of it among the leaves of trees.

But at close range, particularly at the dinner table, it seemed something caught on his upper lip, which he should have had the decency to lick off.

But my uncle doesn't like spinach, especially when it's so full of sand.

Poor uncle, finally in complement to his mustache, slowly gave up his animality. Soon it was no longer uncle, but a hodgepodge of squashes and root plants, leafy and fungal portions, waddling about the house.

Until father cried, my God, cut him up for supper!

After that the difficulty seemed to disappear into the distance of the years . . . lovelier and more distant each of the years that are the distance they create.

A piece of a man had broken off in a road. He picked it up and put it in his pocket.

As he stooped to pick up another piece he came apart at the waist.

His bottom half was still standing. He walked over on his elbows and grabbed the seat of his pants and said, legs go home.

But as they were going along his head fell off. His head yelled, legs stop.

And then one of his knees came apart. But meanwhile his heart had dropped out of his trunk.

As his head screamed, legs turn around, his tongue fell out.

Oh my God, he thought, I'll never get home.

John Haines

The Head on the Table

The enormous head of a bison,
mineral-stained
mottled with sand and rock flour,
lies cushioned on the museum table.

To be here in this bone room
under the soft thunder of traffic;
washed from the ice hills and blue muck,
skull and spine long since
changed to the fiber of stone.

One black, gleaming horn upswept
from the steep forehead,
eyelids sewn shut,
nostrils curled and withered.
The ear thinned down to a clay shell,

listening with the deep presence
of matter that does not die,
while the whole journey of beasts on earth
files without a sound
into the gloom of the catalogues.

The far tundra lying still,
transparent under glass and steel.
Evening of the explorer's lamp,
the wick turned down
in its clear fountain of oil.

In the shadow made there,
a rough blue tongue passes over teeth
stained by thirty thousand years
of swamp water and peat.

The Middle Ages

Always on the point of falling asleep,
the figures of men and beasts.

Faces, deeply grained with dirt,
a soiled finger pointing inward.

Like Dürer's Knight, always haunted
by two companions:

the Devil, with a face like a matted hog,
disheveled and split;

and Death, half dog, half monkey,
a withered bishop with an hourglass.

There's a cold lizard underfoot,
the lancehead glitters in its furry collar;

but it's too late now to storm the silence
on God's forbidden mountain.

You have to go on as the century darkens,
the reins still taut in that armored fist.

―――――

The Stone Harp

A road deepening in the north,
strung with steel,
resonant in the winter evening,
as though the earth were a harp
soon to be struck.

As if a spade
rang in a rock chamber:

in the subterranean light,
glittering with mica,
a figure like a tree turning to stone
stands on its charred roots
and tries to sing.

Now there is all this blood
flowing into the west,
ragged holes at the waterline of the sun—
that ship is sinking.

And the only poet is the wind,
a drifter
who walked in from the coast
with empty pockets.

He stands on the road
at evening, making a sound
like a stone harp
strummed
by a handful of leaves . . .

Judith Hemschemeyer

SKIRMISH

When you attacked with all the weapons I adore,
Wit, charming accent, classic fucked-up past,
Nonchalance bordering on cruelty,
I wanted to rush to all my borders
At once, throw in my best battalions
As the Yugoslavs did in World War Two,
Show you my dream book, my stare, *toute la boutique,*
Use others simply as steppingstones to you.
But I have done that before; each time I wake
To find the front moved on, my heart laid waste,
So I pulled back—the Russian technique—
Ringing my love's core with tough, tight circles
Of pretended calm. I won; I didn't fall.
Now you are gone and I am safe and cold and small.

Garrett Kaoru Hongo

WHAT FOR

At six I lived for spells:
how a few Hawaiian words could call
up the rain, could hymn like the sea
in the long swirl of chambers
curling in the nautilus of a shell,

how Amida's ballads of the Buddhaland
in the drone of the priest's liturgy
could conjure money from the poor
and give them nothing but mantras,
the strange syllables that healed desire.

I lived for stories about the war
my grandfather told over *hana* cards,
slapping them down on the mats
with a sharp Japanese *kiai*.

I lived for songs my grandmother sang
stirring curry into a thick stew,
weaving a calligraphy of Kannon's love
into grass mats and straw sandals.

I lived for the red volcano dirt
staining my toes, the salt residue
of surf and sea wind in my hair,
the arc of a flat stone skipping
in the hollow trough of a wave.

I lived a child's world, waited
for my father to drag himself home,
dusted with blasts of sand, powdered rock,
and the strange ash of raw cement,
his deafness made worse by the clang
of pneumatic drills, sore in his bones
from the buckings of a jackhammer.

He'd hand me a scarred lunchpail,
let me unlace the hightop G.I. boots,
call him the new name I'd invented
that day in school, write it for him
on his newspaper. He'd rub my face
with hands that felt like gravel roads,
tell me to move, go play, and then he'd
walk to the laundry sink to scrub,

rinse the dirt of his long day
from a face brown and grained as koa wood.

I wanted to take away the pain
in his legs, the swelling in his joints,
give him back his hearing,
clear and rare as crystal chimes,
the fins of glass that wrinkled
and sparked the air with their sound.

I wanted to heal the sores that work
and war had sent to him,
let him play catch in the backyard
with me, tossing a tennis ball
past papaya trees without the shoulders
of pain shrugging back his arms.

I wanted to become a doctor of pure magic,
to string a necklace of sweet words
fragrant as pine needles and plumeria,
fragrant as the bread my mother baked,
place it like a lei of cowrie shells
and *pikake* flowers around my father's neck,
and chant him a blessing, a sutra.

WHO AMONG YOU KNOWS THE ESSENCE OF GARLIC?

Can your foreigner's nose smell mullets
roasting in a glaze of brown bean paste
and sprinkled with novas of sea salt?

Can you hear my grandmother
chant the mushroom's sutra?

Can you hear papayas crying
as they bleed in porcelain plates?

I'm telling you that the bamboo
slips the long pliant shoots
of its myriad soft tongues
into your mouth that is full of oranges.

I'm saying that silver waterfalls
of bean threads will burst in hot oil
and stain your lips like zinc.

The marbled skin of the blue mackerel
works good for men. The purple oils
from its flesh perfume the tongues of women.

If you swallow them whole, the rice cakes
soaking in a broth of coconut milk and brown sugar
will never leave the bottom of your stomach.

Flukes of giant black mushrooms
leap from their murky tubs
and strangle the toes of young carrots.

Broiling chickens ooze grease,
yellow tears of fat collect
and spatter in the smoking pot.

Soft ripe pears, blushing
on the kitchen window sill,
kneel like plump women
taking a long, luxurious shampoo,
and invite you to bite their hips.

Why not grab basketfuls of steaming noodles,
lush and slick as the hair of a fine lady,
and squeeze?

The shrimps, big as Portuguese thumbs,
stew among cut guavas, red onions,
ginger root, and rosemary in lemon juice,

the palm oil bubbling to the top,
breaking through layers and layers
of shredded coconut and sliced cashews.

Who among you knows the essence
of garlic and black lotus root,
of red and green peppers sizzling
among squads of oysters in the skillet,
of crushed ginger, fresh green onions,
and pale-blue rice wine simmering
in the stomach of a big red fish?

Barbara Howes
———

AT 79TH AND PARK

A cry!—someone is knocked
Down on the avenue;
People don't know what to do
When a walker lies, not breathing.

I watch, 10 storeys high,
Through the acetylene air:
He has been backed up over;
Still, the accident

Is hard to credit. A group
Of 14 gathers; the Fire
Department rains like bees,
Visored, black-striped on yellow

Batting, *buzz*—they clamber
Around that globule; somebody
Brings out a comforter
For shroud; a woman's puce

Scarf bobs, from my 10th-floor view,
Desperately; by the backed truck
An arm explains, hacks air
In desperation, though no

One takes much notice. As through
A pail of glass, I see—
Far down—an ambulance,
A doctor come; they slide

Away the stretcher . . . In minutes
The piston-arm, the truck,
Puce, police, bees, group
All have been vacuumed up.

David Ignatow
———

GET THE GASWORKS

Get the gasworks into a poem,
and you've got the smoke and smokestacks,
the mottled red and yellow tenements,
and grimy kids who curse with the pungency
of the odor of gas. You've got America, boy.

Sketch in the river and barges,
all dirty and slimy.
How do the seagulls stay so white?
And always cawing like little mad geniuses?
You've got the kind of living
that makes the kind of thinking we do:
gaswork smokestack whistle tooting wisecracks.
They don't come because we like it that way,
but because we find it outside our window each morning,
in soot on the furniture,

and trucks carrying coal for gas,
the kid hot after the ball under the wheel.
He gets it over the belly, all right.
He dies there.

So the kids keep tossing the ball around
after the funeral.
So the cops keep chasing them,
so the mamas keep hollering,
and papa flings his newspaper outward,
in disgust with discipline.

_____

SUNDAY AT THE STATE HOSPITAL

I am sitting across the table
eating my visit sandwich.
The one I brought him stays suspended
near his mouth; his eyes focus
on the table and seem to think,
his shoulders hunched forward.
I chew methodically,
pretending to take him
as a matter of course.
The sandwich tastes mad
and I keep chewing.
My past is sitting in front of me
filled with itself
and trying with almost no success
to bring the present to its mouth.

Donald Justice

COUNTING THE MAD

This one was put in a jacket,
This one was sent home,
This one was given bread and meat
But would eat none,
And this one cried No No No No
All day long.

This one looked at the window
As though it were a wall,
This one saw things that were not there,
This one things that were,
And this one cried No No No No
All day long.

This one thought himself a bird,
This one a dog,
And this one thought himself a man,
An ordinary man,
And cried and cried No No No No
All day long.

SESTINA: HERE IN KATMANDU

We have climbed the mountain.
There's nothing more to do.
It is terrible to come down
To the valley
Where, amidst many flowers,
One thinks of snow,

As formerly, amidst snow,
Climbing the mountain,

One thought of flowers,
Tremulous, ruddy with dew,
In the valley.
One caught their scent coming down.

It is difficult to adjust, once down,
To the absence of snow.
Clear days, from the valley,
One looks up at the mountain.
What else is there to do?
Prayer wheels, flowers!

Let the flowers
Fade, the prayer wheels run down.
What have they to do
With us who have stood atop the snow
Atop the mountain,
Flags seen from the valley?

It might be possible to live in the valley,
To bury oneself among flowers,
If one could forget the mountain,
How, never once looking down,
Stiff, blinded with snow,
One knew what to do.

Meanwhile it is not easy here in Katmandu,
Especially when to the valley
That wind which means snow
Elsewhere, but here means flowers,
Comes down,
As soon it must, from the mountain.

Men at Forty

Men at forty
Learn to close softly
The doors to rooms they will not be
Coming back to.

At rest on a stair landing,
They feel it
Moving beneath them now like the deck of a ship,
Though the swell is gentle.

And deep in mirrors
They rediscover
The face of the boy as he practices tying
His father's tie there in secret

And the face of that father,
Still warm with the mystery of lather.
They are more fathers than sons themselves now.
Something is filling them, something

That is like the twilight sound
Of the crickets, immense,
Filling the woods at the foot of the slope
Behind their mortgaged houses.

Adam LeFevre

Sestina Sestina

The sestina is a difficult form
to master because of the excessive repetition
which usually seems gratuitous or else
makes the speaking voice sound downright mad.

Psychologists say madness characterizes our time.
That may be. For some reason the sestina

is an obsession of mine. My first sestina
was a complete failure. The form
tangled me in a net. By the time
I reached stanza two, the repetition
blabbed like an obnoxious drunk. I got so mad
I swore, and swore I'd write a good sestina or else.

I worked at nothing else,
only the sestina. Day and night, one insipid sestina
after another. Every one I made made me mad.
I should never have strayed from the open forms.
They seem like a fairyland now. Repetition
enchants the mind until time

itself seems to be a sestina. In no time
my universe was bound to six words and nothing else
mattered. That's the danger of repetition.
It creates an illusion of eternity. The sestina
appears to be its own heaven. The form,
fulfilled, has that appeal. So does mad-

ness, psychologists say. But the mad
are their own poems. Their time
is malleable—no need to conform
to architecture designed by someone else.
The maker of sestinas
sulks under the weight of repetition,

flails in a snarl of repetition,
repeating himself like a nervous zodiac for his nomad
mind. So stay away from sestinas.
There are better ways to spend your time.
Write a novel. Take up the guitar. Or else
stifle your creative impulses altogether. Chloroform

the Muse! This form is a hungry monster.
Repetition wants something else every time. Six
mad kings and you, locked in a cell—that's a sestina.

Philip Levine
———

Animals are Passing from Our Lives

It's wonderful how I jog
on four honed-down ivory toes
my massive buttocks slipping
like oiled parts with each light step.

I'm to market. I can smell
the sour, grooved block, I can smell
the blade that opens the hole
and the pudgy white fingers

that shake out the intestines
like a hankie. In my dreams
the snouts drool on the marble,
suffering children, suffering flies,

suffering the consumers
who won't meet their steady eyes
for fear they could see. The boy
who drives me along believes

that any moment I'll fall
on my side and drum my toes
like a typewriter or squeal
and shit like a new housewife

discovering television,
or that I'll turn like a beast
cleverly to hook his teeth
with my teeth. No. Not this pig.

Blasting from Heaven

The little girl won't eat her sandwich;
she lifts the bun and looks in, but the grey beef
     coated with relish is always there.
     Her mother says, "Do it for mother."
Milk and relish and a hard bun that comes off
     like a hat—a kid's life is a cinch.

     And a mother's life? "What can you do
with a man like that?" she asks the sleeping cook
     and then the old Negro who won't sit.
     "He's been out all night trying to get it.
I hope he gets it. What did he ever do
     but get it?" The Negro doesn't look,

     though he looks like he's been out all night
trying. Everyone's been out all night trying.
     Why else would we be drinking beer
     at attention? If she were younger,
or if I were Prince Valiant, I would say that fate
     brought me here to quiet the crying,

     to sweeten the sandwich of the child,
to waken the cook, to stop the Negro from
     bearing witness to the world. The dawn
     still hasn't come, and now we hear
the 8 o'clock whistles blasting from heaven,
     and with no morning the day is sold.

WAKING AN ANGEL

Sparrows quarreled outside our window,
roses swelled, the cherry boughs burst
into fire, and it was spring

in the middle of a bad winter.
We have been good, she said, we have
avoided the fields, tended

our private affairs without complaint,
and this is surely our reward.
I wasn't so sure. There were

hard grey spots on the underbelly
of the ring-tailed coon that died
in the garbage, there was sand

as white as powdered glass overflowing
the vessel of the hyacinth,
there was sand on my own tongue

when I awakened at one or two
in the dark, my nostrils inflamed,
my voice crying out for her.

She wouldn't move. I put my cold hands
on her hips and rocked her gently;
O, O, O, was all she said

through set, dry lips. She was slipping
away from me. I was afraid to look
at what dense wings lifted her

out of my bedroom and my one life,
her voice still trailing O, O, O,
like a raiment of victory.

Susan Mitchell

THE DEAD

At night the dead come down to the river to drink.
They unburden themselves of their fears,
their worries for us. They take out the old photographs.
They pat the lines in our hands and tell our futures,
which are cracked and yellow.
Some dead find their way to our houses.
They go up to the attics.
They read the letters they sent us, insatiable
for signs of their love.
They tell each other stories.
They make so much noise
they wake us
as they did when we were children and they stayed up
drinking all night in the kitchen.

FOR A FRIEND EATING AN APPLE

for Chris

There is nothing I want more
than to watch you eat another apple. So please,
start from the beginning and rub a McIntosh or a Granny Smith
on your sleeve to work up a good shine.
Then, bite into it.
When I hear the first crunch of desire,
my mouth flows with the names of apples. But when I watch
you bite through the skin, my mouth fills with fruit.
Now that I have seen you eat an apple,
there can never be enough apples in the world to satisfy me.
Even if I were to buy bushels of them,
brown paper bags spilling over
with green and red and yellow apples,

there would not be enough.
Now that I have watched you eat an apple
my hand is lonely unless an apple fills it.
Only an apple appreciates what it means to have teeth.
Only an apple understands
how teeth want something to resist them,
though not too much,
how teeth want to make an impression,
then take back the impression they have made,
how teeth really don't want blood,
but only a good fight,
how teeth will go on eating and eating
through an entire lifetime
only to satisfy their secret desire
which is to find something they cannot bite through,
something like a core
they have to spit out,
just so the whole process can start over again.

Marge Piercy

———

THE BUTT OF WINTER

The city lies grey and sopping like a dead rat
under the slow oily rain.
Between the lower east side tenements
the sky is a snotty handkerchief.
The garbage of poor living slimes the streets.
You lie on your bed and think
soon it will be hot and violent,
then it will be cold and mean.
You say you feel as empty
as a popbottle in the street.
You say you feel full of cold water
standing like an old horse trough.

The clock ticks, somewhat wrong,
the walls crack their dry knuckles.
Work is only other rooms where people cough,
only the typewriter clucking like a wrong clock.
Nobody will turn the soiled water into wine,
nobody will shout cold Lazarus alive
but you. You are your own magician.
Stretch out your hand,
stretch out your hand and look:
each finger is a snake of energy,
a gaggle of craning necks.
Each electric finger conducts the world.
Each finger is a bud's eye opening.
Each finger is a vulnerable weapon.
The sun is floating in your belly like a fish.
Light creaks in your bones.
You are sleeping with your tail in your mouth.
Unclench your hands and look.
Nothing is given us but each other.
We have nothing to give
but ourselves.
We have nothing to take but the time
that drips, drips anyhow
leaving a brown stain.
Open your eyes and your belly.
Let the sun rise into your chest and burn your throat,
stretch out your hands and tear the gauzy rain
that your world can be born from you
screaming and red.

THE FRIEND

We sat across the table.
he said, cut off your hands.
they are always poking at things.
they might touch me.
I said yes.

Food grew cold on the table.
he said, burn your body.
it is not clean and smells like sex.
it rubs my mind sore.
I said yes.

I love you, I said.
that's very nice, he said
I like to be loved,
that makes me happy.
Have you cut off your hands yet?

SIMPLE-SONG

When we are going toward someone we say
you are just like me
your thoughts are my brothers
word matches word
how easy to be together.

When we are leaving someone we say
how strange you are
we cannot communicate
we can never agree
how hard, hard and weary to be together.

We are not different nor alike
but each strange in his leather body
sealed in skin and reaching out clumsy hands
and loving is an act
that cannot outlive
the open hand
the open eye
the door in the chest standing open.

David Ray

———

STOPPING NEAR HIGHWAY 80

We are not going to steal the water-tower
in Malcolm, Iowa,
just stop for a picnic right under it.
Nor need they have removed the lightbulb
in the city park
nor locked the toilet doors.
We are at peace, just eating and drinking
our *poco vino* in Malcolm, Iowa,
which evidently once had a band
to go with its bandstand.
We walk down the street, wondering how
it must be to live behind the shades
in Malcolm, Iowa, to peer out,
to remember the town as it was before
the expressway discovered
it, subtracted what would flow
on its river eastwards and westwards.

We are at peace, but when we go into the bar
in Malcolm, Iowa, we find that the aunts
and uncles drinking beer have become
monsters and want to hurt us and we do
not know how they could have ever
taken out the giant breasts
of childhood or cooked the fine biscuits
or lifted us up high on the table
or have told us anything at all
we'd ever want to know
for living lives as gentle as we can.

Vern Rutsala

LATE AT NIGHT

Not willing to exert the mind enough even to sense the quality of the lives of those nearest us, we will, however, late at night, create from scratch around a few random sounds in the cellar—pipes knocking, the furnace working—a whole human being, the prowler come to punish us for lack of love.

LUNCHROOM

The knives on the table are there for a purpose, but their true function has been forgotten over the years. Actually, the lunchroom which now appears so calm and civilized is an arena, the trays and tables converted shields, and we who sit so quietly are gladiators. The man who cleans up, the one who looks so dull, grew tired of the mess and has cleverly diverted us by serving food to slice and eat, thereby satisfying our need to use weapons, which he stealthily reduced in size until they now seem innocuous, just as he has assuaged our desire to kill by teaching us the rudiments of gossip.

The Public Lecture

No matter how good the speaker, the listeners always find him dull. A strange impatience makes its way through the room, a restlessness that shows itself in coughs and a nearly silent shifting of position. The uneasiness rises from the buried fact that this is a trial by ordeal. Far back in time the speaker lived only until he stopped talking; then he was quickly sacrificed and his flesh eaten by the audience. Not really aware of it, audiences today still await restlessly for this climax—it shows itself most clearly when pauses occur, such silence is the audience's disease—and the listeners are forced to dissipate their enormous feelings of frustration by slapping their hands together very hard when the speaker stops.

Harvey Shapiro

National Cold Storage Company

The National Cold Storage Company contains
More things than you can dream of.
Hard by the Brooklyn Bridge it stands
In a litter of freight cars,
Tugs to one side; the other, the traffic
Of the Long Island Expressway.
I myself have dropped into it in seven years
Midnight tossings, plans for escape, the shakes.
Add this to the national total—
Grant's tomb, the Civil War, Arlington,
The young President dead.
Above the warehouse and beneath the stars
The poets creep on the harp of the Bridge.
But see,
They fall into the National Cold Storage Company
One by one. The wind off the river is too cold,

Or the times too rough, or the Bridge
Is not a harp at all. Or maybe
A monstrous birth inside the warehouse
Must be fed by everything—ships, poems,
Stars, all the years of our lives.

Louis Simpson

———

AMERICAN POETRY

Whatever it is, it must have
A stomach that can digest
Rubber, coal, uranium, moons, poems.

Like the shark, it contains a shoe.
It must swim for miles through the desert
Uttering cries that are almost human.

———

ON THE LAWN AT THE VILLA

On the lawn at the villa—
That's the way to start, eh, reader?
We know where we stand—somewhere expensive—
You and I *imperturbes,* as Walt would say,
Before the diversions of wealth, you and I *engagés.*

On the lawn at the villa
Sat a manufacturer of explosives,
His wife from Paris,
And a young man named Bruno,

And myself, being American,
Willing to talk to these malefactors,

The manufacturer of explosives, and so on,
But somehow superior. By that I mean democratic.
It's complicated, being an American,
Having the money and the bad conscience, both at the same time.
Perhaps after all, this is not the right subject for a poem.

We were all sitting there paralyzed
In the hot Tuscan afternoon,
And the bodies of the machine-gun crew were draped over the balcony.
So we sat there all afternoon.

Elizabeth Spires

SALEM, MASSACHUSETTS: 1692

". . . there are accounts of ignorant rustics tying the thumbs and toes of a supposed witch together and throwing her into a pond, where if she floated she was a witch, and if she sank, as was most likely, she usually died from the ill usage. It is gratifying to know that Matthew Hopkins, the notorious witchfinder, met his death in this manner at the hands of some country fellows who believed him to be a wizard."

Robert Fletcher
The Witches' Pharmacopoeia

You also believed, Matthew Hopkins,
that we had a third teat and a *witch's spot*
which, when probed with pins or needles, was insensitive
to pain. How you could disregard the terrible shrieks
from those who knew nothing of our craft,
simple churchgoing women,
as well as our own, even we do not understand.

Perhaps we would have been less vengeful
if our deaths had been by fire—the exhilarating sensation
(after the first scalding) of going up in smoke,
of our grease dropping like rain on our sisters
enabling them
to fly through the night, uneasy shadows on your bedroom wall.
Or even being hung,
a quick snap of the neck, nothing more, then the planting
in the ground, in the crevice near Gallows Hill where
    twenty-two were hung,
and nurturing the mandrake, belladonna, nightshade—
demons from which our powers are derived.

Anything but this jelly to strain through,
the eternal shiver,
the feeling of being in a fog, of never seeing the moon!

We made you look a little strange
to those twisted rustics hungry for another victim.
The earlobes, just a little too pointed,
the hair tinged with trickles of green.
And during the trial,
remember when your nervous laugh and protestations
dissolved into unwilling cackles? So terrifying
the children rolled on the floor foaming at the mouth!
We were responsible for it all.
We were waiting for you, Matthew Hopkins, down there
under the dull pond water. We had all the time in the world
to untie our thumbs and toes,
draw the pins out of our skirts, pricks up,
then wait as you floated down
instead of up,
proving not that you were our kind,
but only a torturer, the weakest sort of man.

Richard Tillinghast

SAILING NEAR SORRENTO

Let the boat luff—jib and main swing free.
Wind drops, wrinkling the green
Tide that shuffles down towards Capri
Burning yellow in the setting sun.
We yawn and stretch and talk of where we've been—
Been all over Europe, tired of the civilized world,
Tired and sleepy, rocking, peacefully lulled.

The US Navy jets drone over again,
Their vapor trails scoring the sky above
The old Etruscan fort set among green
Olive trees. The manic engines rave
And pop the eardrum of the sky as they dive
In practice at the harbor, wrenching sound from sight.
It is rehearsal for the death of light.

Our words hang up in the wind, fused by a flash
Of thought, and powdered dry. We are dumb
As Hiroshima, canceled in the hush
That follows the blast. We shall be made one
With the sea-sucked bones of dead sailors, Ulysses' men
Sunk in the Mediterranean storm—finger
Fused to finger in the neutrons' instant hunger.

Sherley Anne Williams

FLO SHOW

work two ways, baby.
We together and I hear
you breathin, the
air raspin over tongue
and teeth and lips
we come together or apart
and it don't matter.
You mine. I made you
in the private night:
Makin work mo ways than one
and I have put it on yo mind.

I'm cool round yo friends
laugh at yo jive, by-side
you with a smile.
But it is on yo mind
you still feel little pointy
breasts and crisp spiky
hair? Is it what you seen in them
other mens' eyes that make
you have to flo show
me with yo hands
claim me, say this is mine?
"mine" work mo ways than one,
baby.

THE PEACOCK SONG

They don't like to see you with
yo tail draggin low so I
try to hold mines up high. No
one want to know where you go-

in til after you been and
even though I told em ain't
nobody heard. How a peacock
gon speak: I got no tongue.

                        Here
I come with my pigeon-toed
strut and my head is up for
balance and so they can look
in my eyes. See that sty? that
was from beggin; that callus
come from brushin against all
the some ones I met on my
way to been . . . or is it, am?
I never do know. But I
was trying to make em feel
that I need a little heart
rubbin, soul scrubbin; this is
real. But if I'm a peacock
my feathers' s'posed to cover
all hurts and if you want to
stay one then you got to keep
that tail from draggin so mines
is always held up sky high.

Charles Wright

AMERICAN LANDSCAPE

> *For Dick Runyan, in Montana*

   I.

It's April, still winter where
The otter and wolverine, the elk
And porcupine must search for food.

Down in the meadow, along the banks of the creek,
The ghost-weed and Indian paintbrush
Are several months away.

2.

There, in the Yaak, what will they say
As they ease you into your new life,
Indian, gyppo, child of the river's pulse?

What will they say in that small field
Heavy, now, with all of your family?

3.

We enter into the earth like shoots,
Throwing off tendrils, our fingers
Growing, joints loosening like water.

These roots go down forever,
Inch by inch, stone by stone, working
Toward some improbable center.

Above us, our single, unmoving branch
Gathers the sunlight and will not bloom.

4.

Up near Mount-Caribou, the snow-owl
—Almost invisible against a white sky—
Planes down, looking for sleep;

The bear, feeling the new fingers take hold
In that hard earth, turns in his dream,
Thinking a flame has blown through his bones;

And the deer pause; and listen—hearing, it seems,
Your fingers dislodge the sharp stones.

5.
What does one say? What *can* one say:
That death is without a metric,
That it has no metaphor?

That what will remain is what always remains:
The snow; the dark pines, their boughs
Heavy with moisture, and failing;

The clearings we might have crossed;
The footprints we do not leave?

———

APRIL

The plum tree breaks out in bees.
A gull is locked like a ghost in the blue attic of heaven.
The wind goes nattering on,
Gossipy, ill at ease, in the damp rooms it will air.
I count off the grace and stays
My life has come to, and know I want less—

Divested of everything,
A downfall of light in the pine woods, motes in the rush,
Gold leaf through the undergrowth, and come back
As another name, water
Pooled in the black leaves and holding me there, to be
Released as a glint, as a flash, as a spark . . .

THE NEW POEM

It will not resemble the sea.
It will not have dirt on its thick hands.
It will not be part of the weather.

It will not reveal its name.
It will not have dreams you can count on.
It will not be photogenic.

It will not attend our sorrow.
It will not console our children.
It will not be able to help us.

James Wright

AUTUMN BEGINS IN MARTINS FERRY, OHIO

In the Shreve High football stadium,
I think of Polacks nursing long beers in Tiltonsville,
And gray faces of Negroes in the blast furnace at Benwood,
And the ruptured night watchman of Wheeling Steel,
Dreaming of heroes.

All the proud fathers are ashamed to go home.
Their women cluck like starved pullets,
Dying for love.

Therefore,
Their sons grow suicidally beautiful
At the beginning of October,
And gallop terribly against each other's bodies.

A Blessing

Just off the highway to Rochester, Minnesota,
Twilight bounds softly forth on the grass.
And the eyes of those two Indian ponies
Darken with kindness.
They have come gladly out of the willows
To welcome my friend and me.
We step over the barbed wire into the pasture
Where they have been grazing all day, alone.
They ripple tensely, they can hardly contain their happiness
That we have come.
They bow shyly as wet swans. They love each other.
There is no loneliness like theirs.
At home once more,
They begin munching the young tufts of spring in the darkness.
I would like to hold the slenderer one in my arms,
For she has walked over to me
And nuzzled my left hand.
She is black and white,
Her mane falls wild on her forehead,
And the light breeze moves me to caress her long ear
That is delicate as the skin over a girl's wrist.
Suddenly I realize
That if I stepped out of my body I would break
Into blossom.

LYING IN A HAMMOCK AT WILLIAM DUFFY'S FARM IN PINE ISLAND,
MINNESOTA

Over my head, I see the bronze butterfly,
Asleep on the black trunk,
Blowing like a leaf in green shadow.
Down the ravine behind the empty house,
The cowbells follow one another
Into the distances of the afternoon.
To my right,
In a field of sunlight between two pines,
The droppings of last year's horses
Blaze up into golden stones.
I lean back, as the evening darkens and comes on.
A chicken hawk floats over, looking for home.
I have wasted my life.

David Young

ELEGY IN THE FORM OF AN INVITATION

James Wright, b. 1927, Martin's Ferry, Ohio: d. 1980, New York City

Early spring in Ohio. Lines
of thunderstorms, quiet flares
on the southern horizon.
A doctor stares at his hands.
His friend the schoolmaster
plays helplessly with a thread.

I know you have put your voice aside
and entered something else.
I like to think you could come back here now
like a man returning to his body
after a long dream of pain and terror.

It wouldn't be all easy:
sometimes the wind blows birds
right off their wires and branches,
chemical wastes smolder on weedy sidings,
codgers and crones still starve in shacks
in the hills above Portsmouth and Welfare . . .
hobo, cathouse, slagheap, old mines
that never exhaust their veins—
it is all the way you said.

But there is this fierce green
and bean shoots poking through potting soil
and in a month or so the bees
will move like sparks among the roses.
And I like to think
the things that hurt won't hurt you any more
and that you will come back
in the spring, for the quiet,
the dark shine of grackles,
raccoon tracks by the river,
the moon's ghost in the afternoon,
and the black earth behind the plowing.

The University of Wisconsin Press

The University of Wisconsin Press Poetry Series was first proposed in 1978 by Ronald Wallace and Kelly Cherry, who taught in the English department's creative writing program. Although individual editors at the Press were sympathetic, the director was not, and the idea was rejected.

In 1982, a turnover in Press personnel prompted Wallace to try again. This time, Allen Fitchen, the new press director who had been the senior editor at the University of Chicago Press, and Peter Givler, the new humanities editor who had worked for Scribner's in New York, along with several others—Don Anderson, who had started the Poetry Book Club at L.S.U. Press, and Gordon Lester-Massman and Steve Miller, who were themselves poets—enthusiastically approved the project. With a generous grant from the Brittingham Trust (established by Thomas E. Brittingham to benefit the university community), the press announced the series in 1984 and published the first book in 1985. When Givler left to direct the Ohio State University Press in 1985, he was replaced by Barbara Hanrahan as humanities editor.

Manuscripts are screened by writers in the English department and editors at the Press, and the final selection is made by a distinguished outside judge in consultation with Ronald Wallace, the general editor of the series. C. K. Williams, Maxine Kumin, Mona Van Duyn, Charles Wright, and Gerald Stern selected the first five volumes. The winning manuscript of the annual competition receives the $500 Brittingham Prize in Poetry, and is published by the Press in an edition of 500 hardback and 1500 paperback.

Jim Daniels

MAY'S POEM

"I want to write a poem
about something beautiful,"
I tell May, the cook.
On my break from the grill
I stand against the open kitchen door
getting stoned.

"That shit make you stupid."
May wrinkles her forehead
in waves of disapproval.

"I don't need to be smart
to work here."
The grease sticks to my skin
a slimy reminder
of what my future holds.

"I thought you was gonna be
a writer. What about that
beautiful poem?"

I take a long hit
and pinch out the joint.
"You'll end up no good
like my boy Gerald."

"May, I'm gonna make you
a beautiful poem," I say
and I turn and grab her
and hug her to me
pick her up
and twirl her in circles
our sweaty uniforms sticking
together, her large breasts

heaving in my face
as she laughs and laughs
and the waitresses all come back
and the dishwasher who never smiles
makes a noise that could be
half a laugh.

But she's heavy
and I have to put her down.
The manager stands there:
"Play time's over. Break's over."
Everyone walks away
goes back to work.

This isn't my beautiful poem, I know.
My poem would have no manager
no end to breaks.
My poem would have made her lighter.
My poem would have never put her down.

―――――

My Grandfather's Tools

Lifetime tinkerer, fixer upper
always with his shiny tools
in his basement, his workbench
scarred wood blessed with oil
an altar to patience and a steady hand.

My grandfather, the unpaid Mr. Fixit
for the church across the street
and their rectory, convent, school.
My grandfather, no true believer
hedges bets with his tools.

He worked for Packard nearly fifty years,
all his life his joy

that feel of tool in hand—
his knife, his gun, his fistful of bills—
showing the engineers how things
really worked.

His old Packard still runs
despite all logic—
his eternal child
as long as he can get the parts.

Over eighty years, still greasing
his hands under the hood of a car,
black magic balm under his nails,
still a firm grip on the tools.

My grandfather sleeps in his front room
while I pound on the door
a radio apart on the floor
alone with his tools
the reflection of steel.

He replaces a casting in the steering column
and loses reverse gear.
He charges tools on his credit card,
forgets, my father pays the bills.

The logic of dying escapes him,
no wrench or screwdriver to save
his thinning body. I smell death
in his hands: already dirt is gone
from under his nails.

When he dies, we'll all file down
into his basement to sort tools hanging
from hooks, filling drawers, shelves, toolboxes,
and we'll hold them in our hands, feel their weight,
pallbearers carrying off those clean bones,
no one there to carve them back
into tools.

PLACES EVERYONE

"There's a place for everyone in our organization."

The best-looking women
work in bedding.
The fat, wholesome women who smell like cookies
work in kitchen.
In china and silver
the women are fragile, elegant, middle-aged.
In men's
hen-pecked grandfathers
with their pasty smiles
suck ass to sell suits.
The healthy bastards
with sons who have failed them
work in sporting goods.
All the angry people
work downstairs in the stockroom
heaving boxes in and out of trucks.
That's where all the blacks work.
I work down there
tossing boxes with them
not even trying
to match their anger.

Patricia Dobler

APHASIA

for my father

Because scared, because of *have to earn a dollar,*
because for every thing you earned, Grandaddy sat
on your shoulder saying "You're the lucky one,
if you fell into the shithole you'd come up
with a gold piece in your mouth," because traduced,
laughed at, lied to, because you trusted only your hands
and the perfect ribbons of steel rolling out of the mill,
because you never trusted words but filled a house
with the static of stockpiled things, every gadget,
every stick of furniture a barrier to the threat outside,
because you never felt at home in this world
of jokes and silences, because now you think "death"
but say "black feather," here is a garden:
pass your hand over the face of this thing you've forgotten,
this "flower." Whatever you name it, so it will be.
Hello or Forgive Me. I Loved You. Good-bye.

FIELD TRIP TO THE MILL

Sister Monica has her hands full
timing the climb to the catwalk
so the fourth-graders are lined up
before the next heat is tapped, "and no
giggling no jostling, you monkeys!
So close to the edge!" She passes out
sourballs for bribes, not liking
the smile on the foreman's face,

the way he pulls at his cap,
he's not Catholic. Protestant madness,
these field trips, this hanging from catwalks
suspended over an open hearth.

Sister Monica understands Hell
to be like this. If overhead cranes clawing
their way through layers of dark air
grew leathery wings and flew screeching
at them, it wouldn't surprise her.
And the three warning whistle blasts,
the blazing orange heat pouring out
liquid fire like Devil's soup
doesn't surprise her. She understands
Industry and Capital and Labor,
the Protestant trinity. That is why
she trembles here, the children clinging
to her as she watches them learn their future.

_____

UNCLE RUDY EXPLAINS THE EVENTS OF 1955

We laid the last course of firebrick
in the big 3-storey kiln when something broke upstairs.
Us brickies on the kiln bottom held our breath
at the first whiff of lime, we knew that stuff
could blind you, burn your lungs.
Each man found another man's hand
before shutting his eyes, so we inched out
that way—like kids, eyes shut tight
and holding hands. Climbed the ladder, finally up
to sweet air, the lime falling like snow
and burning our skin all the way.
That was the winter I found a rabbit
in one of my traps still alive.
The noise he made. "Quit it quit it quit it."
Lord, just like a person. So I quit.

David Kirby

THE COWS ARE GOING TO PARIS: A PASTORAL

The cows are going to Paris;
when they boarded the train
at Corbeil and Fontainebleau
the people were frightened
and ran out into the fields and meadows
and chewed the grass in terror,

and now the cows are gong to
shop at the Galeries Lafayette,
stroll in the Louvre and the Jeu de Paume,
see plays produced and directed by cows,
a farce in the manner
of Georges Feydeau, for example,

in which a certain Monsieur Bull
wishes to deceive his wife,
so he arranges to meet the wife
of a friend in a hotel of low repute.
The only one who can betray him
is another monsieur who stutters

whenever it rains.
And of course it rains:
"M-m-mooo!" he says, "M-m-m-moooo!"
The cows are delighted;
they have never thought of the rain
as having so much meaning until now.

And when the deceived monsieur
grabs a sword in order to
pierce the innards of his false friend,
the cows are absolutely enthralled,
it having never occurred to them
that the slaughter of their species

413

could be occasioned by anything
other than the desire to eat
or make money, that it could have
rage as its cause,
a feeling of betrayal,
the breaking of a heart.

Meanwhile, the people from the train
have made themselves comfortable
under the trees;
the diet of the cows
is nourishing and unrefined,

and somehow it seems natural
to stand in small groups for hours,
saying nothing. Indeed,
when the cows return
to the fields and meadows,

the people will not get back on board
and must be prodded
before they enter the cars.
Having been to the city, the cows understand;
to them, the people are like

the nymphs and shepherds in the painting
by Watteau who are made to leave
the isle of forgetfulness and so set out
for the fallen world, but slowly,
and not without a mournful backward glance.

THE LATE NEWS

The anchorwoman is unsmiling, even somber,
for her biggest stories are about death,
and even when she has a feature
on a twelve year-old college student
or a gorilla who understands sign language,
there is something tentative about her relief:
she knows that the Great Antagonist
will strike again, and soon.

The weatherman smiles a lot,
but he is making the best of a bad thing,
for the weather is necessary, yes,
but boring. As for the actors
in the commercials, they are jovial
yet insincere, for they do not love the lotions,
sprays, and gargles they urge us to buy,
products that are bad for us anyway and overpriced.

Only the sportscaster is happy, for sports news
is good news: money always changes hands,
and if someone has lost that day, someone else has won.
Should anyone die, that's death, not sports,
and death is the anchorwoman's department.
Even if the Soviets should fire all their missiles at us
and vice versa, the sportscaster will still be happy:
you can't cover everything in a half hour,

for crissakes, and sports will be all that is left.
There will be no jobs to go to, and our cars won't work,
and there will be no electricity,
but you can make a ball out of anything,
and then all you need is a line to get it across
or a hoop to put it through. The sportscaster knows
how the world will end: not with a whimper,
not with a bang, but with a cheer.

THEOLOGY FROM THE VIEWPOINT OF A YOUNGER SON

My younger son, still in kindergarten,
wants to now how Jesus died.
I give him the biblical version,
but talk of scourging and crucifixion
only confuses him, and finally he says,
"I thought he was fooling around with a knife."
If that were the case, I say,
the New Testament would be another story altogether,
and the magnificent cathedrals of Europe
would be so different, the crosses over the altar
replaced with great shiny blades. . . .

Listen, you little heresiarch,
you're not the first comedian in church history.
Take St. Martin: the crippled beggars
of Touraine took flight at the approach
of his miraculous corpse, fearing the saint
would heal and thus impoverish them,
which he did anyway, just to teach them a lesson.
Or St. Brendan the Navigator, who made camp
on the back of a whale, discovering his mistake
only after he had lit a fire for supper.

The devil is grim, he does not laugh,
but we do. It's not easy, being a younger son,
having so many masters. "We too must write bibles,"
says Emerson. Besides, the world is so stupid.
No amount of explanation is sufficient, sonny.
You're right: he was fooling around with a knife.

Lisa Zeidner

A BOMB

Afterwards, we'll all remember
having seen it coming.
A trick of mind, like déjà-vu:
how sometimes, while being witty
over drinks, with dishes
in the sink or hand on the door
of a cabinet wherein lie
the last cashews dusted with salt
at the bottom of a jar
when you're not even hungry,
the mind summons a picture of a place
shocking in its specificity—

a certain block, a house belonging
to no one you knew in the old
neighborhood, or turning a corner
in a city you visited once
on business years ago
and haven't thought about since.
So hard to accept
irrelevance, irregularity.

Much easier to think the picture means
to tell you something, warn you,
but of what? Of where you'll die?
Maybe, since all your death will be—

all anybody's—is that shudder
like a random memory, not a burglar
at the back door but something
on the house's own quirky,
undecipherable Richter Scale,
so minor you must have imagined it.

───────

HAPPINESS

What it is
is the absence of pain. Nothing more.

Over a decade of life in the bull's eye
of troubled cities in the Northeastern corridor

and I've never been raped,
never stabbed, burglarized, or even mugged

though I hate to say or even think
I never get colds

or hear a sportscaster brag
about a basketball player's percentage from the line

before the foul shot that would win the game:
why wave a red flag in the bull's face

if the bull is God
in happy pastures, chewing the grass?

Infinite disasters and fender-benders lurk
around each corner

like the black holes that claim stray socks
at the laundromat.

Best to notice happiness peripherally,
the way walking in a city

you take in a pretty weed
growing from a sidewalk crack

or a woman with slim ankles
passing briskly—to meet someone for a drink

perhaps, a man she has not seen,
back whole from a treasure hunt or war.

You, too, have someone waiting at home
and for a goosebumped second you know

that you are loved. That nothing,
at least today, has gone wrong.

Yale University Press

The oldest university press poetry series in the country, the Yale Series of Younger Poets was begun in 1919 when Clarence Day (author of *Life With Father*) proposed it to his brother, George Parmly Day (the first director of the Press). The series was designed to publish first books only, and, with some exceptions, that policy has continued to the present. Early editors of the series were typically Yale English professors, but as the series gained in prestige, established poets were appointed to make the selections. Over the past forty years the series has been edited by W. H. Auden (1946–58), Dudley Fitts (1959–69), Stanley Kunitz (1970–76), Richard Hugo (1977–82), and James Merrill (1983–present). Manuscripts, solicited in an annual open competition, are screened by Press readers who send finalists on to the series editor for a decision.

Yale publishes one first book per year in an edition of 800 cloth and 2,200 paper.

Thomas Bolt, *Out of the Woods*, 1988
Julie Agoos, *Above the Land*, 1987
George Bradley, *Terms To Be Met*, 1986
Pamela Alexander, *Navigable Waterways*, 1985
Richard Kenney, *The Evolution of the Flightless Bird*, 1984
Cathy Song, *Picture Bride*, 1983
David Wojahn, *Icehouse Lights*, 1982
John Bensko, *Green Soldiers*, 1981
William Virgil Davis, *One Way To Reconstruct the Scene*, 1980
Leslie Ullman, *Natural Histories*, 1979
Bin Ramke, *The Difference Between Night and Day*, 1978
Olga Broumas, *Beginning With O*, 1977
Carolyn Forché, *Gathering the Tribes*, 1976
Maura Stanton, *Snow on Snow*, 1975
Michael Ryan, *Threats Instead of Trees*, 1974

Robert Hass, *Field Guide*, 1973
Michael Casey, *Obscenities*, 1972
Peter Klappert, *Lugging Vegetables to Nantucket*, 1971
Hugh Seidman, *Collecting Evidence*, 1970
Judith Johnson Sherwin, *Uranium Poems*, 1969
Helen Chasin, *Coming Close and Other Poems*, 1968
James Tate, *The Lost Pilot*, 1967
Daniel G. Hoffman, *An Armada of Thirty Whales*, 1966
Jean Valentine, *Dream Barker*, 1965
Peter Davison, *The Breaking of the Day*, 1964
Sandra Hochman, *Manhattan Pastures*, 1963
Jack Gilbert, *Views of Jeopardy*, 1962
Alan Dugan, *Poems*, 1961
George Starbuck, *Bone Thoughts*, 1960
William Dickey, *Of the Festivity*, 1959
John Hollander, *A Crackling of Thorns*, 1958
James Arlington Wright, *The Green Wall*, 1957
John Ashbery, *Some Trees*, 1956
W. S. Merwin, *The Dancing Bears*, 1954
Edgar Bogardus, *Various Jangling Keys*, 1953
W. S. Merwin, *A Mask for Janus*, 1952
Adrienne Cecile Rich, *A Change of World*, 1951
Rosaline Moore, *The Grasshopper's Man*, 1949
Robert Horan, *A Beginning*, 1948
Joan Murray, *Poems*, 1947
Eve Merriam, *Family Circle*, 1946
Charles Edward Butler, *Cut is the Branch*, 1945
William Meredith, *Love Letter From an Impossible Land*, 1944
Margaret Walker, *For My People*, 1943
Jeremy Ingalls, *The Metaphysical Sword*, 1941
Norman Rosten, *Return Again, Traveler*, 1940
Reuel Denney, *The Connecticut River*, 1939
Joy Davidman, *Letter To a Comrade*, 1938
Margaret Haley, *The Gardener Mind*, 1937
Edward Weismiller, *The Deer Come Down*, 1936

Muriel Rukeyser, *Theory of Flight*, 1935
James Agee, *Permit Me Voyage*, 1934
Shirley Barker, *The Dark Hills Under*, 1933
Paul H. Engle, *Worn Earth*, 1932
Dorothy Belle Flanagan, *Dark Certainty*, 1931
Louise Owen, *Virtuosa*, 1930
Henri Faust, *Half-light and Overtones*, 1929
Francis M. Frost, *Hemlock Wall*, 1929
Mildred Bowers, *Twist O' Smoke*, 1928
Francis Clairborne Mason, *This Unchanging Mask*, 1928
Ted Olson, *A Stranger and Afraid*, 1928
Lindley Williams Hubbell, *Dark Pavilion*, 1927
Thomas Hornsby Ferril, *High Passage*, 1926
Eleanor Slater, *Quest*, 1926
Dorothy E. Reid, *Coach into Pumpkin*, 1925
Elizabeth Jessup Blake, *Up and Down*, 1924
Hervey Allen, *The Blindman: A Ballad of Noqent l'Artaud*, 1923
Marion M. Boyd, *Silver Wands*, 1923
Beatrice E. Harmon, *Mosaics*, 1923
Dean Belden Lyman, Jr., *The Last Lutanist*, 1923
Paul Tanaquil (Jacques Georges Clemenceau LeClercq), *Sotto Voce: A Poet's Pack*, 1923
Amos Niven Wilder, *Battle-retrospect*, 1923
Medora C. Addison, *Dreams and a Sword*, 1922
Bernard Raymund, *Hidden Waters*, 1922
Harold Vinal, *White April*, 1922
Theodord Howard Banks, Jr., *Wild Geese*, 1921
Viola Chittenden White, *Horizons*, 1921
Oscar Williams, *The Golden Darkness*, 1921
Alfred Raymond Bellinger, *Spires and Poplars*, 1920
Darl Macleod Boyle, *Where Lilith Dances*, 1920
Thomas Caldecot Chubb, *The White God*, 1920
David Osborne Hamilton, *Four Gardens*, 1920
Howard Swazey Buck, *The Tempering*, 1919
John Chipman Farrar, *Forgotten Shrines*, 1919

John Ashbery

THE PAINTER

Sitting between the sea and the buildings
He enjoyed painting the sea's portrait.
But just as children imagine a prayer
Is merely silence, he expected his subject
To rush up the sand, and, seizing a brush
Plaster its own portrait on the canvas.

So there was never any paint on his canvas
Until the people who lived in the buildings
Put him to work: "Try using the brush
As a means to an end. Select, for a portrait,
Something less angry and large, and more subject
To a painter's moods, or, perhaps, to a prayer."

How could he explain to them his prayer
That nature, not art, might usurp the canvas?
He chose his wife for a new subject,
Making her vast, like ruined buildings,
As if, forgetting itself, the portrait
Had expressed itself without a brush.

Slightly encouraged, he dipped his brush
In the sea, murmuring a heartfelt prayer:
"My soul, when I paint this next portrait
Let it be you who wrecks the canvas."
The news spread like wildfire through the buildings:
He had gone back to the sea for his subject.

Imagine a painter crucified by his subject!
Too exhausted even to lift his brush,
He provoked some artists leaning from the buildings
To malicious mirth: "We haven't a prayer
Now, of putting ourselves on canvas,
Or getting the sea to sit for a portrait!"

Others declared it a self-portrait.
Finally all indications of a subject
Began to fade, leaving the canvas
Perfectly white. He put down the brush.
At once a howl, that was also a prayer,
Arose from the overcrowded buildings.

They tossed him, the portrait, from the tallest of the buildings;
And the sea devoured the canvas and the brush
As though his subject had decided to remain a prayer.

SOME TREES

These are amazing; each
Joining a neighbor, as though speech
Were a still performance.
Arranging by chance

To meet as far this morning
From the world as agreeing
With it, you and I
Are suddenly what the trees try

To tell us we are:
That their merely being there
Means something; that soon
We may touch, love, explain.

And glad not to have invented
Such comeliness, we are surrounded:
A silence already filled with noises,
A canvas on which emerges

A chorus of smiles, a winter morning.
Placed in a puzzling light, and moving,
Our days put on such reticence
These accents seem their own defense.

George Bradley

Aubade

Once in a great while, you might open your eyes
Into bright sunlight and think you are somewhere else.
Say Sardegna in '76, early one morning in Olbia—
The sun is red and huge, rising over the bay,
And the day is already warm; the town is weathered,
Worn to the colors of a pastel sketch, like the eyes
Of a man who has been drunk most of his life—
Bleached by the sun, or washed out by memory? There
Is no way of knowing, and of course you can never go back.
To speak the same words, to stand the same ground
Will not suffice, and the thought itself accomplishes
Nothing. All of it, Olbia, that sun, yourself one morning,
Is whirling away like the speed of light, and you
Are borne into a life irretrievably infused with a reality
Beyond recall, so that there is no telling how you arrived
In the sunshine, confused, waking as from dreams.

In Suspense

at the Verrazano Narrows Bridge

The composition of many particulars
Held the broad promise of our beginning
And so we set out calmly into the sky,
Out over sheer space and distant waters
Where other travellers had found harbor;
It was the gothic grandeur, the bright towers,
By which we knew the magnitude of our attempt,
Rushing forward into the expanding light.

The structure of our adventure, the road
We went by, protected us from the view
Beneath us, and it was the monumental
Objects, distant caricatures of themselves,
Which tried to occupy our attention.
Having come so far, we reached the summit:
A surprise, we hadn't been paying attention
To much besides a perception of ourselves
As puny and audacious, caught in a monumental
Undertaking; but now the panoramic view
Of our accomplishment, the end of the road,
Presented itself in the soft, reflected light.
We felt, of course, elevated in our attempt,
Inspired by the reach of the last aspiring tower,
Felt fulfilled in the wish each of us harbors
To journey and return safely off the waters;
And so we were set down out of the sky
According to the prescriptions of our beginning
Into a difficult place, though we weren't particular.

Olga Broumas

ARTEMIS

Let's not have tea. White wine
eases the mind along
the slopes
of the faithful body, helps

any memory once engraved
on the twin
chromosome ribbons, emerge, tentative
from the archaeology of an excised past.

I am a woman
who understands
the necessity of an impulse whose goal or origin
still lie beyond me. I keep the goat

for more
than the pastoral reasons. I work
in silver the tongue-like forms
that curve round a throat

an arm-pit, the upper
thigh, whose significance stirs in me
like a curviform alphabet
that defies

decoding, appears
to consist of vowels, beginning with O, the O-
mega, horseshoe, the cave of sound.
What tiny fragments

survive, mangled into our language.
I am a woman committed to
a politics
of transliteration, the methodology

of a mind
stunned at the suddenly
possible shifts of meaning—for which
like amnesiacs

in a ward on fire, we must
find words
or burn.

CINDERELLA

. . . the joy that isn't shared I heard, dies young.
            —Anne Sexton, 1928–1974

Apart from my sisters, estranged
from my mother, I am a woman alone
in a house of men
who secretly
call themselves princes, alone
with me usually, under cover of dark. I am the one allowed in

to the royal chambers, whose small foot conveniently
fills the slipper of glass. The woman writer, the lady
umpire, the madam chairman, anyone's wife.
I know what I know.
And I once was glad

of the chance to use it, even alone
in a strange castle, doing overtime on my own, cracking
the royal code. The princes spoke
in their fathers' language, were eager to praise me
my nimble tongue. I am a woman in a state of siege, alone

as one piece of laundry, strung on a windy clothesline a
mile long. A woman co-opted by promises: the lure
of a job, the ruse of a choice, a woman forced
to bear witness, falsely
against my kind, as each
other sister was judged inadequate, bitchy, incompetent,
jealous, too thin, too fat. I know what I know.

What sweet bread I make
for myself in this prosperous house
is dirty, what good soup I boil turns
in my mouth to mud. Give
me my ashes. A cold stove, a cinder-block pillow, wet
canvas shoes in my sisters', my sisters' hut. Or I swear

I'll die young
like those favored before me, hand-picked each one
for her joyful heart.

Peter Davison

FINALE: PRESTO

"I think I'm going to die," I tried to say.
My husband, standing over the bed, labored
To hear words in the sounds as they emerged.
He shook his head as briskly as a dog
Taking its first steps on land, and acted deaf
To the words he knew he might have heard me speak.
Throughout this evil month I've said the same
To every visitor. It comes out gibberish.
The night nurse, hiding in my room to smoke,
My daughter, prattling anxiously of clothes,
My son, weary from four hundred miles
Of travel every weekend—all escape
By smiling, talking, plumping up my pillows.
I wrack myself to utter any word;
They reply, "Dear, I cannot understand you."
If I could move this hand, this leg, I'd write
Or stamp a fury on the sterile floor.
I'd act the eagle. I, who winced at death
If the neighbor's second cousin passed at ninety,

Who bore an ounce of pain so awkwardly
It might have been a ton, who fed myself
With visions of good order in a future
Near enough to reach for—I am cumbered
With armlessness, with leglessness, with silence.
To say the word so anyone could hear it!
Death, do you hear me, death? The room is empty.
Only the one word now, hearers or no.
I batter at it with convulsive shouts
That resonate like lead. Again. And now—
Listen—it rings out like a miracle.
No one stands near. The corridor is dark.
"Death." I sing the lovely word again,
And footsteps start to chatter down the hall
Towards my bed. Smiling at every sound,
I see that no one can arrive in time,
And I, emptying like water from a jug,
Will be poured out before a hand can right me.
That word raised echoes of a halleluia.
Death, do you hear me singing in your key?

_____

THE KEEPSAKE

What a jewel he had won for his treasury!
A memory thorny as porcupines,
Hard as a gallstone. His bad dream, distilled
From such ingredients as moonshine, lovers' sweat,
And the purr of voices husky with self-deception,
Slept like a tumor—arrested, of course, or no hope
To survive at all. Yet, though the growth lay still
And was hard to remember at the best of times,
It wakened to supply him with a twinge when
He was tired, a bleeding in despair,
A paralysis when prostrate. Could any man
So burdened not cringe with pride, possessor of
So shining, so ineradicable a sorrow?

Late Summer Love Song

The evening's first cricket
Shrank from your passage
As your feet whispered
Past where he pastured.

Now the sun steals
A last look through the orchard
Where you lie low,
Fragrant in meadow.

Hear my blood welcome you,
Giddy with gratitude
For what shall pass
In the intricate grass.

Alan Dugan

Love Song: I and Thou

Nothing is plumb, level or square;
   the studs are bowed, the joists
are shaky by nature, no piece fits
   any other piece without a gap
or pinch, and bent nails
   dance all over the surfacing
like maggots. By Christ
   I am no carpenter. I built
the roof for myself, the walls
   for myself, the floors
for myself, and got
   hung up in it myself. I
danced with a purple thumb
   at this house-warming, drunk
with my prime whiskey: rage.

Oh I spat rage's nails
into the frame-up of my work:
    it held. It settled plumb,
level, solid, square and true
    for that great moment. Then
it screamed and went on through,
    skewing as wrong the other way.
God damned it. This is hell,
    but I planned it, I sawed it,
I nailed it, and I
    will live in it until it kills me.
I can nail my left palm
    to the left-hand cross-piece but
I can't do everything myself.
    I need a hand to nail the right,
a help, a love, a you, a wife.

Carolyn Forché
———————

TAKING OFF MY CLOTHES

I take off my shirt, I show you.
I shaved the hair out under my arms.
I roll up my pants, I scraped off the hair
on my legs with a knife, getting white.

My hair is the color of chopped maples.
My eyes dark as beans cooked in the south.
(Coal fields in the moon on torn-up hills)

Skin polished as a Ming bowl
showing its blood cracks, its age, I have hundreds
of names for the snow, for this, all of them quiet.

In the night I come to you and it seems a shame
to waste my deepest shudders on a wall of a man.

You recognize strangers,
think you lived through destruction.
You can't explain this night, my face, your memory.

You want to know what I know?
Your own hands are lying.

Year at Mudstraw

Listen to the pine splits
crack in the stove.
Clouds down our roof like
burnt pine, milk.
The smell of come in the shack.

A breeze on the wall
from boiling tomatoes.
A baby snorts air
while it sucks me.

It was time to put apricots
out in the sun,
cover them with cheesecloth.

Nothing but the whine of bad mud
between the cabin logs.
I hum Cold Blew The Bliss
to the child, touch fattened dough.
I wait for the sound of his truck
hoeing a splutter of thawed ditch.

And when he comes he points his rifle
at the floor, lets the dog
smell his pants.

Soup's about done, my breasts
dropping from pot steam.
He slides a day's beard down my neck.
I open my clothes to his hands.

One buck in the woods, but too quick.
My nipples stiffen, his touch.
I want to swallow down his come,
something in his heart
freezes in a dead run.

Robert Hass
————

GRAVEYARD AT BOLINAS

Yews as tall as pines
and lonelier
lean to the weather there
dark against the sky.
Gulls hover,
herons ride the wind
across the bluff,
their great wings wide.

The markers are scattered like teeth
or bones among wild violets
and reedy onion grass:
Eliab Streeter,
Gamaliel St. John.
At the end of their world
these transplanted Yankees
put down roots at last
and give a sour fragrance to the air.

Sarah Ransom,
all her days an upright wife.

Velorous Hodge,
done with the slaughtering of seals.

In the shadow of a peeling eucalyptus
Eliza Granger Binns is
"With Christ, which is better"
(1852–1858).

The delicate
light green leaves of monkey flowers
(or Indian lettuce)
are tangled on her grave
in thick small curls.
I picked a bunch
thinking to make
a salad of Eliza Binns.

Afterwards I walked along the beach,
remembering how the oldest markers,
glazed by sea wind,
were effaced, clean
as driftwood, incurious
as stone. The sun was on my neck.
Some days it's not so hard to say
the quick pulse of blood
through living flesh
is all there is.

ON THE COAST NEAR SAUSALITO

1
I won't say much for the sea
except that it was, almost
the color of sour milk.

The sun in that clear
unmenacing sky was low,
angled off the grey fissure of the cliffs,
hills dark green with manzanita.

Low tide: slimed rocks
mottled brown and thick with kelp
like the huge backs of ancient tortoises
merged with the grey stone
of the breakwater, sliding off
to antediluvian depths.
The old story: here filthy life begins.

2
Fish-
ing, as Melville said,
"to purge the spleen,"
to put to task my clumsy hands
my hands that bruise by
not touching
pluck the legs from a prawn,
peel the shell off,
and curl the body twice about a hook.

3
The cabezone is not highly regarded
by fishermen, except Italians
who have the grace
to fry the pale, almost bluish flesh
in olive oil with a sprig
of fresh rosemary.

The cabezone, an ugly atavistic fish,
as old as the coastal shelf
it feeds upon
has fins of duck's-web thickness,
resembles a prehistoric toad,
and is delicately sweet.

Catching one, the fierce quiver of surprise
and the line's tension
are a recognition.

4
But it's strange to kill
for the sudden feel of life.
The danger is
to moralize
that strangeness.
Holding the spiny monster in my hands
his bulging purple eyes
were eyes and the sun was
almost tangent to the planet
on our uneasy coast.
Creature and creature,
we stared down centuries.

Peter Klappert

———

Ellie Mae Leaves in a Hurry

There's some who say she put death up her dress
and some who say they saw her pour it down.
It's not the sort of thing you want to press

so we just assumed she planned on leaving town
and gave her money for the first express.
She had some family up in Puget Sound.

Well we are married men. We've got interests.
You can't take children out like cats to drown.
It's not the sort of thing you want to press.

We didn't know she'd go and pour death down,
though most of us had heard of her distress.
We just assumed she planned on leaving town.

There's some of us who put death up her dress
but she had family up in Puget Sound.
We gave her money for the first express.

Well we are married men. We've got interests.
Though most of us had heard of her distress.
You can't take children out like cats to drown,
it's just the sort of news that gets around.

———————

PHOTOGRAPHS OF OGUNQUIT

*Abbot Lot came to Abbot Joseph and said: Father, according as I am able, I keep
my little rule, and my little fast, my prayer, meditation and contemplative silence;
and according as I am able I strive to cleanse my heart of thoughts: now what
more should I do? The elder rose up in reply and stretched out his hands to
heaven, and his fingers became like ten lamps of fire. He said: why not be totally
changed into fire?*

(The Wisdom of the Desert, *translated by Thomas Merton*)

I.

On the last day you would not
let me take your picture. The sun
was shattering on glass,
the stonewharf hurt my eyes. I was angry
and the sky would not cloud over.

You were only twenty. It was the beginning
of the last day. The fishermen
refused to see the air between us,
the full face of your smile, the full
mouth, spitting. They sat eyeing the sea.

The wind ignited your hair. I resisted
your flight and walked away
way down the beach. The beach was full
of families. Your eyes were bluegreen.
Your distress was wild and anonymous.

I resisted your flight, now what more
must I do? The rocks hurt my eyes.
I was angry. I turned. The beach
was full of families. The fishermen
looked at their lines. Children are singing.

II.

The curtains stood up and watched us,
the swollen door was forced shut, we were
warped against each other. I could not
tell you from the humid air. I wanted
to say I will not want to take your
picture to tell the truth I wanted to say
the sheets are smothering I
wanted to refuse to sleep against
the door I wanted to say the room
is standing in the corners holding its breath.
When it was over, neither of us laughed.

III.

It was one o'clock. I'm not sure
how far I walked. You walked the wharf.
We walked back.

What you've given you cannot take
out of my hands, and what I've
given is still mine to give.
I take it with me, there is sand
in the shutter. Perhaps you meant
to leave it on the chair.

                    We will fight back
with anger and recriminations,
with demands and ultimatums.
The camera is set on #4. The fishermen
saw nothing.
                I hope the bus has brought you
safely to yourself.
                    When you wouldn't pose
you said "Now what more must I do?"
Children were singing.

                    The camera
           is at the bottom of the suitcase.

W. S. Merwin

PROTEUS

By the splashed cave I found him. Not
(As I had expected) patently delusive
In a shape sea-monstrous, terrible though sleeping,
To scare all comers, nor as that bronze-thewed
Old king of Pharos with staring locks,
But under a gray rock, resting his eyes
From futurity, from the blinding crystal
Of that morning sea, his face flicked with a wisp
Of senile beard, a frail somnolent old man.

Who would harness the sea-beast
To the extravagant burden of his question
Must find him thus dreaming of his daughters,
Of porpoises and horses; then pitiless
Of an old man's complaints, unawed
At what fierce beasts are roused under his grasp,
Between the brutal ignorance of his hands
Must seize and hold him till the beast stands again
Manlike but docile, the neck bowed to answer.

I had heard in seven wise cities
Of the last shape of his wisdom: when he,
Giver of winds, father as some said
Of the triple nightmare, from the mouth of a man
Would loose the much-whistled wind of prophecy.
The nothing into which a man leans forward
Is mother of all restiveness, drawing
The body prone to falling into no
Repose at last but the repose of falling.

Wherefore I had brought foot to his island
In the dead of dawn, had picked my way
Among the creaking cypresses, the anonymous
Granite sepulchres; wherefore, beyond these,
I seized him now by sleeping throat and heel.
What were my life, unless I might be stone
To grasp him like the grave, though wisdom change
From supposition to savage supposition;
Unless the rigor of mortal hands seemed deathly?

I was a sepulchre to his pleadings,
Stone to his arguments, to his threats;
When he leapt in a bull's rage
By horn and tail I held him; I became
A mad bull's shadow, and would not leave him;
As a battling ram he rose in my hands;
My arms were locked horns that would not leave his horns;
I was the cleft stick and the claws of birds
When he was a serpent between my fingers.

Wild as heaven erupting into a child
He burst under my fists into a lion;
By mane and foot I grappled him;
Closer to him than his own strength I strained
And held him longer. The sun had fought
Almost to noon when I felt the beast's sinews
Fail, the beast's bristles fall smooth
Again to the skin of a man. I loosed him then.
The head he turned toward me wore a face of mine.

Here was no wisdom but my own silence
Echoed as from a mirror; no marine
Oracular stare but my own eyes
Blinded and drowned in their reflections;
No voice came but a voice we shared, saying,
"You prevail always, but, deathly, I am with you
Always." I am he, by grace of no wisdom,
Who to no end battles the foolish shapes
Of his own death by the insatiate sea.

Adrienne Rich

A CHANGE OF WORLD

Fashions are changing in the sphere.
Oceans are asking wave by wave
What new shapes will be worn next year;
And the mountains, stooped and grave,
Are wondering silently range by range
What if they prove too old for the change.

The little tailors busily sitting
Flashing their shears in rival haste
Won't spare time for a prior fitting—
In with the stitches, too late to baste.
They say the season for doubt has passed:
The changes coming are due to last.

AUNT JENNIFER'S TIGERS

Aunt Jennifer's tigers prance across a screen,
Bright topaz denizens of a world of green.
They do not fear the men beneath the tree;
They pace in sleek chivalric certainty.

Aunt Jennifer's fingers fluttering through her wool
Find even the ivory needle hard to pull.
The massive weight of Uncle's wedding band
Sits heavily upon Aunt Jennifer's hand.

When Aunt is dead, her terrified hands will lie
Still ringed with ordeals she was mastered by.
The tigers in the panel that she made
Will go on prancing, proud and unafraid.

————

Storm Warnings

The glass has been falling all the afternoon,
And knowing better than the instrument
What winds are walking overhead, what zone
Of gray unrest is moving across the land,
I leave the book upon a pillowed chair
And walk from window to closed window, watching
Boughs strain against the sky

And think again, as often when the air
Moves inward toward a silent core of waiting,
How with a single purpose time has traveled
By secret currents of the undiscerned
Into this polar realm. Weather abroad
And weather in the heart alike come on
Regardless of prediction.

Between foreseeing and averting change
Lies all the mastery of elements
Which clocks and weatherglasses cannot alter.
Time in the hand is not control of time,
Not shattered fragments of an instrument
A proof against the wind; the wind will rise,
We can only close the shutters.

I draw the curtains as the sky goes black
And set a match to candles sheathed in glass
Against the keyhole draught, the insistent whine
Of weather through the unsealed aperture.
This is our sole defense against the season;
These are the things that we have learned to do
Who live in troubled regions.

Cathy Song

IKEBANA

To prepare the body,
aim for the translucent perfection
you find in the sliced shavings
of a pickled turnip.
In order for this to happen,
you must avoid the sun,
protect the face
under a paper parasol
until it is bruised white
like the skin of lilies.
Use white soap
from a blue porcelain
dish for this.

Restrict yourself.
Eat the whites of things:
tender bamboo shoots,
the veins of the young iris,
the clouded eye of a fish.

Then wrap the body,
as if it were a perfumed gift,

in pieces of silk
held together with invisible threads
like a kite, weighing no more
than a handful of crushed chrysanthemums.
Light enough to float in the wind.
You want the effect
of koi moving through water.
When the light leaves
the room, twist lilacs
into the lacquered hair
piled high like a complicated shrine.
There should be tiny bells
inserted somewhere
in the web of hair
to imitate crickets
singing in a hidden grove.

Reveal the nape of the neck,
your beauty spot.
Hold the arrangement.
If your spine slacks
and you feel faint,
remember the hand-picked flower
set in the front alcove,
which, just this morning,
you so skillfully wired into place.
How poised it is!
Petal and leaf
curving like a fan,
the stem snipped and wedged
into the metal base—
to appear like a spontaneous accident.

The Youngest Daughter

The sky has been dark
for many years.
My skin has become as damp
and pale as rice paper
and feels the way
mother's used to before the drying sun
parched it out there in the fields.

     Lately, when I touch my eyelids,
my hands react as if
I had just touched something
hot enough to burn.
My skin, aspirin colored,
tingles with migraine. Mother
has been massaging the left side of my face
especially in the evenings
when the pain flares up.

This morning
her breathing was graveled,
her voice gruff with affection
when I wheeled her into the bath.
She was in a good humor,
making jokes about her great breasts,
floating in the milky water
like two walruses,
flaccid and whiskered around the nipples.
I scrubbed them with a sour taste
in my mouth, thinking:
six children and an old man
have sucked from these brown nipples.

I was almost tender
when I came to the blue bruises
that freckle her body,

places where she has been injecting insulin
for thirty years. I soaped her slowly,
she sighed deeply, her eyes closed.
It seems it has always
been like this: the two of us
in this sunless room,
the splashing of the bathwater.

In the afternoons
when she has rested
she prepares our ritual of tea and rice,
garnished with a shred of gingered fish,
a slice of pickled turnip,
a token for my white body.
We eat in the familiar silence.
She knows I am not to be trusted,
even now planning my escape.
As I toast to her health
with the tea she has poured,
a thousand cranes curtain the window,
fly up in a sudden breeze.

Maura Stanton

THE ALL-NIGHT WAITRESS

for Gail Fischer

To tell the truth, I really *am*
a balloon, I'm only rubber, shapeless,
smelly on the inside . . .
I'm growing almost invisible.
Even the truckers admire my fine
indistinctiveness, shoving their fat hands
through my heart as they cry,
"Hey, baby! You're really weird!"
Two things may happen: if the gas

explodes at the grill some night,
I'll burst through the greasy ceiling
into black, high air,
a white something children point at
from the bathroom window at 3 A.M.
Or I'll simply deflate.
Sweeping up, the day shift will find
a blob of white substance
under my uniform by the door.
"Look," they'll say, "what a strange
unnatural egg, who wants to touch it?"
Actually, I wonder how I'd
really like being locked into orbit
around the earth, watching
blue, shifting land forever—
Or how it would feel to disappear
unaccountably in the arms of some welder
who might burst into tears
& keep my rubbery guts inside his lunch box
to caress on breaks, to sing to . . .
Still it would mean escape
into a snail's consciousness, that muscular
foot which glides a steep shell
over a rocky landscape, recording passage
on a brain so small how could it hurt?

THE FISHERMAN'S WIFE

The fisherman said I was his third wish.
He washed off the salt, taught me to breathe,
kick my scissory legs & doze
trembling in the sharp straw beside him.
Now he had boots, a boat, a wife with gill-
silver skin who peered at the sky for fish.
I couldn't speak: The nets in my throat
trapped the shiny movements of words;

the new hands, glimmering in the dark,
only stuttered like ice across his back
while I gulped for the water! the water!
needing the density of his mouth.
When I mended sails, the needle pricked
seawater from my veins; the other wives
scurried out of their clogs for the priest
who rubbed me with garlic against the devil.
A pelican dipped & angled for my eyes—
yet I couldn't drown: the angry water
shoved me into the light, I washed inland,
shellfish clamped in my streaming hair.
The fisherman plucked leeches from my neck,
crying, "You're the last wish!" I saw torn
boots, the boat shattered on a rock.
I dreamed I was out at sea, but the shapes
went blue, blurred, I wasn't anything,
a chill, a wish, his wife stirring in sleep.

James Tate

THE LOST PILOT

    for my father, 1922–1944

Your face did not rot
like the others—the co-pilot,
for example, I saw him

yesterday. His face is corn-
mush: his wife and daughter,
the poor ignorant people, stare

as if he will compose soon.
He was more wronged than Job.
But your face did not rot

like the others—it grew dark,
and hard like ebony;
the features progressed in their

distinction. If I could cajole
you to come back for an evening,
down from your compulsive

orbiting, I would touch you,
read your face as Dallas,
your hoodlum gunner, now,

with the blistered eyes, reads
his braille editions. I would
touch your face as a disinterested

scholar touches an original page.
However frightening, I would
discover you, and I would not

turn you in; I would not make
you face your wife, or Dallas,
or the co-pilot, Jim. You

could return to your crazy
orbiting, and I would not try
to fully understand what

it means to you. All I know
is this: when I see you,
as I have seen you at least

once every year of my life,
spin across the wilds of the sky
like a tiny, African god,

I feel dead. I feel as if I were
the residue of a stranger's life,
that I should pursue you.

My head cocked toward the sky,
I cannot get off the ground,
and, you, passing over again,

fast, perfect, and unwilling
to tell me that you are doing
well, or that it was mistake

that placed you in that world,
and me in this; or that misfortune
placed these worlds in us.

Leslie Ullman

Breakfast

Your husband has just thrown a cup.
Your kitchen fills with sunlight.

Your hands grow
massive, capable of anything.

The folds of his beard
arrange themselves over the mouth

inside, the real mouth that never
moves. He sits down

and you face one another
and you see nothing, like people

who sit down in public.
The cup's round sides crash

gently behind your eyes. *Again and again*
you come down to the cold kitchen

and watch the steam rise from his hands.
He emptied the cup, standing at the window.

You came downstairs
thinking at first the room was empty.

You had dreamed you weren't dreaming
as he traced the line where the dark

flame of your hair touched
his face. The cup hit the floor.

Now the house shifts its weight.
The ferns in the window darken

and melt, and soon he will disappear
as usual, for good.

Your daughter enters the kitchen
not fully awake, her bare feet

missing the barely visible pieces.

David Wojahn

Heaven for Railroad Men

You're still a young man,
he says, not to his son,
it's his bitterness he's
talking to and
at the restaurant
he orders a fourth round
before dinner.
With Mother wiping
her glasses at the table,

I help him from his chair
to the john. He pees slowly,
fingers like hams
on his fly, a complex
test of logic
for a man this drunk.
I'm splashing cold water in his face

and he tells me he's dying.
Don't say a thing to your Mother,
and please, Dave,
don't ever remember me like this.

I remember how you said you
needed to ride
the baggage cars forever,
passing prairie towns
where silos squat like
pepper shakers on dry earth.

I want to be six again
and sway with you
down the sagging rails
to Minot, Winnipeg, and beyond,
your mailsacks piled
like foothills of the Rockies.

You're unloading your government Colt,
unzipping your suitcase
for Canadian inspectors.
Father, when I touched you
I was trembling.

Heaven for railroad men
begins with a collapsed trestle.
The engine goes steaming
off into nothing.
There are no rails to hold you.
You're singing country-western
at the top of your lungs.
You go flying forever,
the door pulled open,
mailsacks scattered
into space like seed.

Biographies of Poets

Guidelines for
Submissions
of Manuscripts to
University Presses

Acknowledgments

Biographies of Poets

Jack Anderson was born in Milwaukee on June 15, 1935. The author of seven books of poetry, including *The Invention of New Jersey* and *Toward the Liberation of the Left Hand,* he is a dance critic for the *New York Times.* In 1980 he received the de la Torre Bueno Prize for dance writing. (Pp. 258–61)

John Ashbery was born in Rochester, New York, in 1927, and was educated at Harvard, Columbia, and New York University. His books include *Some Trees, The Double Dream of Spring, Shadow Train,* and *Self-Portrait in a Convex Mirror,* which won the Pulitzer Prize and the National Book Award. He is currently art critic for *Newsweek.* (Pp. 358–59, 424–25)

Susan Astor was born in New York City in 1946. Her poetry has appeared widely in such magazines as *Confrontation, The Paris Review, Partisan Review,* and *Poet Lore,* and in her first book, *Dame.* She teaches full time as a freelance Poet in the Schools. In 1985 she won the Award of Excellence of Composers and Songwriters International for the lyrics to a song trilogy. (Pp. 99–100)

Michael Benedikt was born in New York City. His books include *The Badminton at Great Barrington, Sky,* and *The Body,* as well as five anthologies of twentieth-century literature in translation. He has had grants from NEA and the Guggenheim Foundation, and has been a contributing editor for *Art News* and *Art International.* (Pp. 359–60)

Beth Bentley was born in St. Paul, Minnesota, in 1926. Her books include *Phone Calls From the Dead* and *Country of Resemblances,* as well as a selection of the *Poems of Hazel Hall.* She spent an NEA grant in France, and has since published translations of contemporary French poets. She teaches at the University of Washington. (P. 248)

Robert Bly was born in Madison, Minnesota, in 1926. His books include *Silence in the Snowy Fields* and *The Light Around the Body,* which won the National Book Award, as well as translations of Neruda, Vallejo, Lorca, Jimenez, and others. He has had fellowships from the Guggenheim Foundation and the Rockefeller Foundation. (Pp. 360–61)

George Bradley was born in Roslyn, New York, in 1953. His poems have appeared widely in such magazines as *The New Yorker, Poetry, The Paris Review, The American Poetry Review,* and others. His first book, *Terms to be Met,* won the Yale Younger Poets Prize, and he has received awards from the Academy of American Poets and the Ingram Merrill Foundation. (Pp. 426–27)

Olga Broumas was born in Syros, Greece, in 1949, and came to the United States in 1967. She is the author of six collections of poetry, including *Beginning with O* and *Black Holes, Black Stockings,* coauthored with Jane Miller. The recipient of Guggenheim and NEA fellowships, she is currently translating the work of Odysseas Elytis. (Pp. 427–30)

Debra Bruce was born in Albany, New York, in 1951. The recipient of grants from NEA, NEH, and the Illinois Arts Council, she has published two books of poetry, *Pure Daughter* and *Sudden Hunger.* She teaches English and Women's Studies at Northeastern Illinois University. (P. 48)

Sharon Bryan was born in 1943. She received a B.A. in Philosophy from the University of Utah, an M.A. in Anthropology from Cornell University, and an M.F.A. from the University of Iowa. Her poems appear in *The Atlantic, The Nation,* and *Poetry Northwest,* among others, and in two books, *Salt Air* and *Objects of Affection.* She teaches at the University of Washington. (P. 362)

Ralph Burns was born in Norman, Oklahoma, in 1949, and grew up in Tulsa. His three books of poems are *Us, Windy Tuesday Nights,* and *Any Given Day.* He has been writer-in-residence at Southcentral Community Mental Health Center in Bloomington, Indiana. (Pp. 42–43)

Kathryn Stripling Byer was born in south Georgia in 1944, and was educated at Wesleyan College and the University of North Carolina–Greensboro. Her poems have appeared in *Poetry, Georgia Review, Southern Review,* and others. She has published two chapbooks, *Search Party* and *Alma,* and one full-length collection, *The Girl in the Midst of the Harvest.* She lives in Cullowhee, North Carolina. (Pp. 328–30)

William Carpenter was born in Cambridge, Massachusetts, in 1940. He received the Associated Writing Programs award for his first book, *The Hours of Morning,* and the Samuel French Morse Prize for his second book, *Rain.* He is currently dean of faculty at the College of the Atlantic in Bar Harbor, Maine. (Pp. 234–36, 342–43)

Siv Cedering was born in Oeverkalix, Sweden, in 1939, and came to the United States in 1953. A photographer and a poet, her books include *Cup of Cold Water, Mother Is,* and *Letters from the Floating World*. She has taught at the University of Massachusetts and Columbia University. (Pp. 261–63)

Fred Chappell was born in Canton, North Carolina, in 1936. His books include five novels, a collection of short stories, and numerous volumes of poetry. He has been awarded the Sir Walter Raleigh Prize, The Prix de Meilleur des Lettres Etrangers from the Academie Française, and the Bollingen Prize in Poetry. A selection of his work is collected in *The Fred Chappell Reader*. (Pp. 156–59)

Kelly Cherry was born in Baton Rouge, but grew up in Ithaca, New York, and Richmond, Virginia. She has published three books of poetry, *Lovers and Agnostics, Relativity: A Point of View,* and *Natural Theology,* as well as four novels and two chapbooks. The recipient of an NEA fellowship, a Pushcart Prize, and a PEN/Syndicated Fiction Award, she teaches at the University of Wisconsin–Madison. (Pp. 160–62)

John Ciardi was born in Boston in 1916, and was educated at Bates College, Tufts College, and the University of Michigan. His many books include *As If: Poems New and Selected, I Marry You: A Sheaf of Love Poems, Person to Person,* and the influential text, *How Does a Poem Mean?* Poetry editor of *The Saturday Review* for many years, he taught at Harvard and Rutgers. (Pp. 48–51)

David Citino was born in Cleveland, and was educated at Ohio State University. His books include *The Gift of Fire, The Appassionata Doctrines,* and *Last Rites and Other Poems,* as well as two anthologies of Ohio poetry. The recipient of an NEA fellowship and an Alumni Distinguished Teaching Award, he teaches at Ohio State University. (Pp. 51–52, 241–43)

Lucille Clifton was born in Depew, New York, in 1936, and completed two years of college at Howard University in Washington, D.C. The author of six books of poetry and many children's books, she is former poet laureate of Maryland and recipient of two NEA fellowships. She teaches at the University of California at Santa Cruz. (Pp. 195–96)

Peter Cooley was born in Detroit in 1940. He is the author of four books of poetry, *The Company of Strangers, The Room Where Summer Ends, Nightseasons,* and *The Van Gogh Notebook*. Since 1970 he has been poetry editor of *North American Review,* and he currently teaches at Tulane University. (P. 68)

Gerald Costanzo was born in Portland, Oregon, in 1945, and was educated at Harvard and Johns Hopkins. He is the author of two books of poetry, *In the Aviary* and *Wage the Improbable Happiness,* as well as poems and articles in *The Nation, American Poetry Review,* and *The Georgia Review,* among others. The recipient of an NEA fellowship, he is director of the creative writing program at Carnegie Mellon University, and poetry editor for Carnegie Mellon University Press. (Pp. 213–14)

Robert Creeley was born in Arlington, Massachusetts, in 1926, and was educated at Harvard and The University of New Mexico. He has lived in France, Spain, Canada, and Guatemala, and since 1966 has taught at SUNY–Buffalo where he holds the David Gray Chair of Poetry and Letters. He is the recipient of Guggenheim fellowships and a Rockefeller grant, and has published *For Love, Pieces,* and *Collected Poems 1945–75,* among others. (Pp. 58–59)

Philip Dacey was born in St. Louis in 1939, and was educated at St. Louis University, Stanford, and the University of Iowa. The author of four books of poems, including *How I Escaped from the Labyrinth* and *The Man Under the Bed,* as well as several chapbooks, he has received two NEA fellowships and two Pushcart Prizes. He teaches at Southwest State University in Marshall, Minnesota. (Pp. 68–70, 146–47)

Jim Daniels was born in Detroit in 1956, and was educated at Alma College and Bowling Green State University. The recipient of an NEA fellowship and of the Brittingham Prize in Poetry for his first book, *Places/Everyone,* he has worked as a soda jerk, short-order cook, janitor, assembly-line worker, and bank bookkeeper. He currently teaches at Carnegie Mellon University. (Pp. 407–11)

Thulani Davis lives in New York City. She is the author of *All the Renegade Ghosts Rise* and *Playing the Changes.* (Pp. 362–63)

Peter Davison was born in New York City in 1928, and was educated at Harvard. His work has appeared widely in anthologies and magazines, including *The New Yorker, Poetry, Harper's,* and *Kenyon Review,* and in many books, including *The Breaking of the Day, and Other Poems, Walking the Boundaries, A Voice in the Mountain,* and *Praying Wrong.* He is poetry editor of *The Atlantic,* and senior editor of the Atlantic Monthly Press. (Pp. 430–32)

Carl Dennis was born in St. Louis in 1939, and attended Oberlin, the University of Chicago, the University of Minnesota, and the University of California at Berkeley. He has published four books of poems: *A House of My Own, Climbing*

Down, Signs and Wonders, and *The Near World.* The recipient of a Guggenheim fellowship, he teaches at SUNY-Buffalo. (Pp. 305–6)

Babette Deutsch was born in 1895 in New York City, and was educated at Barnard College. A poet, fiction writer, critic, translator, and editor, she published many books including *Banners, Animal, Vegetable, Mineral, Poetry in Our Time,* and *The Collected Poems of Babette Deutsch.* She taught at Columbia University. (P. 129)

James Dickey was born in Atlanta in 1923, and was educated at Clemson College and Vanderbilt University. The recipient of many awards, he has worked in advertising and taught at Reed College, the University of Wisconsin, and Washington University, among others. His books include *Drowning with Others, Buckdancer's Choice,* which won the National Book Award, *Poems: 1957–1967,* and the novel, *Deliverance.* (Pp. 363–67)

William Dickey was born in Bellingham, Washington, in 1928, and was educated at Reed, Harvard, Iowa, and Oxford. His ten books of poetry include *Of the Festivity, More Under Saturn,* and *The Rainbow Grocery.* The recipient of Woodrow Wilson, Fullbright and NEA fellowships, he teaches at San Francisco State University, and is working on the subject of computers and poetry. (Pp. 196–98)

Annie Dillard is the author of seven books, most recently *An American Childhood.* Her *Pilgrim at Tinker Creek* won the Pulitzer Prize in general nonfiction in 1974. She has received grants from the NEA and the Guggenheim Foundation, as well as a New York Press Club Award and a Washington governor's award for literature. Her poems appear widely in *The Atlantic Monthly, Harper's, Poetry, Field,* and others. (Pp. 214–15)

Patricia Dobler was born in Middletown, Ohio, in 1939, and was educated at Xavier College and the University of Pittsburgh. Her poems have appeared in *Kayak, Prairie Schooner,* and *The Ohio Review,* among others, and her first book, *Talking to Strangers,* won the Brittingham Prize for 1986. The recipient of an NEA fellowship and a Pushcart Prize, she is director of the Woman's Creative Writing Center of Carlow College. (Pp. 411–12)

Susan Donnelly was born and brought up near Boston, and graduated from Mount Holyoke College. Her poems have appeared in *Ploughshares, Yankee, Prairie Schooner,* and *Poetry Northwest,* among others, and her first book, *Eve Names the Animals,* won the Samuel French Morse Poetry Prize. An administrator at Harvard, she lives in Cambridge, Massachusetts. (Pp. 237–38)

Rita Dove was born in Akron, Ohio, in 1952, and was educated at Miami (Ohio) and Iowa. She has published three books of poetry: *The Yellow House on the Corner, Museum,* and *Thomas and Beulah,* which won the Pulitzer Prize for Poetry in 1987. The recipient of NEA, Guggenheim, and Fullbright fellowships, she is currently president of the Associated Writing Programs and teaches at Arizona State University. (Pp. 70–71)

Alan Dugan was born in Brooklyn, New York, in 1923, and was educated at Queens College and Mexico City College. The recipient of the Pulitzer Prize and Guggenheim and Rockefeller fellowships, he has worked in advertising and publishing, and as a model maker for a medical supply house. His books include *Poems, Poems 2, Poems 3,* and *Poems 4.* (Pp. 432–33)

Stephen Dunn is the author of six collections of poetry, including *Looking for Holes in the Ceiling, A Circus of Needs,* and *Local Time,* which won the National Poetry Series Open Competition for 1986. The recipient of two NEA fellowships and the Theodore Roethke Prize, his work appears widely in *The New Yorker, The Nation, The Atlantic,* and others. He teaches at Stockton State College and Columbia University. (Pp. 71–73, 198–200)

Stuart Dybek was born in Chicago in 1942, and was educated at Loyola University and the University of Iowa. He has published two books, *Brass Knuckles* and *Childhood and Other Neighborhoods,* and has received numerous prizes including the O. Henry Award, the Nelson Algren Award, and fellowships from the NEA and the Guggenheim Foundation. He teaches at Western Michigan University. (Pp. 264–65)

Russell Edson is the author of many books of poetry, including *The Clam Theater, The Intuitive Journey and Other Works, The Reason Why the Closet-Man Is Never Sad,* and *The Wounded Breakfast.* He writes, "Information as to how I scratched, and where, will make interesting twitterings after I'm dead; not while I still live, and still scratch." He still lives and scratches in Stamford, Connecticut. (Pp. 367–69)

Lynn Emanuel was born in New York in 1949, and was educated at Bennington, City College of New York, and the University of Iowa. Her first book, *Hotel Fiesta,* won the Great Lakes Colleges Association New Writers' Award, and she is the author of two chapbooks. The recipient of an NEA fellowship, she teaches at the University of Pittsburgh. (Pp. 100–101)

John Engels was born in South Bend, Indiana, in 1931, and was educated at Notre Dame, University College, Dublin, and the University of Iowa. He is the author of seven books of poetry, including *Cardinals in the Ice Age,* a National Poetry Series selection for 1987. The recipient of NEA, Guggenheim, and Fulbright fellowships, he teaches at St. Michael's College in Winooski, Vermont. (Pp. 101–2)

Jane Flanders was born in Waynesboro, Pennsylvania, in 1940, and was educated at Bryn Mawr and Columbia. Her two books of poetry are *Leaving and Coming Back* and *The Students of Snow,* and her awards include a Discovery Award, an NEA fellowship, and three Pushcart Prizes. She lives in Pelham, New York. (Pp. 200–201)

Carolyn Forché was born in Detroit in 1950. Her books include *Gathering the Tribes,* which received the Yale Younger Poets Prize, *The Country Between Us,* which received the Lamont Prize, and *Flowers From The Volcano,* translations of the poetry of Claribel Alegria. The recipient of NEA and Guggenheim fellowships, she currently lives in Vermont. (Pp. 433–35)

Alice Fulton was born in Troy, New York, in 1952, and was educated at Empire State College and Cornell. Her first book, *Dance Script with Electric Ballerina,* won the Associated Writing Programs Award, and her second book, *Palladium,* was a National Poetry Series selection. She has been a disc jockey, a photolab technician, and a telephone operator, and she currently teaches at the University of Michigan. (Pp. 113–15)

Brendan Galvin was born in Everett, Massachusetts, in 1938. His books include *No Time for Good Reasons, Atlantic Flyway,* and *Seals in the Inner Harbor.* The recipient of an NEA fellowship, he teaches at Central Connecticut University, and divides the year between homes in Durham, Connecticut, and Truro, Massachusetts. (Pp. 102–3)

George Garrett was born in 1929. Novelist and story writer, he is the author of seven books of poetry, most recently *The Collected Poems of George Garrett.* He was poetry editor of *The Transatlantic Review,* and is currently an editor for the parody magazine *Poultry: A Magazine of Voice.* His honors include fellowships from the Guggenheim Foundation, the Ford Foundation, and the NEA. (Pp. 52–53)

Margaret Gibson was born in Philadelphia in 1944, and was educated at Hollins College and the University of Virginia. Her three books of poems are *Signs, Long Walks in the Afternoon,* and *Memories of the Future, the Daybooks of Tina Modotti.* The recipient of Woodrow Wilson and NEA fellowships, she lives in Preston, Connecticut. (Pp. 163–66)

Sandra M. Gilbert was born in New York City in 1936. Her four books of poems are *In the Fourth World, The Summer Kitchen, Emily's Bread*, and *Blood Pressure*. She is also coauthor of *The Madwoman in the Attic: The Woman Writer and the Nineteenth-Century Literary Imagination*, and *No Man's Land: The Place of the Woman Writer in the Twentieth Century*. She teaches at Princeton University. (Pp. 43–45)

Gary Gildner was born in West Branch, Michigan, in 1938, and educated at Michigan State. His five books of poetry include *First Practice, Nails, The Runner*, and *Blue Like the Heavens: New & Selected Poems*. The recipient of a National Magazine Award for Fiction, a Pushcart Prize, and two NEA fellowships, he has taught at Northern Michigan University, Drake, Reed, and Michigan State. (Pp. 265–68)

Elton Glaser teaches at the University of Akron. His two books are *Relics* and *Tropical Depressions*. (Pp. 142–43)

Patricia Goedicke was born in Boston in 1931, brought up in Hanover, New Hampshire, and educated at Middlebury and Ohio University. Her eight books of poetry include *Between Oceans, Crossing the Same River, The Wind of Our Going*, and *Listen, Love*. The recipient of many prizes, she lived for twelve years in Mexico, and now teaches at the University of Montana. (Pp. 201–2)

Jorie Graham was raised in Italy and attended the Sorbonne, Columbia University, and the University of Iowa. She has published three collections of poetry: *Hybrids of Plants and of Ghosts, Erosion*, and *The End of Beauty*. Her honors include an Ingram Merrill grant, a Bunting fellowship, an NEA fellowship, and a Guggenheim grant. She teaches at the University of Iowa. (Pp. 306–9)

Debora Greger was born in 1949. She is the author of *Movable Islands* and *And,* and has been awarded the Amy Lowell Traveling Poetry Scholarship, a Bunting fellowship, two NEA fellowships, and an Ingram Merrill Foundation grant. Educated at the University of Washington and the University of Iowa, she now teaches at the University of Florida. (Pp. 310–11)

John Haines was born in Norfolk, Virginia, in 1924, and spent many years as a homesteader in the Fairbanks, Alaska, area. His books include *Winter News, News from the Glacier, The Stone Harp*, and *Stories We Listened to*. Although he has taught at the Universities of Washington, Alaska, and Montana, he is presently self-employed as a writer and lecturer. (Pp. 369–71)

Patricia Hampl was born in St. Paul, Minnesota, and attended the University of Minnesota and the University of Iowa. Her two volumes of poetry are *Woman Before an Aquarium* and *Resort and Other Poems,* and she is the author of a prose memoir, *A Romantic Education.* The recipient of grants from the NEA, the Bush Foundation, and the Ingram Merrill Foundation, she teaches at the University of Minnesota. (P. 268)

Cathryn Hankla was born in Tazewell County, Virginia, in 1958, and was educated at Hollins College, where she currently teaches. Her books include a collection of poems, *Phenomena,* a collection of stories, *Learning the Mother Tongue,* and a novel, *A Blue Moon in Poorwater.* (Pp. 216–17)

Michael S. Harper was born in Brooklyn in 1938, and was educated in Los Angeles and at the University of Iowa. His nine books of poetry include *Dear John, Dear Coltrane, Nightmare Begins Responsibility, Images of Kin,* and *Healing Song for the Inner Ear.* Recently honored with a Doctor of Letters honorary degree at Trinity College (Hartford), he is currently Israel J. Kapstein Professor of English at Brown. (Pp. 115–16, 269)

Robert Hass was born in San Francisco in 1941, and was educated at St. Mary's College of California and Stanford. The recipient of Guggenheim and MacArthur fellowships, he has taught at Columbia, SUNY–Buffalo, and the University of California–Berkeley. His books include *Field Guide, Praise,* and *Twentieth-Century Pleasures.* (Pp. 435–38)

William Hathaway was born in Madison, Wisconsin, in 1944, and grew up in Ithaca, New York. He is the author of four books of poetry, the most recent being *Fish, Flesh, & Fowl.* He has taught at Louisiana State University, Cornell University, Union College, and Wichita State University, and has worked as a bellman at the Ramada Hotel in Saratoga Springs, New York. His work has never been funded by the federal government. (Pp. 166–67)

Michael Heffernan was born in Detroit in 1942, and was educated at the University of Detroit and the University of Massachusetts. His books of poetry include *Booking Passage, A Figure of Plain Force, The Cry of Oliver Hardy, To the Wreakers of Havoc,* and *Central States.* The recipient of grants from NEA and NEH, he lives in Arkansas. (Pp. 104–6)

Judith Hemschemeyer was born in Sheboygan, Wisconsin, in 1935. Her books of poems are *I Remember the Room Was Filled With Light, Very Close and Very Slow,* and *The Ride Home.* A fiction writer and translator as well as a poet, she teaches at the University of Central Florida. (P. 372)

Conrad Hilberry was born in Illinois in 1928, grew up in Michigan, studied at Oberlin College and the University of Wisconsin, and currently teaches at Kalamazoo College. The recipient of fellowships from Breadloaf, the MacDowell Colony, and NEA, he has published five books of poetry: *Encounter on Burrows Hill, Rust, Man in the Attic, Housemarks,* and *The Moon Seen as a Slice of Pineapple.* (Pp. 106–7, 249–51)

Linda Hogan is a member of the Chickasaw Nation. She is the author of several books of poetry and a collection of short stories. Her book, *Seeing through the Sun,* received an American Book Award from the Before Columbus Foundation. The recipient of several other grants and awards, she teaches at the University of Minnesota and works part time in wildlife rehabilitation. (Pp. 202–4)

Jonathan Holden was born in New Jersey in 1941, and was educated at Oberlin, San Francisco State, and the University of Colorado. His eight books include *Design for a House,* which won the Devins Award, *Leverage,* which won the AWP Award, *The Names of the Rapids,* which won the Juniper Prize, and *Style and Authenticity in Postmodern Poetry.* He teaches at Kansas State University. (Pp. 204–6, 343–44)

Garrett Kaoru Hongo was born in Hawaii in 1951. Educated at Pomona College and the University of California–Irvine, he is the recipient of an NEA fellowship and the author of several books, including *Yellow Light* and *The River of Heaven.* He currently teaches at the University of Missouri and is poetry editor of *The Missouri Review.* (Pp. 372–76)

Barbara Howes was born in New York City in 1914, and was educated at Bennington. Her books of poetry include *The Undersea Farmer, Light & Dark, Looking up at Leaves, The Blue Garden,* and *A Private Signal: Poems New & Selected.* She has also edited several anthologies, and published one book of short stories, *The Road Commissioner & Other Stories.* (Pp. 376–77)

Harry Humes was born in Girardville, Pennsylvania, in 1935, and was educated at Bloomsburg State College and the University of North Carolina–Greensboro. His several books include *Winter Weeds,* which won the Devins award, and *Ridge Music,* which was a finalist in the AWP competition. He edits the poetry journal, *Yarrow,* and teaches at Kutztown University. (Pp. 218–19)

Terry Hummer is the author of *The Angelic Orders* and *The Passion of the Right-Angled Man.* He is also the coeditor of *The Imagination as Glory: The Poetry of James Dickey.* Born in Macon, Mississippi, in 1950, he was educated at the University of Southern Mississippi and the University of Utah. He currently teaches at Kenyon College. (Pp. 166–67)

David Ignatow was born in Brooklyn, New York, in 1914. He has published fourteen books of poetry, including *Poems: 1934–1969* and *New and Collected Poems: 1970–1985*. His prizes include the Bollingen Prize, the Shelley Memorial Award, and the National Institute of Arts and Letters Award, among others. Poet-in-residence at the Walt Whitman Birthplace Association, he teaches part-time at Columbia University. (Pp. 377–78)

Colette Inez was born in Brussels, Belgium, in 1931, and was educated at Hunter College. Her books include *The Woman Who Loved Worms, Alive and Taking Names, Eight Minutes from the Sun,* and *Family Life.* The recipient of Guggenheim, Rockefeller, and NEA fellowships, she teaches at Columbia University. (Pp. 251–52)

Phyllis Janowitz teaches at Cornell University. Her first book, *Rites of Strangers,* won the Associated Writing Programs Award, and her second book, *Visiting Rites,* was named one of the outstanding books of 1982 by the New York Times Book Review. The recipient of NEA, Bunting Institute, and Hodder fellowships, she has published widely in such magazines as *The New Yorker, The Atlantic,* the *Nation,* and others. (Pp. 345–48)

Donald Justice was born in Miami in 1925. His first book, *The Summer Anniversaries,* was the Lamont Poetry Selection for 1959, and was followed by *Night Light, Departures, Selected Poems,* and *The Sunset Maker.* The recipient of the Pulitzer Prize in poetry in 1980, he now teaches at the University of Florida. (Pp. 379–81)

X. J. Kennedy was born in Dover, New Jersey, in 1929, and attended Columbia, the University of Paris, and the University of Michigan. His first collection of poetry, *Nude Descending a Staircase,* received the Lamont Award; his most recent, *Cross Ties,* won a *Los Angeles Times* Book Award. A freelance writer, he has published textbooks, anthologies, and numerous books for children. (P. 107)

David Kirby was born in Baton Rouge in 1944, and was educated at Louisiana State University and Johns Hopkins University. His books include *The Opera Lover, Sarah Bernhardt's Leg, Diving for Poems: Where Poetry Comes From and How to Write It,* and *Saving the Young Men of Vienna.* The recipient of the Brittingham Prize in Poetry for 1986 and of an NEA fellowship, he teaches at Florida State University in Tallahassee. (Pp. 413–17)

Peter Klappert was born in Rockville Center, New York, in 1942. His six collections of poetry include *Lugging Vegetables to Nantucket, Circular Stairs, Distress in the Mirrors,* and *The Idiot Princess of the Last Dynasty.* The recipient of fellowships from the NEA and the Ingram Merrill Foundation, he currently teaches at George Mason University. (Pp. 438–41)

Etheridge Knight was born in Corinth, Mississippi, in 1931. He attended high school for two years, and was educated "at various prisons, jails." His books include *Poems from Prison, Belly Song and Other Poems,* and *The Essential Etheridge Knight.* The recipient of a Guggenheim fellowship, he has taught at the University of Pittsburgh and Lincoln University. (P. 270)

Ronald Koertge was born in Olney, Illinois, in 1940. He is the author of thirteen books of poetry, mostly from independent presses like Sumac, Wormwood Review, and Little Caesar. He is also the author of two novels, *The Boogeyman* and *Where the Kissing Never Stops.* He teaches at Pasadena City College. (Pp. 53–55)

John Koethe was born in San Diego, California, in 1945, and was educated at Princeton and Harvard. His three books of poetry are *Blue Vents, Domes,* and *The Late Wisconsin Spring.* The recipient of the Frank O'Hara Award for Poetry and the Bernard F. Conners Prize from *The Paris Review,* he teaches at the University of Wisconsin–Milwaukee. (Pp. 311–33)

Ted Kooser was born in Ames, Iowa, in 1939, and was educated at Iowa State University and the University of Nebraska. His poetry has appeared widely in *Poetry, The New Yorker, The Nation,* and *Field,* among others, and in twelve books and chapbooks. He is the editor and publisher of Windflower Press, and Second Vice President-Marketing Administration for Lincoln Benefit Life Company in Lincoln, Nebraska. (Pp. 271–272)

Jeanne Larsen was born in Washington, D.C., in 1950, and attended Oberlin College, Hollins College, the University of Iowa, and Nagasaki University. She is the author of *James Cook in Search of Terra Incognita* and *Brocade River Poems: Selected Works of the Tang Dynasty Courtesan Xue Tao.* She teaches at Hollins College. (Pp. 348–50)

Sydney Lea was born in eastern Pennsylvania in 1942, and educated at Yale. His poetry collections include *Searching the Drowned Man, The Floating Candles,* and *No Sign,* and he has published a novel, *Last of the Light,* and a critical study, *Gothic to Fantastic.* The editor of *New England Review and Bread Loaf Quarterly,* he teaches at Middlebury College. (Pp. 116–17)

Adam Lefevre was born in Albany, New York, in 1950, and was educated at Williams College and the University of Iowa. Having worked as a laborer, warehouseman, and teacher, he currently is a professional actor on stage, screen, and television. His plays have been produced in Manhattan, Dallas, and Louisville, and he lives in New Paltz, New York. (Pp. 381–83)

Philip Levine was born in Detroit in 1928 of Russian-Jewish immigrants. After a series of jobs including plater of plumbing parts, breaker of old roads, loader of boxcars, and advertising writer, he taught at Fresno State and Tufts. His dozen books include *The Names of the Lost,* which won the Lenore Marshall Award, *Ashes* and *Seven Years from Somewhere,* each of which won the National Book Critics Circle Award, and *A Walk with Tom Jefferson.* (Pp. 383–85)

Larry Levis was born in Fresno, California, in 1946, and was educated at California State University–Fresno, Syracuse University, and the University of Iowa. He is the author of *Wrecking Crew, The Afterlife,* and *Winter Stars.* The recipient of fellowships from the NEA and the Guggenheim Foundation, he teaches at the University of Utah. (Pp. 273–74)

Elizabeth Libbey was born in Arlington, Virginia, and was educated at the Universities of Montana and Iowa. Her poems have appeared in *The New Yorker, Ploughshares, Poetry Northwest,* and *Ascent,* and in two books, *The Crowd Inside* and *Songs of a Returning Soul.* She has taught at the University of Chicago and the University of Kentucky. (P. 73)

Susan Ludvigson was born in Wisconsin and currently lives in North Carolina, where she teaches at Winthrop College. Her books include *The Beautiful Noon of No Shadow, The Swimmer, Northern Lights,* and *The Wisconsin Women.* She is the recipient of fellowships from NEA, Guggenheim, and Fulbright. (Pp. 168–69)

Charles Martin was born in 1942, and was educated at Fordham University and SUNY–Buffalo. He is the author of *Steal the Bacon, Room for Error, Passages from Friday,* and a translation, *The Poems of Catullus.* The recipient of an Ingram Merrill Award and the Bess Hokin Award from *Poetry,* he teaches at Queensborough Community College. (P. 108)

Dan Masterson was born in Buffalo in 1934. Having worked as a disc jockey, missionary, and theatrical public relations director, he currently directs the Poetry Writing Program at Rockland Community College and the Poetry Writing Workshops at Manhattanville College. The recipient of several awards and prizes, he has published two books: *On Earth as It Is,* and *Those Who Trespass.* (Pp. 117–18)

Mekeel McBride was born in Pittsburgh in 1950, and was educated at Mills College and Indiana University. She is the author of two books of poetry, *Ordinary World* and *The Going Under of the Evening Land.* The recipient of an NEA fellowship, she teaches at the University of New Hampshire. (Pp. 74–75)

Linda McCarriston was born in Chelsea, Massachusetts, in 1943, and attended Goddard College and Boston University. Her poems have appeared in *Poetry, Poetry Northwest, Poetry NOW,* and *Ploughshares,* among others, and in one book, *Talking Soft Dutch.* The recipient of an NEA fellowship, the Grolier Prize, and the Consuelo Ford Prize, she teaches at Norwich University. (Pp. 330–31)

Walter McDonald was born in Lubbock, Texas, in 1934, and educated at Texas Tech College and the University of Iowa. His books include *Burning the Fence, The Flying Dutchman,* and *After the Noise of Saigon.* A pilot in the United States Air Force from 1957–1971, he currently teaches at Texas Tech University. (Pp. 206–8, 243–44)

Sandra McPherson was born in San Jose, California, in 1943, and was educated at San Jose College and the University of Washington. Her books include *Elegies for the Hot Season, Radiation, The Year of Our Birth,* and *Patron Happiness.* She has taught at the Universities of Iowa and California–Berkeley, and has been the recipient of NEA and Guggenheim fellowships. (Pp. 130–31)

Peter Meinke was born in Brooklyn in 1932, and educated at Hamilton College, the University of Michigan, and the University of Minnesota. His poetry collections include *The Night Train and the Golden Bird, Trying to Surprise God,* and *Night Watch on the Chesapeake.* His short story collection, *The Piano Tuner,* won the Flannery O'Connor Award. He teaches at Eckerd College in St. Petersburg, Florida. (Pp. 275–76)

W. S. Merwin was born on Sept. 30, 1927, in New York City. Educated at Princeton, he is the recipient of numerous honors, including a Rockefeller fellowship, a Ford Foundation grant, a Guggenheim fellowship, and the Pulitzer Prize. His many books of poetry, prose, and translations include *The Dancing Bears, The Carrier of Ladders,* and *Opening the Hand.* (Pp. 441–43)

Gary Miranda is the author of *Grace Period* and *Listeners at the Breathing Place.* Born in Bremerton, Washington, and raised in the Pacific Northwest, he has taught at the University of Athens, Greece, and at Reed College in Portland, Oregon. (Pp. 313–15)

Susan Mitchell was born in New York in 1944, and was educated at Wellesley and Georgetown University. Her poems have appeared in *The New Yorker, The Atlantic, The Nation,* and other magazines, and in one book, *The Water Inside the Water.* The recipient of a Henry Hoynes fellowship and an NEA fellowship, she teaches at Vermont College. (Pp. 386–87)

Lisel Mueller was born in Germany and came to America just before World War II. She is the author of *The Private Life,* which won the Lamont Prize, *The Need to Hold Still,* which won the American Book Award, and *Second Language,* as well as several chapbooks and two volumes of translation from the work of Marie Luise Kaschnitz. She lives in the Chicago area and teaches in the Warren Wilson M.F.A. Program. (Pp. 170–73)

Carol Muske was born in St. Paul, Minnesota, in 1945, and was educated at Creighton University, the State University of California at San Francisco, and the University of Paris. She has published three books: *Camouflage, Skylight,* and *Wyndmere.* The recipient of many grants and awards, including fellowships from NEA and Guggenheim, she teaches at the University of Southern California. (Pp. 277–79)

Leonard Nathan was born in Los Angeles in 1924, and attended UCLA and Berkeley. He is the recipient of a Guggenheim fellowship and a National Institute of Arts and Letters award, and the author of numerous books including *Returning Your Call,* which was nominated for a National Book Award. He teaches at Berkeley. (Pp. 315–16)

Howard Nemerov graduated from Harvard in 1941 and went on to teach at Hamilton College, Bennington College, the University of Minnesota, and Brandeis University. He is currently the Edward Mallinckrodt Distinguished University Professor of English at Washington University. The author of numerous collections of poetry, fiction, and essays, he has received the National Book Award, the Pulitzer Prize, and the Bollingen Award, among many others. (Pp. 85–87)

Joyce Carol Oates was born in Lockport, New York, in 1938, and was educated at Syracuse University and the University of Wisconsin–Madison. Her numerous books include *A Garden of Earthly Delight, Expensive People, Crossing the Border, Bellefleur, The Fabulous Beasts, Solstice,* and *On Boxing.* She has taught at the Universities of Detroit and Windsor, Canada. (P. 174)

Ed Ochester was born in Brooklyn, New York, in 1939, and was educated at Cornell, Harvard, and the University of Wisconsin. His nine collections of poetry include *Changing the Name to Ochester, Weehawken Ferry, Miracle Mile,* and *Dancing on the Edges of Knives,* which won the Devins Award. He is poetry editor at the University of Pittsburgh Press, past president of the Associated Writing Programs, and director of the writing program at the University of Pittsburgh. (Pp. 75–78, 219–20)

Diana O'Hehir is the author of three books of poetry—*Summoned, The Power to Change Geography,* and *Home Free*—and of two novels—*I Wish This War Were Over* and *Running Away from Home.* The recipient of an NEA fellowship, a Guggenheim fellowship, and five MacDowell Resident Fellowships, she teaches at Mills College. (P. 317)

Sharon Olds was born in San Francisco in 1942, and was educated at Stanford and Columbia. Her books are *Satan Says, The Dead and the Living,* which won the Lamont Prize and the National Book Critics Circle Award, and *The Gold Cell.* The recipient of grants from CAPS, NEA, and Guggenheim, she has taught at Brandeis and Columbia. She lives in New York City. (Pp. 279–84)

Carole Oles was born in New York City in 1939, and was educated at Queens College and Berkeley. Her books of poetry are *The Loneliness Factor, Quarry,* and *Night Watches: Inventions on the Life of Maria Mitchell.* The recipient of an NEA grant, the Gertrude B. Claytor Prize, and others, she has taught at the University of Massachusetts and Hollins College. (P. 336)

Charles Olson was born in 1910, in Worcester, Massachusetts, and died in 1970. The author of an influential essay on "projective verse," he taught at Harvard, the State University of New York at Buffalo, and at Black Mountain College, where he was rector in the early 1950s. His many books include *The Maximus Poems, The Distances,* and *Selected Writings of Charles Olson.* (Pp. 60–63)

Alicia Ostriker was born in New York City in 1937, and studied at Brandeis and the University of Wisconsin. She is the author of six books of poems, including *A Woman Under the Surface* and *The Imaginary Lover,* as well as several critical books, including *Vision and Verse in William Blake, Writing Like a Woman,* and *Stealing the Language: The Emergence of Women's Poetry in America.* She teaches at Rutgers University. (Pp. 318–20)

Molly Peacock was born in Buffalo in 1947, and attended SUNY–Binghamton and Johns Hopkins. She has published two collections of poetry, *And Live Apart* and

Raw Heaven, and her work appears widely in *The New Yorker, The Paris Review, The Nation,* and others. The recipient of fellowships from the Ingram Merrill Foundation and the New York Foundation for the Arts, she teaches at Friends Seminary. (Pp. 220–23)

Michael Pettit is assistant professor of English at Mount Holyoke College. Recipient of a National Endowment for the Arts fellowship in 1985, he is the author of *American Light* and *Cardinal Points.* (Pp. 143–44)

Marge Piercy was born in Detroit in 1936, and was educated at the University of Michigan and Northwestern University. She is the author of ten books of poetry including *The Moon Is Always Female, Circles on the Water: Selected Poems,* and *My Mother's Body,* and nine books of fiction including *Woman on the Edge of Time,* and *Gone to Soldiers.* She lives in Wellfleet, Massachusetts. (Pp. 387–90)

Robert Pinsky was born in Long Branch, New Jersey, in 1940. His books of poetry are *Sadness and Happiness, An Explanation of America,* and *History of My Heart,* which was awarded the William Carlos Williams Prize. He is also the author of *The Situation of Poetry, Poetry and the World,* and an interactive computer narrative, *Mindwheel.* He teaches at the University of California. (Pp. 321–23)

Stanley Plumly was born in Barnesville, Ohio, in 1939, and was educated at Wilmington College and Ohio University. The recipient of NEA and Guggenheim fellowships, he has published *In the Outer Dark: Poems, Giraffe, Out-of-the-Body Travel,* and *Summer Celestial.* He has taught at Ohio University, Columbia University, and the University of Houston, among others. (Pp. 175–76)

Wyatt Prunty was born in 1947, and attended the University of the South, Johns Hopkins, and LSU. His books include *The Times Between, What Women Know, What Men Believe, River of January,* and *Fallen from the Symboled World: Modes of Thought in Contemporary Poetry.* The recipient of fellowships from the Brown Foundation and the Breadloaf Writers Conference, he teaches at Virginia Polytechnic Institute. (Pp. 147–149)

Bin Ramke was born in Port Neches, Texas, in 1947. His three books are *The Difference Between Night and Day, White Monkeys,* and *The Language Student.* He is the director of the graduate writing program at the University of Denver, poetry editor of *The Denver Quarterly,* and poetry editor for the University of Georgia Press. (Pp. 108–9)

Paula Rankin was born in Newport News, Virginia, in 1945, and was educated at the College of William and Mary and at Vanderbilt. Her poetry has appeared widely in such magazines as *The Nation, Poetry Northwest,* and *North American Review,* and she has published three books: *By the Wreckmaster's Cottage, Augers,* and *To The House Ghost.* She teaches at Baldwin-Wallace College. (Pp. 78–79)

David Ray was born in Oklahoma in 1932, and has lived in Greece, Italy, Spain, and France. The author of many collections of poetry and a book of short stories, he is the recipient of the William Carlos Williams Award, an Arvon Award, a Woursell fellowship, and an NEA fellowship. He teaches at the University of Missouri–Kansas City. (Pp. 390–91)

James Reiss was born in New York City in 1941, and was educated at the University of Chicago. His work appears in such magazines as *The New Yorker, Poetry, Esquire,* and *The Nation,* and in two books, *The Breathers* and *Express.* The recipient of an NEA fellowship and the Consuelo Ford Award, he lives in New York City and teaches at Miami University in Ohio. (Pp. 284–85)

Adrienne Rich was born in Baltimore in 1929, and was educated at Radcliffe. Her books include *A Change of World, Diving Into the Wreck, The Dream of a Common Language, The Fact of a Doorframe: Poems Selected and New,* and *Of Woman Born: Motherhood as Experience and Institution.* She is the recipient of numerous prizes and awards. (Pp. 443–45)

Theodore Roethke was born in Saginaw, Michigan, in 1908, and was educated at Michigan and Harvard. His books include *The Lost Son and Other Poems, The Waking: Poems, Words for the Wind, The Far Field,* and several collections for children. The recipient of a Guggenheim fellowship, the Pulitzer Prize, two National Book Awards, and other honors, he taught at the University of Washington. (Pp. 132–33)

Pattiann Rogers was born in Joplin, Missouri, in 1940, and was educated at the University of Missouri and the University of Houston. The recipient of an NEA grant and a Guggenheim fellowship, she is the author of two books, *The Expectations of Light* and *The Tattooed Lady in the Garden.* She lives in Stafford, Texas. (Pp. 323–26)

William Pitt Root was born in Austin, Minnesota, in 1941, and was educated at the University of North Carolina–Greensboro. The recipient of Rockefeller, Guggenheim, and NEA grants, he has published a number of books, including

Faultdancing, Invisible Guests, and *Reasons for Going It On Foot.* He teaches at Hunter College, New York City. (Pp. 285–86)

Liz Rosenberg was born and raised on Long Island, New York. She attended Bennington College and Johns Hopkins. Her first book of poems, *The Fire Music,* won the Agnes Starrett Prize, and she has published a chapbook, *The Angel Poems.* She teaches at the State University of New York at Binghamton. (Pp. 286–88)

Gibbons Ruark was born in North Carolina in 1941, and educated at the Universities of North Carolina and Massachusetts. His books include *A Program for Survival, Reeds,* and *Keeping Company,* which won the Saxifrage Prize. The recipient of two NEA fellowships, he teaches at the University of Delaware. (Pp. 149–50)

Marieve Rugo was born in Romania and brought up in England during World War II. Her first book, *Fields of Vision,* appeared in 1983, and she is currently working on a second manuscript entitled *Unfinished Business.* (P. 45)

Vern Rutsala was born in McCall, Idaho, in 1934, and was educated at Reed College and the University of Iowa. His books of poetry include *Paragraphs, Walking Home from the Icehouse, Backtracking,* and *Ruined Cities.* The recipient of Guggenheim and NEA fellowships, he teaches at Lewis and Clark College. (Pp. 391–92)

David St. John was born in California in 1949, and currently teaches at the University of Southern California. He is the author of five limited edition books and three collections of poetry: *Hush, The Shore,* and *No Heaven.* He has received grants and fellowships from the Ingram Merrill Foundation, the Guggenheim Foundation, and the NEA. He is poetry editor of *The Antioch Review.* (P. 151)

Grace Schulman is the author of several books, including *Burn Down the Icons, Hemispheres,* and *Marianne Moore: The Poetry of Engagement,* and is the translator of T. Carmi's *At the Stone of Losses.* Her poems have appeared in many magazines, including *Grand Street, The New Yorker,* and the *American Poetry Review.* Poetry editor of *The Nation,* she teaches at Baruch College. (P. 326)

Alan Shapiro was born in Boston in 1952, and was educated at Brandeis and Stanford. He is the author of three books of poetry: *After the Digging, The Courtesy,* and *Happy Hour.* The recipient of NEA and Guggenheim fellowships, he teaches at Northwestern University. (Pp. 88–89)

Harvey Shapiro was born in Chicago in 1924, and was educated at Yale and Columbia. His books of poetry include *The Eye, Battle Report, This World,* and *The Light Holds.* Although he has taught at Cornell and Bard, he has made his living mostly as a journalist, at *Commentary, The New Yorker,* and *The New York Times,* where he is an editor of the *Magazine.* (Pp. 392–93)

Janet Beeler Shaw was born in Springfield, Illinois, in 1937, and attended Stephens College, Goucher College, and Cleveland State University. Her books include *Dowry* (poems), *Some of the Things I Did Not Do* (short stories), and *Taking Leave* (novel). Her work appears in *The Atlantic, Redbook, Esquire,* and others, and she teaches periodically at the University of Wisconsin. (Pp. 223–24)

Richard Shelton has published eight books of poetry, including *The Tattooed Desert, The Bus to Veracruz, Selected Poems: 1969–1981,* and *Hohokam.* The recipient of an NEA fellowship and three Borestone Mountain Awards, he teaches at the University of Arizona. (Pp. 288–90)

Jane Shore was born in New Jersey in 1947, and was educated at Goddard College and the University of Iowa. Her first books of poems, *Eye Level,* won the Juniper Prize, and her second collection, *The Minute Hand,* won the Lamont Prize. The recipient of an NEA fellowship and the Bess Hokin Prize, she has taught at the University of Washington and Tufts. (Pp. 208–9)

Peggy Shumaker was born in La Mesa, California, in 1952, and educated at the University of Arizona. The author of *Esperanza's Hair* and *The Circle of Totems,* she is director of the writing program at Old Dominion University. (Pp. 45–46)

Robert Siegel was educated at Wheaton College, Johns Hopkins, and Harvard. His two books of poetry are *The Beasts & the Elders* and *In A Pig's Eye,* and he has published several fantasy novels, including *Alpha Centauri* and *Whalesong.* The recipient of awards from the Ingram Merrill Foundation and the NEA, he teaches at the University of Wisconsin–Milwaukee. (Pp. 95–96)

Louis Simpson was born in the West Indies, and emigrated to the United States at the age of seventeen. He is the author of nine books of poetry, including *At the End of the Open Road,* which won the Pulitzer Prize, *People Live Here: Selected Poems 1949–1983,* and *The Best Hour of the Night.* The recipient of many prizes and awards, he teaches at SUNY–Stony Brook. (Pp. 393–94)

David R. Slavitt was educated at Yale and Columbia. The author of over three dozen books of poetry and fiction, he has taught at many colleges and universities, and currently teaches at Rutgers. His poetry collections include *The Walls of Thebes, Big Nose, Dozens,* and *Rounding the Horn.* (Pp. 177–79)

Dave Smith was born in Portsmouth, Virginia, in 1942, and was educated at the University of Virginia, Southern Illinois University, and Ohio University. His many books include *The Roundhouse Voices: Selected and New Poems, Local Assays: On Contemporary American Poetry,* and *The Morrow Anthology of Younger American Poets.* The recipient of NEA and Guggenheim fellowships, he teaches at Virginia Commonwealth University. (Pp. 118–23)

Paul Smyth was born in Boston in 1944, and was educated at Harvard. His books include *Conversions, Thistles and Thorns,* and *Antibodies,* and his work has appeared in *Redbook* and *Kenyon Review,* among others. He currently lives in the Berkshire hilltown of Cummington. (P. 109)

Cathy Song was born in Honolulu in 1955, and studied at Wellesley and Boston University. Her first book, *Picture Bride,* won the Yale Younger Poets Prize, and her work appears in many anthologies including *The Norton Anthology of Modern Poetry.* (Pp. 445, 447)

Barry Spacks was born in Philadelphia in 1931, and was educated at the University of Pennsylvania, Indiana University, and Cambridge University. He has taught at the Universities of Florida and Kentucky, and recently at the University of California at Santa Barbara, after retiring from M.I.T. He has published two novels and five books of poetry, most recently *Spacks Street: New and Selected Poems.* (P. 110)

Elizabeth Spires was born in Lancaster, Ohio, in 1952, and was educated at Vassar and Johns Hopkins. She has published three books of poetry, *Globe, Swan's Island,* and *Annonciade,* and has been the recipient of an NEA fellowship, an Ingram Merrill Foundation Award, and an Amy Lowell Travelling Poetry Scholarship. She teaches at Goucher College. (Pp. 394–95)

Maura Stanton was born in Evanston, Illinois, in 1946, and was educated at the University of Minnesota and the University of Iowa. She is the author of two books of poetry, *Snow on Snow* and *Cries of Swimmers,* and a novel, *Molly Companion.* She directs the program in creative writing at Indiana University. (Pp. 337, 448–50)

David Steingass was born in Elyria, Ohio, in 1940, and was educated at the University of Maine and the University of California–Irvine. His poems appear widely in magazines, and in two books, *Body Compass* and *American Handbook*. He has taught at the Universities of Maine, Louisiana State, and Wisconsin, and supports himself through readings, writing, and school residency programs. (Pp. 291–93)

Adrien Stoutenberg was born in Darfur, Minnesota, in 1916. A librarian, reporter, editor, and freelance writer, she won the Lamont Prize for *Heroes, Advise Us*. Her other books include *A Short History of the Fur Trade* and *Greenwich Mean Time*. (Pp. 338–39)

James Tate was born in Kansas City, Missouri, in 1943, and was educated at Kansas State College and the University of Iowa. His books include *The Lost Pilot, Viper Jazz, Absences,* and *Reckoner*. He teaches at the University of Massachusetts. (Pp. 450–52)

Henry Taylor was born in Loudon County, Virginia, in 1942, and was educated at the University of Virginia and Hollins College. He has published a number of books, including *The Horse Show at Midnight, An Afternoon of Pocket Billiards,* and *The Flying Change,* which won the Pulitzer Prize. The recipient of two NEA fellowships and the Witter Bynner Prize, he teaches at the American University in Washington, D.C. (Pp. 180–83, 339)

Richard Tillinghast was born in Memphis in 1940, and was educated at the University of the South and Harvard, where he studied with Robert Lowell. His books are *Sleep Watch, The Knife and Other Poems,* and *Our Flag Was Still There*. An amateur cook, fly fisherman, and gardener, he teaches at the University of Michigan. (P. 396)

Leslie Ullman was born in Chicago in 1947, and was educated at Skidmore and the University of Iowa. Her first book, *Natural Histories,* won the Yale Younger Poets Prize and the Great Lakes College Association New Writers Award. The recipient of an NEA fellowship, she teaches in El Paso, Texas, and at Vermont College. (Pp. 452–53)

Constance Urdang was born in New York City, and was educated at Smith College and the University of Iowa. Her books include *The Picnic in the Cemetery, The Lone Woman and Others, Only the World,* and a novel, *Natural History*. A widely published poet, she has also written articles on gypsies, shopping malls, food fads, and witchcraft, and was coordinator of the writers program at Washington University. (Pp. 293–94)

Mona Van Duyn was born in Waterloo, Iowa, in 1921, and was educated at Iowa State Teachers College and the State University of Iowa. Her books include *A Time of Bees, To See, To Take,* and *Letters from a Father, and Other Poems.* The recipient of NEA and Guggenheim fellowships, the Bollingen Prize, and the National Book Award, she has taught at Washington University. (Pp. 229–32)

Michael Van Walleghen was born in Detroit in 1938, and was educated at Wayne State University and the University of Iowa. His two books of poems are *The Wichita Poems* and *More Trouble with the Obvious.* The recipient of two NEA fellowships, he teaches at the University of Illinois. (Pp. 123–24)

David Wagoner was born in Massilon, Ohio, in 1926, and grew up in Whiting, Indiana. He is the author of fourteen books of poetry, including *Through the Forest: New and Selected Poems,* and ten novels, one of which, *The Escape Artist,* was made into a feature film. The editor of *Poetry Northwest,* and a chancellor of the Academy of American Poets, he teaches at the University of Washington. (Pp. 134–38)

Robert Wallace was born in Springfield, Missouri, in 1932, and was educated at Harvard and Cambridge. His books of poems include *Views from a Ferris Wheel, Ungainly Things, Critters, Swimmer in the Rain,* and *Girlfriends and Wives.* A founder of Bits Press, he edits the biennial of light verse and funny poems, *Light Year.* He teaches at Case Western Reserve University. (Pp. 79–80)

Ronald Wallace was born in Cedar Rapids, Iowa, in 1945, and grew up in St. Louis. His seven books include *Plums, Stones, Kisses & Hooks, Tunes for Bears to Dance To, People and Dog in the Sun,* and *God Be With the Clown: Humor in American Poetry.* His poems appear widely in *The Atlantic, The New Yorker, The Nation, Poetry,* and others. He is director of creative writing at the University of Wisconsin–Madison. (Pp. 225, 295–96)

Marilyn Nelson Waniek was born in Cleveland in 1946 and was educated at the Universities of California (Davis), Pennsylvania, and Minnesota. Her books include *For the Body* and *Mama's Promises,* and she has had fellowships from the Danforth Foundation and the NEA. She teaches at the University of Connecticut (Storrs). (Pp. 183–85)

James Whitehead was born in St. Louis in 1936, and was raised in Mississippi. Educated at Vanderbilt and the University of Iowa, he has published three collections of poetry, *Domains, Local Men,* and *Local Men and Domains,* and one novel, *Joiner.* He teaches at the University of Arkansas in Fayetteville. (P. 125)

Dara Wier was born in New Orleans. She is the author of four books of poems: *The Book of Knowledge, All You Have in Common, The 8-Step Grapevine,* and *Blood, Hook & Eye.* A past president of the Associated Writing Programs, she currently directs the writing program at the University of Massachusetts. (Pp. 80–81)

Miller Williams has taught at the Universities of Chile and Mexico, and for seven years at Breadloaf. A fellow of the American Academy in Rome, he currently is director of the University of Arkansas Press, and professor of English and Foreign Languages at Arkansas. His books include a history of American railroads, critical works, translations, and several volumes of poetry, and he has been honored by numerous awards. (Pp. 185–90)

Sherley Anne Williams was born on August 25, 1944, in Bakersfield, California. Educated at California State University–Fresno and Brown University, she is the author of several books, including *Give Birth to Brightness* and *The Peacock Poems,* which was a National Book Award nominee. (Pp. 397–98)

Eleanor Wilner is the author of two books of poems, *Shikhinah* and *maya,* and a book on visionary imagination, *Gathering the Winds.* The recipient of an NEA grant and two Borestone Mountain Awards, she has taught at the University of Iowa, the University of Chicago, and Temple University Japan, among others. (Pp. 89–92)

David Wojahn was born in St. Paul, Minnesota in 1953. His poems have appeared in *Poetry, The New Yorker,* and *The Missouri Review,* among others, and in two books, *Icehouse Lights* and *Glassworks.* The recipient of an NEA fellowship and the Amy Lowell Travelling Poetry Scholarship, he is Lilly Professor of Poetry at Indiana University. (Pp. 454–55)

John Woods was born in Martinsville, Indiana, in 1926. He is the author of eight books and six shorter collections of poetry, including *Turning to Look Back, Striking the Earth,* and *The Salt Stone.* The recipient of numerous awards and prizes, he has given readings and workshops at over two hundred colleges and universities. He teaches at Western Michigan University. (Pp. 138–39)

Charles Wright was born in Pickwick Dam, Tennessee, in 1935, and grew up in Tennessee and North Carolina. He is the author of seven books of poetry, including *China Trace, The Southern Cross, Country Music: Selected Early Poems,* and *The Other Side of the River.* The recipient of numerous awards and prizes, including NEA and Guggenheim fellowships, he teaches at the University of Virginia. (Pp. 398–401)

James Wright was born in 1927 in Martins Ferry, Ohio and was educated at Kenyon College and the University of Washington. His books include *The Green Wall*, *The Branch Will Not Break*, and *Collected Poems*, which won the Pulitzer Prize. He taught at the University of Minnesota, Macalester College, and SUNY–Buffalo, among others. (Pp. 401–3)

Robert Wrigley was born in the midwest, but is now a confirmed westerner. The recipient of an NEA fellowship and the Celia B. Wagner Award, he is the author of two books, *The Sinking of Clay City* and *Moon in a Mason Jar*. He has taught since 1977 at Lewis and Clark State College, and served as Idaho's state writer-in-residence from 1986 to 1988. (Pp. 125–26)

Al Young was born in Ocean Springs, Mississippi, in 1939, and was educated at the University of Michigan, Stanford University, and the University of California-Berkeley. The recipient of NEA and Guggenheim fellowships, he has published *The Song Turning Back into Itself*, *Geography of the Near Past*, and *The Blues Don't Change*, among others. (Pp. 190–191)

David Young was born in Davenport, Iowa, in 1936, and grew up in Minneapolis and Omaha. Educated at Carleton and Yale, he has taught at Oberlin College since 1961. He is the author of six books of poetry, three books of criticism, five books of translation, and four anthologies. His most recent books are *Foraging*, a collection of poems, and *Troubled Mirror*, a study of Yeats. He edits *Field*. (Pp. 297, 403–4)

Lisa Zeidner was born in Washington, D.C., in 1955, and was educated at Carnegie-Mellon University, Johns Hopkins, and Washington University. Winner of the 1988 Brittingham Prize in Poetry for *Pocket Sundial*, she is also the author of *Talking Cure* (poems) and two novels, *Customs* and *Alexandra Freed*. She lives in Philadelphia and teaches at Rutgers University. (Pp. 332–33, 417–19)

Paul Zimmer was born in Canton, Ohio, in 1934. He attended Kent State University, worked as a steel mill electrician, warehouseman, shoe clerk, bill collector, technical writer, and bookstore manager before beginning his career in scholarly publishing with the Universities of Pittsburgh, Georgia, and Iowa. He has published five books and four chapbooks of poetry, and is currently director of the University of Iowa Press. (Pp. 297–301)

Guidelines for Submitting Manuscripts
to University Presses

Because submissions guidelines change periodically, poets are advised to contact the presses directly before submitting manuscripts.

The University of Alabama Press awards a $1000 prize and publication to each of two manuscripts submitted in an open competition. Manuscripts should be submitted in standard form: 48–75 numbered pages in addition to the table of contents and acknowledgments, single- or double-spaced, on one side of letter-sized paper. Manuscripts must be accompanied by a $5 reading fee (made payable to the University of Alabama) and a self-addressed stamped envelope stamped with sufficient postage for return. Manuscripts must be unpublished with the exception of individual poems in magazines and chapbooks in editions of fewer than 500 copies. Inform the editors of simultaneous submissions. Manuscripts should be sent between September 1 and November 1. Send to: Series Editors, The Alabama Poetry Series, Department of English, Drawer AL, The University of Alabama, University, Alabama 35486.

The University of Arkansas Press invites enquiries about submitting manuscripts. Send to: The University of Arkansas Press, McIlroy House, 201 Ozark, Fayetteville, Arkansas 72701.

The Associated Writing Programs Award Series awards a $1000 prize to the winning submission in an open competition. Finalists' manuscripts are often published by one of the participating university presses as well. Unpublished manuscripts of at least 48 pages in length are eligible; individual poems may have been previously published. A $10 reading and handling fee is required. One self-addressed, stamped envelope or mailer large enough to accommodate the manuscript is required for return of submission. Manuscripts should be typed double-spaced on good quality paper (photocopies are acceptable), and must be bound securely. Each manuscript must include a cover page with the author's name, address, phone number, and manuscript title. The author's name must not appear anywhere but on the cover page. Manuscripts should be mailed between January 1 and February 28. Include a self-addressed, stamped postcard for acknowledgment of the receipt of the manuscript. Send to: AWP Award Series in Poetry, Associated Writing Programs, Old Dominion University, Norfolk, Virginia 23508–8510.

Carnegie Mellon University Press considers manuscripts in October. A $7.50 reading fee, and SASE are required. Write to the press about specific dates and guidelines: Carnegie Mellon University Press, P.O. Box 21, Schenley Park, Pittsburgh, Pennsylvania 15213.

The University of Georgia Press considers manuscripts twice each year. Poets who have not yet published a full-length book of poems should submit manuscripts in September. Poets who have published at least one-full length book of poems should submit manuscripts in January. Individual poems may have been previously published in magazines or anthologies. Manuscripts must be typewritten (photocopies are acceptable) and must be at least 50 pages in length. A submission fee of $10 is required, as is a stamped, self-addressed book-mailer or envelope of appropriate size for return of manuscript. Send to: Contemporary Poetry Series, University of Georgia Press, Athens, Georgia 30602.

The University of Illinois Press considers manuscripts periodically. Include a $5 handling fee. Send to: Poetry Editor, The University of Illinois Press, 54 E. Gregory Drive, Champaign, Illinois 61820.

The University of Iowa Press awards two $1,000 prizes annually to poets who have published at least one book. Manuscripts of from 50 to 120 pages may be submitted during the months of February and March, and must be accompanied by stamped, self-addressed return packaging. The series is intended to encourage mature poets and their work. No reading fee is required. Send to: The Iowa Poetry Prizes, The University of Iowa Press, Iowa City, Iowa 52242.

The Johns Hopkins University Press does not consider unsolicited manuscripts. Send enquiries to: Poetry Editor, The Johns Hopkins University Press, 701 West 40th Street, Suite 275, Baltimore, Maryland 21211.

Louisiana State University Press considers manuscripts periodically. Enquiries, accompanied by some sample poems, should be sent to: Ms. Beverly Jarrett, Poetry Editor, Louisiana State University Press, Baton Rouge, Louisiana 70893.

The University of Massachusetts Press awards the Juniper Prize of $1000 to the winning manuscript in an open competition. The prize is granted annually, alternately to first and subsequent books. In 1989 the Press will consider only manuscripts by poets who have not yet published a book of poems, and in 1990 the Press will consider only manuscripts by poets who have published at least one previous book. Manuscripts should be approximately 60 pages in length. Previously published poems must be acknowledged. A $10 reading fee, and a manuscript-size, self-addressed, stamped envelope, are required. Submissions must be postmarked not later than October 1. Send to: Juniper Prize, University of Massachusetts Press, c/o Mail Office, University of Massachusetts, Amherst, Massachusetts 01003.

The University of Missouri Press considers first books of poetry only, for its Breakthrough Books series, and Devins Award for Poetry ($500). Submissions must be made between February 1 and March 31, and must be accompanied by a form obtainable from the press. A $10 reading fee and a manuscript-size, self-addressed, stamped envelope are required. Poetry collections should support from 64 to 104 pages in estimated print length. Simultaneous submissions are not acceptable. Manuscripts must be double-spaced and numbered sequentially. For entry form send to: Breakthrough Editor, University of Missouri Press, 200 Lewis Hall, Columbia, Missouri 65211.

Northeastern University Press sponsors the Samuel French Morse Poetry Prize. The contest is open to American poets who have published no more than one book of poems. Manuscripts must be between 50 and 70 pages in length, typed, bound, and submitted in duplicate. Manuscripts should include a list of acknowledgments and a brief biography of the entrant. The poet's name should not appear on the binders, the title pages, or on any of the poems themselves. An entry fee of $7.50 should be made payable to the English Department, Northeastern University. Include a large, self-addressed, stamped envelope for return of manuscript. The submissions deadline is September 15. Send to: Professor Guy Rotella, Chair, Morse Poetry Prize Committee, English Department, 406 Holmes Hall, Northeastern University, Boston, Massachusetts 02115.

Ohio State University Press in conjunction with *The Journal: The Literary Magazine of Ohio State University* awards a $750 prize annually to a manuscript selected in an open competition. Manuscripts of at least 48 pages must be submitted during the month of September. Manuscripts must be typed, double-spaced. Previously published poems must be acknowledged. A handling fee of $10 is required, and entitles the entrant to a one-year subscription of *The Journal*. Include a stamped, self-addressed, manuscript-size envelope. Send to: David Citino, Poetry Editor, The Ohio State University Press, 175 Mount Hall, 1050 Carmack Road, Columbus, Ohio 43210-1002.

The University of Pittsburgh Press solicits the work of new and established poets. Poets who have not yet published a book of over 48 pages in an edition of 750 copies may submit manuscripts in March and April for the Agnes Lynch Starrett Prize ($2,000 and publication by the Press). Include self-addressed stamped return packaging, a self-addressed stamped postcard, and a handling fee of $10. Manuscripts may be from 48 to 120 typescript pages. Poets who have already published one or more books may submit manuscripts in September and October. For complete guidelines write to: Poetry Editor, University of Pittsburgh Press, 127 North Bellefield Avenue, Pittsburgh, Pennsylvania 15260.

Princeton University Press considers poetry manuscripts during June and December of each year. Manuscripts should be about 60 or more pages in length. Manuscripts should be submitted in simple folders (without metal brackets or rings), and the poet's name should appear on the title page only. A stamped, self-addressed mailing envelope is appreciated, and a list of previous poetry publications is requested. Send to: Poetry Editor, Princeton Series of Contemporary Poets, Princeton University Press, 41 William Street, Princeton, New Jersey 08540.

The University of Utah Press selects one book of poetry a year for the University of Utah Poetry Series. Manuscripts may be submitted in March, must be at least 60 pages in length, and accompanied by return packaging. For further information write: Poetry Editor, University of Utah Press, Salt Lake City, Utah 84112.

Wesleyan University Press considers books by new and established poets separately. First book manuscripts should be sent to the Press at least six weeks prior to September and April when the New Poets Board meets to make selections. A $15 administrative fee, and a self-addressed, stamped envelope are required. Manuscripts must be typed and should be between 60 and 80 pages in length. Established poets (who have published one or more full length books) may submit manuscripts at any time. There is no handling fee, but a self-addressed, stamped envelope is required for return of manuscript. Established poets should include a list of previously published books, with names of publishers and dates of publication. It is also helpful to include photocopies of reviews of these books. Two copies of the manuscript are required. Send manuscripts to: Wesleyan University Press, 110 Mt. Vernon Street, Middletown, Connecticut 06457.

The University of Wisconsin Press awards the Brittingham Prize in Poetry ($500 and publication) to the winning manuscript selected in an open annual competition. Manuscripts must be typed, preferably double-spaced, and must be accompanied by a $10 reading fee and a self-addressed, manuscript-size, unpadded manila envelope. Manuscripts should not be bound or placed in a folder of any kind. Manuscripts should be approximately 50–80 pages in length, and should include a list of all previously published poems. Manuscripts must be received by the Press during the month of September only. Send to: Ronald Wallace, Series Editor, The Brittingham Prize in Poetry, The University of Wisconsin Press, 114 North Murray Street, Madison, Wisconsin 53715.

Yale University Press considers manuscripts by poets under the age of forty who have not yet published a book of poems. Manuscripts should be from 48 to 64 pages in length, with no more than one poem per page. Manuscripts must be typewritten, either single- or double-spaced (photocopies are acceptable). There should be a title page with author's name, telephone number, and address, a table of contents, and a page of biographical data. Pages should be numbered consecutively, beginning with the title page. The deadline for submission is February 28. A submission fee of $5 is required, as is a self-addressed stamped mailer for return of manuscript. Send to: the Editor, Yale Series of Younger Poets, Yale University Press, 92A Yale Station, New Haven, Connecticut 06520.

Acknowledgments

Permission to publish the poems included in this anthology has been granted by the university presses listed below and by other copyright holders as indicated.

The University of Alabama Press

Ralph Burns, "And Leave Show Business?," from *Any Given Day* (1985).
Sandra M. Gilbert, "Her Last Sickness," from *In the Fourth World* (1979). Reprinted by permission of the author and The New Yorker Magazine, Inc., © 1969 The New Yorker Magazine, Inc. "The Suits", from *In the Fourth World* (1979), first appeared in *Poetry*. Reprinted by permission of the author and the Editor of *Poetry*, © 1972 The Modern Poetry Association.
Mariève Rugo, "Translation," from *Fields of Vision* (1983), first appeared in *Hubbub* (Vol. 1, Issue 1, Spring, 1983). Reprinted by permission of the author and *Hubbub*, © 1983 *Hubbub*.
Peggy Shumaker, "Calvinism", from *Esperanza's Hair* (1985).

The University of Arkansas Press

Debra Bruce, "Hey Baby," from *Pure Daughter* (1983). Reprinted by permission of the author.
John Ciardi, "True or False," from *The Birds of Pompeii* (1985). "Two Egrets" and "Was a Man," from *Selected Poems* (1984). Reprinted by permission of Miller Williams, Literary Executor, Estate of John Ciardi.
David Citino, "Einstein, Placenta, the Caves of Lascaux," from *The Gift of Fire* (1986). Reprinted by permission of the author.
George Garrett, "Little Movie Without a Middle," from *The Collected Poems of George Garrett* (1984). Reprinted by permission of the author.
Ronald Koertge, "Gretel," "Sidekicks," and "Two Men," from *Life on the Edge of the Continent* (1982). Reprinted by permission of the author.

The University of California Press

Robert Creeley, "I Know a Man," "Joy," and "The Language," from *The Collected Poems of Robert Creeley, 1945–1975* © 1982 by the Regents of The University of California. Reprinted by permission of the author.
Charles Olson, "I, Maximus of Gloucester, To You," from *The Maximus Poems*. © 1983 The Regents of the University of California.

Carnegie Mellon University Press

Peter Cooley, "Last Conversation," from *The Room Where Summer Ends* (1979). Reprinted by permission of the author.

Philip Dacey, "Form Rejection Letter," from *How I Escaped from the Labyrinth* (1977). Reprinted by permission of the author.

Rita Dove, "Pomade," from *Thomas and Beulah* (1986). Originally published in *Poetry*. Reprinted by permission of the author.

Stephen Dunn, "Weatherman," from *A Circus of Needs* (1978). Reprinted by permission of the author.

Elizabeth Libbey, "Helpmate," from *The Crowd Inside* (1978). Originally published in *Out There*.

Mekeel McBride, "A Blessing," from *The Going Under of the Evening Land* (1983). Originally published in *The New Yorker*.

Ed Ochester, "Cooking," from *Miracle Mile* (1984). Reprinted by permission of the author. "The Heart of Owl Country," from *Changing the Name to Ochester* (1984). Reprinted by permission of the author.

Paula Rankin, "Sideshows," from *By the Wreckmaster's Cottage* (1977). Originally published in *Back Door*. Reprinted by permission of the author.

Robert Wallace, "I Go On Talking to You," from *Swimmer in the Rain* (1979). Originally published in *The Denver Quarterly*. Reprinted by permission of the author.

Dara Wier, "Lucille's Kumquat-Colored Kimono" and "Midge in the Morning," from *The 8-Step Grapevine* (1980). Reprinted by permission of the author.

The University of Chicago Press

Howard Nemerov, "Adoration" and "Because You Asked About the Line Between Prose and Poetry," from *Sentences* (1980). Reprinted by permission of the author. "Beginner's Guide," from *Gnomes and Occasions* (1973). Reprinted by permission of the author.

Alan Shapiro, "Mezuzah," from *The Courtesy* (1983). Reprinted by permission of the author.

Eleanor Wilner, "The Continuous is Broken, and Resumes," from *Shekhinah* (1984). Originally published in *The Third Wind* 1, No.1, Winter 1983. Reprinted by permission of the author. "Emigration," from *Shekhinah* (1984). Originally published in *Ms.*, June, 1980. Reprinted by permission of the author.

The University Presses of Florida

Robert Siegel, "In A Pig's Eye," from *In a Pig's Eye* (1980). Originally published as "To Market, To Market," in *Prairie Schooner,* © 1976 The University of Nebraska Press. Reprinted by permission of the author.

The University of Georgia Press

Susan Astor, "The Coupling," from *Dame* (1980). Reprinted by permission of the author.

Lynn Emanuel, "The Photograph of Ramona Posing While Father Sketches Her in Charcoal," from *Hotel Fiesta* (1984). Reprinted by permission of the author.

John Engels, "Joyce Vogler in 1948" from *Vivaldi in Early Fall* (1981). Reprinted by permission of the author.

Brendan Galvin, "The Birds," from *Atlantic Flyway* (1980). Reprinted by permission of the author.

Michael Heffernan, Sonnet #6 from "The Crazyman's Revival," "Daffodils," and "Famous Last Words," from *The Cry of Oliver Hardy* (1979). Reprinted by permission of the author.

Conrad Hilberry, "The Woman Who Was Ready to Die," from *The Moon Seen as a Slice of Pineapple* (1984). Reprinted by permission of the author.

X. J. Kennedy, "Ars Poetica" and "Nude Descending a Staircase," from *Cross Ties* (1985). Reprinted by permission of the author.

Charles Martin, "Terminal Colloquy," from *Room for Error* (1978). Reprinted by permission of the author.

Bin Ramke, "The Obscure Pleasure of the Indistinct," from *White Monkeys* (1981). Reprinted by permission of the author.

Paul Smyth, "Road Construction," from *Conversions* (1974). Reprinted by permission of the author.

Barry Spacks, "Malediction," from *Imagining a Unicorn* (1978). Reprinted by permission of the author.

The University of Illinois Press

Alice Fulton, "Everyone Knows the World Is Ending," from *Palladium* (1986). Originally published in *Epoch*. Reprinted by permission of the author. "Plumbline," from *Palladium* (1986). Originally published in *Poetry*. Reprinted by permission of the author.

Michael S. Harper, "Nightmare Begins Responsibility," from *Images of Kin: New and Selected Poems* (1977). Reprinted by permission of the author, © 1974 Michael S. Harper.

Sydney Lea, "For My Father, Who Hunted," from *Searching the Drowned Man* (1980). Originally published in *Ascent*. Reprinted by permission of the author.

Dan Masterson, "For a Child Going Blind," from *On Earth as It Is* (1978). Reprinted by permission of the author and The New Yorker Magazine, Inc., © 1976 The New Yorker Magazine, Inc.

Dave Smith, "Night Fishing for Blues," from *Cumberland Station* (1976). Originally published in *Shenandoah*. Reprinted by permission of the author. "On a Field Trip at Fredericksburg," from *Cumberland Station* (1976). Reprinted by permission of the author and The New Yorker Magazine, Inc., © 1975 The New Yorker Magazine, Inc.

Michael Van Walleghen, "More Trouble With the Obvious," from *More Trouble With the Obvious* (1981). Originally published in *The Hudson Review*. Reprinted by permission of the author.

James Whitehead, "A Local Man Remembers Betty Fuller," from *Local Men* (1979). Originally published in *The Hollins Critic*. Reprinted by permission of the author.

Robert Wrigley, "Heart Attack," from *Moon in a Mason Jar* (1986). Originally published in *Anthology of Magazine Verse and Yearbook of American Poetry 1984*. Reprinted by permission of the author.

Indiana University Press

Babette Deutsch, "Disasters of War: Goya at the Museum," from *Collected Poems: 1919–1962* (1963). Reprinted by permission of Adam Yarmolinsky, Executor, The Estate of Babette Deutsch.

Sandra McPherson, "Keeping House" and "Resigning from a Job in a Defense Industry," from *Elegies for the Hot Season* (1970). Reprinted by permission of the author, © 1970 Sandra McPherson; and by The Ecco Press, 1982.

Theodore Roethke, "Elegy for Jane," "My Papa's Waltz," and "The Waking," from *Words for the Wind* (1958). Reprinted by permission of Doubleday & Company, Inc.

David Wagoner, "Beauty and the Beast," from *Collected Poems* (1976). Originally published in *The Iowa Review*. Reprinted by permission of the author. "The Poets Agree to Be Quiet by the Swamp," and "Report From a Forest Logged by the Weyerhaeuser Company," from *Collected Poems* (1976). Reprinted by permission of the author.

John Woods, "I Only Have One Cavity," from *Striking the Earth* (1976). Originally pub-

David R. Slavitt, "Broads," from *Big Nose* (1983). Originally published in *Poultry: A Magazine of Voice*. Reprinted by permission of the author. "Eczema," from *Rounding the Horn* (1978). Reprinted by permission of the author.

Henry Taylor, "Artichoke," and "At the Swings," from *The Flying Change* (1985). Reprinted by permission of the author.

Marilyn Waniek, "Emily Dickinson's Defunct," from *For the Body* (1978). Reprinted by permission of the author. "Women's Locker Room," from *Mama's Promises* (1985). Reprinted by permission of the author.

Miller Williams, "A Poem for Emily," from *Imperfect Love* (1986). Originally published in *Poetry*. Reprinted by permission of the author. "Ruby Tells All," from *Imperfect Love* (1986). Reprinted by permission of the author. "Why God Permits Evil: For Answer to This Question of Interest to Many Write Bible Answers Dept. E–7," from *Why God Permits Evil* (1977). Originally published in *Best Poems of 1976* (Borestone Mountain Poetry Awards). Reprinted by permission of the author.

Al Young, "W. H. Auden and Mantan Moreland," from *The Blues Don't Change: New And Selected Poems* (1982). Reprinted by permission of the author.

The University of Massachusetts Press

Lucille Clifton, "forgiving my father," and "homage to my hips," from *Two-Headed Woman* (1980). Reprinted by permission of the author.

William Dickey, "Face-Paintings of the Caduveo Indians," from *The Rainbow Grocery* (1978). Originally published in *New Letters*. Reprinted by permission of author. "The Food of Love," and "Happiness," from *The Rainbow Grocery* (1978). Reprinted by permission of the author.

Stephen Dunn, "At Every Gas Station There Are Mechanics," from *Looking for Holes in the Ceiling* (1974). Reprinted by permission of the author. "Day and Night Handball," from *Looking for Holes in the Ceiling* (1974). Originally published in *Three Rivers Poetry Journal*, 1973. Reprinted by permission of the author.

Jane Flanders, "Heavenly Bodies," from *The Students of Snow* (1982). Originally published in *West Branch*. Reprinted by permission of the author.

Patricia Goedicke, "Like Animals," from *Crossing the Same River* (1980) and *Listen, Love*, (Barnwood Press, 1986). Originally published in *Waves*. Reprinted by permission of the author.

Linda Hogan, "The Truth Is," from *Seeing Through the Sun* (1985). Reprinted by permission of the author.

Jonathan Holden, "Casino," from *The Names of the Rapids* (1985). Originally published in *Quarterly West*. Reprinted by permission of the author. "'The Swing,' by Honoré Fragonard," from *The Names of the Rapids* (1985). Originally published in *Minnesota Review*. Reprinted by permission of the author.

Walter McDonald, "The Food Pickers of Saigon," from *After the Noise of Saigon* (1987). Originally published in *TriQuarterly*, 1986. Reprinted by permission of the author.

Jane Shore, "Lot's Wife," from *Eye Level* (1977). Reprinted by permission of the author.

University of Missouri Press

Gerald Costanzo, "At Irony's Picnic," and "Vigilantes," reprinted from *In the Aviary* by Gerald Costanzo, by permission of the University of Missouri Press. © 1974 by Gerald Costanzo. "At Irony's Picnic" originally published in *Kayak*. "Vigilantes" originally published in *Poetry Now*. Reprinted by permission of the author.

Annie Dillard, "The Man Who Wishes to Feed on Mahogany," reprinted from *Tickets For a Prayer Wheel* by Annie Dillard, by permission of the University of Missouri Press. © 1974 by Annie Dillard. Reprinted by permission of the author.

Cathryn Hankla, "The Night-Father Was Found Alive," reprinted from *Phenomena* by Cathryn Hankla, by permission of the University of Missouri Press. © 1983 by Cathryn Hankla. Originally published in *Mississippi Valley Review*. Reprinted by permission of the author.

Harry Humes, "The Man Who Carves Whales," and "The New Site of the Calvary Temple," reprinted from *Winter Weeds* by Harry Humes, by permission of the University of Missouri Press. © 1983 by Harry Humes. "The Man Who Carves Whales" originally published in *Kansas Quarterly*. "The New Site of the Calvary Temple" originally published in *Graham House Review*. Reprinted by permission of the author.

Ed Ochester, "James Wright Walks into a Sumac Patch near Aliquippa, Pennsylvania," reprinted from *Dancing on the Edges of Knives* by Ed Ochester, by permission of the University of Missouri Press. © 1973 by Ed Ochester. Originally published in *Crazy Horse*. Reprinted by permission of the author.

Molly Peacock, "The Life of Leon Bonvin," reprinted from *And Live Apart* by Molly Peacock, by permission of the University of Missouri Press. © 1980 by Molly Peacock. Reprinted by permission of the author.

Janet Beeler Shaw, "Burial Day" and "Missouri Bottomland," reprinted from *Dowry* by Janet Beeler, by permission of the University of Missouri Press. © 1978 by Janet Beeler. "Burial Day" originally published in *New Orleans Review*. Reprinted by permission of the author.

Ronald Wallace, "Oranges," reprinted from *Plums, Stones, Kisses & Hooks* by Ronald Wallace, by permission of the University of Missouri Press. © 1981 by Ronald Wallace. Originally published by *The New Yorker*. Reprinted by permission of the author.

The University of North Carolina Press

Mona Van Duyn, "The Gardener to His God," and "Recovery" from *Merciful Disguises: Published and Unpublished Poems*. © 1973 Mona Van Duyn. Reprinted by permission of the Atheneum Publishers and the author.

Northeastern University Press

William Carpenter, "Fire," from *Rain* (1985). Originally published in *Poets: In their Work, About Their Work*, 1983. Reprinted by permission of the author. "Something is Adrift in the Water," from *Rain* (1985). Originally published in *Quarterly West*. Reprinted by permission of the author.

Susan Donnelly, "Eve Names the Animals," from *Eve Names the Animals* (1985). Originally published in *The Beloit Poetry Journal*. Reprinted by permission of the author.

The Ohio State University Press

David Citino, "Grynszpan, 1938," and "Mary's Second Child," from *Last Rites and Other Poems* by David Citino, The Ohio State University Press, 1980. Reprinted by permission of the author.

Walter McDonald, "Hauling Over Wolf Creek Pass in Winter," from *The Flying Dutchman*, by Walter McDonald, The Ohio State University Press, 1987. Originally published in *TriQuarterly* 1984. Reprinted by permission of the author.

Leonard Nathan, "The Penance" originally published in *The New Republic.* "The Penance" and "Great" from *Returning Your Call: Poems.* Reprinted by permission of the author and Princeton University Press.

Diana O'Hehir, "Illinois Central Hospital," from *The Power to Change Geography* (1979). Reprinted by permission of the author and Princeton University Press.

Alicia Ostriker, "The Exchange," "Homecoming," and "Those Who Know Do Not Speak, Those Who Speak Do Not Know," from *A Woman Under the Surface: Poems and Prose Poems* (1982). Reprinted by permission of the author and Princeton University Press.

Robert Pinsky, "A Love of Death," from "Part Two: Its Great Emptiness," from *An Explanation of America* (1979). Reprinted by permission of the author and Princeton University Press.

Pattiann Rogers, "Portrait" and "How the Body in Motion Affects the Mind," from *Expectations of Light* (1981). Reprinted by permission of the author and Princeton University Press. "Portrait" originally published in *Poetry.*

Grace Schulman, "Bill Flanagan at Maryknoll," from *Burn Down the Icons* (1976). Reprinted by permission of the author and Princeton University Press.

Texas Tech University Press

Kathryn Stripling Byer, "Solstice," and "Wide Open, These Gates," from *The Girl in the Midst of the Harvest* (1986). Reprinted by permission of the author.

Linda McCarriston, "Barn Fire" and "Trouble" from *Talking Soft Dutch* (1984). Reprinted by permission of the author. "Barn Fire" originally published in *The Ohio Review.*

Lisa Zeidner, "Audience," from *Talking Cure* (1982). Reprinted by permission of the author.

University of Utah Press

Carole Oles, "Better Vision," from *Quarry* (1983). Reprinted by permission of the author.

Maura Stanton, "Childhood," from *Cries of Swimmers* (1984). Originally published in *Poetry.* Reprinted by permission of the author.

Adrien Stoutenburg, "Hypochondria," from *Greenwich Mean Time* (1979). Originally published in *Poetry Northwest.*

Henry Taylor, "Bernard and Sarah," from *An Afternoon of Pocket Billiards* (1975). Reprinted by permission of the author.

The University Press of Virginia

William Carpenter, "California," from *The Hours of Morning* (1981). Reprinted by permission of the author.

Jonathan Holden, "Fate," from *Leverage* (1983). Reprinted by permission of the author.

Phyllis Janowitz, "A Family Portrait" and "Veal," from *Rites of Strangers* (1978). Reprinted by permission of the author. "Veal" originally published in *Centering* and *Event.*

Jeanne Larsen, "A Natural History of Pittsburgh," from *James Cook in Search of Terra Incognita* (1979). Reprinted by permission of the author.

Wesleyan University Press

John Ashbery, "Faust," copyright © 1962 by John Ashbery. Reprinted from *The Tennis Court Oath.*

Michael Benedikt, "Fred, The Neat Pig," copyright © 1976 by Michael Benedikt. Reprinted from *Night Cries* by permission of the author.